W9-AVI-836

KAREN BROWN'S

French

Country Inns & Itineraries

KAREN BROWN'S

French Country Inns & Itineraries

Written by

KAREN BROWN & JUNE BROWN

Illustrations by Barbara Tapp
Cover Painting by Jann Pollard

Travel Press
Karen Brown's Country Inn Series

Editors: Clare Brown, June Brown, Karen Brown, Louise Vierra
Illustrations: Barbara Tapp; Maps: Susanne Lau Alloway—Greenleaf Design & Graphics
Cover painting: Jann Pollard; Aide-de-camp: William Brown; Technical support: William Brown III
Written in cooperation with Town & Country-Hillsdale Travel, San Mateo, CA 94401

Copyright © 1977, 1981, 1985, 1986, 1988, 1990, 1992, 1994 by Karen Brown's Guides.
All rights reserved

This book or parts thereof may not be reproduced in any form without obtaining written
permission from the publisher: Travel Press, P.O. Box 70, San Mateo, CA 94401, tel: 415-342-9117

Distributed USA & Canada: The Globe Pequot Press
Box 833, Old Saybrook, CT 06475-0833, tel: (203)395-0440, fax: (203) 395-0312

Distributed Europe: Springfield Books Ltd., tel: (0484) 864 955, fax: (0484) 865 443
Norman Road., Denby Dale, Huddersfield HD8 8TH, W. Yorkshire, England,
A catalog record for this book is available from the British Library

Distributed Australia: Little Hills Press Pty. Ltd., tel: (02) 437-6995, fax: (02) 438-5762
1st Floor, Regent House, 37-43 Alexander St, Crows Nest NSW 2065, Australia

Distributed New Zealand: Tandem Press Ltd., tel: (0064) 9 480-1452, fax: (0064) 9 480 1455
P.O. Box 34-272, Birkenhead, Auckland 10, New Zealand

Library of Congress Cataloging-in-Publication Data
Brown, Karen.
   Karen Brown's French country inns & itineraries / written by Karen
Brown ; sketches by Barbara Tapp ; cover painting by Jann Pollard. -
-- 7th rev. ed.
        p. cm. - (Karen Brown's country inn series)
        Includes index.
   ISBN 0-930328-18-3 : $14.95
     1. Hotels--France--Guidesbooks. 2. Castles--France--Guidebooks.
3. France--Guidebooks. I. Title. II. Title: French country inns &
itineraries.   III. Title: French country inns and itineraries.
IV. Title: Karen Brown's French country inns and itineraries.
V. Series.
TX907.5.F7B76   1994
647.944401--dc20   93-29584
                                                             CIP

with love to

NANCY

a wonderful mother-in-law
and
traveling companion

KAREN BROWN TITLES

California Country Inns & Itineraries

English Country Bed & Breakfasts

English, Welsh & Scottish Country Hotels & Itineraries

French Country Bed & Breakfasts

French Country Inns & Itineraries

German Country Inns & Itineraries

Irish Country Inns & Itineraries

Italian Country Bed & Breakfasts

Italian Country Inns & Itineraries

Spanish Country Inns & Itineraries

Swiss Country Inns & Itineraries

Contents

Introduction

Yes, you can fly to Paris, eat hamburgers, stay in a generic chain hotel and return home with stacks of snapshots or you can follow our driving itineraries and venture into the ever-changing French countryside. You can eat, sleep, and drink France, enjoy lovely scenery and unusual sights, mingle with the French, and return home with special memories as well as snapshots to recall them. To further tempt you we have selected magnificent places to lay your head each night: elegant châteaux, cozy inns, scenic mills and refined manors owned and managed by warm and fascinating people. Many of these were designed and built centuries ago as private residences and are set in beautiful surroundings. As travelers, you can take full advantage of this opportunity to live France every minute, twenty-four hours a day.

Fremeil

PURPOSE OF THIS GUIDE

This guide is written with two main objectives: to describe the most charming, beguiling lodging throughout France and to "tie" them together with itineraries to enable travelers to plan their own holiday. The aim is not simply to inform you of the fact that these places exist, but to encourage you to go and see for yourself: explore towns and villages not emphasized on tours and stay at hotels that truly reflect the French lifestyle. This book contains all of the necessary ingredients to assist you with your travel arrangements: easy-to-follow driving itineraries that take you deep into the lovely French countryside and most importantly a selective listing of hotels that we have seen and enjoy. It might be an elegant château dominating a bank of the Loire River or a cozy mill tucked into the landscape of the Dordogne Valley, but there is a common denominator from country cottage to stately mansion—they all have charm. Our theory is that where you stay each night matters. Your hotels should add the touch of perfection that makes your holiday very special, the memories you bring home should be of more than just museums, landmarks and palace tours. Such sights are important, but with this guide you can add a romantic element to your trip: traveling the enchanting back roads of France and staying in picturesque hideaways. If you prefer to travel the bed and breakfast way, we suggest you refer to our companion guide *French Country Bed & Breakfasts*. We encourage you to buy new editions of our guide and throw away old ones because in each new edition we add new listings, update prices, phone and fax numbers and delete places that no longer meet our standards.

CLOTHING

France stretches some 1,200 kilometers from Calais on the north coast to Nice on the Riviera in the south so expect changes in the weather, regardless of the season. For winter bring warm coats, sweaters, gloves, snug hats and boots. The rest of the year a layered effect will equip you for any kind of weather: skirts or trousers combined with blouses or shirts that can be "built upon" with layers of sweaters depending upon the chill of the day. A raincoat is a necessity, along with a folding umbrella. Sturdy, comfortable walking shoes are recommended not only for roaming the countryside and mountain trails, but also for negotiating cobbled streets. Daytime dress is casual, but in the evening it is often appropriate to dress for dinner at your hotel.

CREDIT CARDS

When a hotel welcomes plastic payment, the type of card is identified by the following abbreviations: AX: American Express; VS: Visa; MC: MasterCard; or simply—all major.

CURRENT

If you are taking any electrical appliances made for use in the United States, you will need a transformer plus a Continental two-pin adapter. A voltage of 220 AC current at 50 cycles per second is almost country-wide, though in remote areas you may encounter 120V. The voltage is often displayed on the socket.

DRIVING

BELTS: It is mandatory and strictly enforced in France that every passenger wear a seat belt. Children under ten years of age must sit in the back seat.

CAR RENTAL: All major car rental companies are represented throughout France at airports, train stations and in major cities, but it is wise to consult your travel agent for rates and details. Car companies in collaboration with airlines sometimes offer a variety of rental packages which often have to be booked and paid for in conjunction with the airline reservation. Rail Europe is currently offering four packages that combine train, air and car rental for travel within France. If traveling between Paris and Provence, for example, you might want to consider taking the train or a connecting flight one direction and covering the other direction by car, or simply bridging any longer distances by train and using a rental car for side trips. Be sure to investigate all options available before you leave home. Reservation and pre-payment are not necessarily cheaper but will ensure your price. Remember to ask the cost of taxes, insurance and any surcharges for picking up the vehicle in one location and dropping it off in another.

DRIVER'S LICENSE: A valid driver's license is accepted in France if a stay does not exceed one year. The minimum driving age is eighteen.

GASOLINE: Americans are shocked by the high price of gasoline in Europe. *Faîtes le plein, s'il vous plaît* translates as "Fill her up, please." At some self-service stations you must pay in advance, before using the pumps. Credit cards such as MasterCard and Visa are often accepted.

PARKING: It is illegal to park a car in the same place for more than twenty-four hours. In larger towns it is often customary that on the first fifteen days of a month parking is permitted on the side of the road whose building addresses are odd numbers, and from the sixteenth to the end of the month on the even-numbered side of the road. Parking is prohibited in front of hospitals, police stations and post offices. Blue Zones restrict parking to just one hour and require that you place a disc in your car window on Monday to Saturday from 9 am to 12:30 pm and again from 2:30 pm to 7 pm. Discs can be purchased at police stations and tobacco shops. Gray Zones are metered zones and a fee must be paid between the hours of 9 am and 7 pm.

ROADS: The French highway network consists of *autoroutes* (freeways/motorways), *péages* (autoroutes on which a toll is charged) and secondary roads (also excellent highways). Charges on toll roads are assessed according to the distance traveled. A travel ticket is issued on entry and the toll is paid on leaving the autoroute. The ticket will outline costs for distance traveled for various types of vehicles. It is expensive to travel on toll roads, so carefully weigh the advantage of time versus cost. If you have unlimited time and a limited budget you may prefer the smaller highways and country roads. A suggestion would be to use the autoroutes to navigate in and out of, or bypass, large cities and then return to the country roads. At toll booths French francs are the only acceptable form of payment.

SPEED: Posted speed limits are strictly enforced and fines are hefty. Traffic moves fast on the autoroutes and toll roads with speed limits of 130 kph (81 mph). On the secondary highways the speed limit is 90 kph (56 mph). The speed limit within city and town limits is usually 60 kph (38 mph).

HOTELS

HOTEL DESCRIPTIONS: In the third section of this guide you will find a selective listing of hotels that are referenced alphabetically by town. No hotel ever pays to be included. Every hotel recommended has been personally visited by us. It is impossible to revisit every hotel on a research trip as there are always new hotels to investigate, but we try to "check up" on as many as possible. We also rely on feedback from readers, follow up on any complaints and eliminate hotels that do not maintain their quality of service, accommodation and welcome. Places to stay include château-hotels, hôstelleries, hotels, old mills, manors, country inns and restaurants with rooms. The accommodation varies from luxurious to country-cozy, but it is all charming, quaint and typically French. People who seek personal experiences and unforgettable accommodation rather than predictable motel-like rooms will appreciate the country inns and château-hotels recommended in this book. The appeal of a little inn with simple furnishings will beckon some, while the glamour of ornate ballrooms dressed with crystal chandeliers and gilt mirrors will appeal to others. We have tried to describe as clearly and accurately as possible what each hotel has to offer so that you can make a choice to suit your preferences. However, no matter how careful we are, sometimes we misjudge a hotel's merits, or the ownership changes, or unfortunately sometimes hotels just do not maintain their standards. If you find a hotel is not as we have indicated, please let us know, and accept our sincere apologies.

HOTEL RATES: We quote high season, 1994 rates as provided by the hotels. The rates given are for the **least** expensive to the **most** expensive double room inclusive of tax for two persons **excluding breakfast**. If hotels have suites we have included their least expensive rate. Please **always check prices and terms** with hotels when making bookings.

HOTEL RESERVATIONS & CANCELLATIONS: People often ask, "Do I need a hotel reservation?" The answer really depends on how flexible you want to be, how tight your schedule is, during which season you are traveling, and how disappointed you would be if your first choice were unavailable. Reservations are confining and lock you into a solid framework. Most hotels will want a deposit to hold your room and frequently refunds are difficult should you change your plans—especially at the last minute. In France a hotel is not required by law to refund a deposit regardless of the cancellation notice given. Although reservations can be restrictive, it is nice not to spend a part of your vacation day searching for available accommodation and it is also important to realize that major tourist cities can be completely sold out during the peak season of June to September. Hotel space in the cities is especially crowded during annually scheduled events. So unless you don't mind taking your chances on a last-minute cancellation, staying in larger hotels or on the outskirts of a town, it is best to make a reservation. Generally, space in the countryside is a little easier. Several options for making hotel reservations are discussed on the following page. However, in each case, when making a reservation be sure to consider the following: Be specific as to what your needs are, such as a ground-floor room, ensuite bathroom or twin beds. Check the prices that may well have changed from those given in the book (summer 1994). Ask what type of deposit is required, either a check or perhaps, more simply, a credit card number. Advise them as to your anticipated arrival time. Discuss dining options if so desired. Ask for a confirmation letter with brochure and map to be sent to you.

LETTER: If you write for reservations, state clearly and exactly what you want, how many people are in your party, how many rooms you require, the category of room you prefer (standard, superior, deluxe), and your date of arrival and departure and inquire about deposit requirements. The important point, because of the language difference, is to be brief in your request. Although most hotels can understand a letter written in English, opposite we have provided a reservation request letter in French and English.

FAX: Faxing is a very quick way to reach a hotel. If the hotel has a fax we have included the number in the listing. As you are communicating with a machine, you also don't have to concern yourself with time of day or be concerned with disturbing someone's sleep.

TELEPHONE: A very efficient way for making a reservation is by telephone—the cost is minimal and you have your answer immediately—so if space is not available, you can then choose an alternate. (If calling from the United States, allow for the time difference [France is five hours ahead of New York] so that you can call during their business day. Dial 011 [the international code], 33 [France's code], and the telephone number.)

SAMPLE RESERVATION REQUEST LETTER

Madame/Monsieur:

Nous sommes _____ personnes.
We have   (number)   of persons in our party

Nous voudrions réserver pour _____ nuit(s), du _____ au _____
We would like to reserve for (number of) nights, from (arrival date) to (departure date)

_____ *chambre(s) à deux lits*
a room(s) with twin beds

_____ *chambre(s) avec un grand lit*
room(s) with double bed

_____ *chambre(s) avec un lit supplémentaire*
room(s) with an extra bed

_____ *avec toilette et baignoire ou douche privée.*
with a private toilet and bathtub or shower.

Veuillez confirmer la réservation en nous communicant le prix de la chambre, et le montant des arrhes que vous souhaitez. Dans l'attente de vos nouvelles, nous vous prions d'agréer, Madame, Monsieur, l'expression de nos sentiments distingués.
Please advise availability, rate of room and deposit needed. We will be waiting for your confirmation and send our kindest regards.

Your Name & Address

HOTEL RESTAURANTS: French cuisine is incomparable in creativity and price. It is not uncommon to pay more for dinner than for a room. Where hotels are concerned the price you pay for your meal is usually a reflection of the price you pay for your room: i.e., expensive hotels usually have expensive restaurants. We do not discuss restaurants in depth but we note whether a hotel has a restaurant. Some of France's most charming hotels are actually "restaurants with rooms," principally restaurants that offer rooms to patrons of their restaurant. Restaurants often have a tourist menu or menu of the day. These are set meals that usually include specialties of the house, are good value for your money, and offer you a meal where the courses complement one another. Restaurants known for their gourmet cuisine often offer a *menu dégustation* (tasting menu), so that you can sample the chef's many artful creations. Many hotels prefer overnight guests to dine at their restaurant. To avoid misunderstandings, inquire about a hotel's dining policy when making your room reservation.

INFORMATION

Syndicat d'Initiative is the name for the tourist offices (symbolized by a large "I") found in all larger towns and resorts in France. Tourist offices are pleased to give maps, brochures and advice on local attractions and events. They often close for two hours for lunch in the middle of the day. In Paris the main tourist office is located at 127, Avenue Champs Élysées, 75008 Paris near the George V métro stop. (Open all year 9 am to 8 pm, tel: (01) 47.23.61.72, fax: (01) 47.23.56.91.) There are also 45 regional *Accueil de France* (French Welcome) offices that will make reservations at hotels in their area no more than eight days in advance.

Information can be obtained before you leave for France by writing to the French Government Tourist Office at the following addresses:

AUSTRALIA
BNP Building 12th floor, 12 Castlereagh Street, Sydney NSW 2000

GREAT BRITAIN
178 Piccadilly, London WIV 0AL

UNITED STATES
610 Fifth Street, New York, New York 10020
9454 Wilshire Boulevard, Beverly Hills, California 90212
645 North Michigan Avenue, Chicago, Illinois 60611

Or information can be obtained by phoning France-On-Call-Hotline at: (900) 990-0040 (9 am to 6 pm EST Monday to Friday). Callers pay 50 cents per minute for the service and can receive additional information by mail free of charge.

ITINERARIES

Eleven driving itineraries are included in this guide to help you map a route through the various regions of France. An overview map that shows all 11 itineraries is on page 15. At the beginning of each itinerary we suggest our recommended pacing for the itinerary to help you decide the amount of time to allocate to each region.

MAPS

Each driving itinerary is preceded by a map showing the route and each hotel listing is referenced to a map at the back of the book. These are an artist's renderings and are not intended to replace detailed commercial maps. We very much enjoy the *Michelin Motoring Atlas of France,* a book of maps with a scale of 1:200, 000 (1 cm = 2 km) and use highlight pens to outline our route. We also find the yellow Michelin maps very useful and we state which Michelin 200 series map each hotel town is found on in the hotel description. While the atlas and yellow maps are invaluable for detailed plans we find it too detailed for getting an overview of our trip and rely upon a one-page map of France to outline our journey. French hotel maps in this book can be cross-referenced with those in our companion guide *French Country Bed & Breakfasts*.

Introduction

MONEY

The unit of currency is the French Franc, abbreviated to F (1F = 100 centimes). It is generally best to cash travelers' checks at a bank with a *bureau de change* desk—remember to take your passport for identification. There can be quite large variations in the exchange rates and service charges offered by banks even on the same street. *Bureaux de change* are open twenty-four hours at the Paris Charles de Gaulle, Le Bourget and Orly airports, and are normally open from 7:30 am to midnight at major railway stations. Some hotels will exchange money as a service to their guests, but they will approximate the exchange in their favor to guard against daily currency fluctuations.

BANKS: Banking hours vary, but in most large towns and cities banks are open Monday to Friday, 9 am to 4:30 pm. Banks close at midday on a day prior to a national holiday and all day on a Monday if a holiday falls on a Tuesday. In small towns banks are often closed on Mondays instead of on Saturdays.

POST OFFICES

Post offices are open in most towns from 8 am to 7 pm Monday to Friday and from 8 am to midday on Saturdays. There is a post office in Paris that is open twenty-four hours a day, located at 52, Rue du Louvre, 75001 Paris. In addition to the standard services that are typically provided by post offices, domestic and international telephone calls can be placed efficiently and relatively inexpensively.

TRAINS

France has an excellent train system that serves major towns and cities. However, it is often necessary to supplement your travel arrangements with either taxi or car rental to reach the small countryside towns and isolated inns. If you decide to travel by train, in addition to point-to-point tickets, a variety of travel passes and options in conjunction with car rental and airline passage are available. Information, reservations and tickets are offered by Rail Europe and can only be obtained through your travel agent. If flying into Paris and continuing immediately onto a countryside location, you might want to consider an airline connection as opposed to travel by train or car. You will find it more efficient in terms of time and cost to fly as the train stations for Paris are inside the city limits and it is necessary to spend time and money getting to the city center from the airport. After concluding your countryside travels if you want to spend time in Paris, you might consider dropping your rental car at a station and traveling by train directly into the heart of the city.

Itineraries—Overview Map

Rouen

Champagne

Reims

Mont St Michel

Épernay

Alsace

Caen

Normandy

Strasbourg

St Malo

PARIS

Colmar

Rennes

Brittany

Angers

Vézelay

Tours

Dijon

Orléans

Nantes

Châteaux Country

Burgundy

Beaune

Dordogne & Lot River Valleys

Brantôme

Grand Gorges du Verdon

Sarlat

Moustiers Ste Marie

Conques

Trigance

Cahors

Ste Enimie

Avignon

Vence

Millau

Gordes

Nîmes

Nice

Gorges du Tarn

Arles

Grasse

Aix

Hilltowns of the Riviera

Carcassonne

Provence

15

Normandy

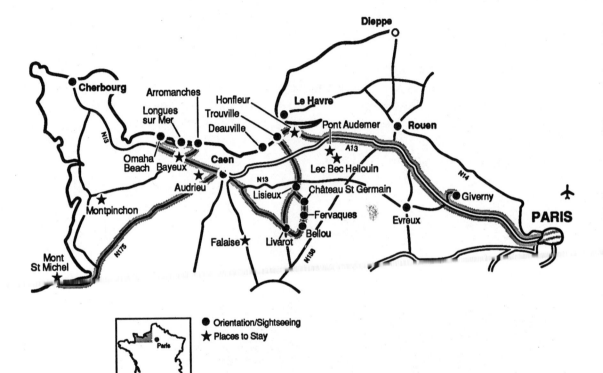

Dieppe

Cherbourg

Arromanches

Honfleur

Le Havre

Longues
sur Mer

Trouville

Deauville

Pont Audemer

Rouen

N13

Omaha
Beach

Bayeux

Caen

A13

Lec Bec Hellouin

N14

Audrieu

N13

Château St Germain

Montpinchon

Lisieux

Fervaques

Giverny

Evreux

PARIS

N175

Falaise

Livarot

Bellou

N138

Mont
St Michel

● Orientation/Sightseeing
★ Places to Stay

Paris

Normandy

This itinerary heads north from Paris to Monet's wonderful gardens at Giverny, on to the coast with the picturesque port of Honfleur, and to the world-famous D-Day beaches where on June 6, 1944 the Allies made their major offensive, reinforcing the turnaround in World War II. Decades have passed but abandoned pillboxes remain, the floating harbor endures, and museums document the events of the war. Turning inland you visit historic Bayeux to marvel at its almost thousand-year-old tapestry and the hinterland of Normandy with rolling farmland and villages of half-timbered houses—an area famous for its cheese. We conclude this itinerary, and begin the Brittany itinerary, at Normandy's most famous sight, Mont St Michel, a sightseeing venue that has attracted legions of visitors for hundreds of years.

Giverny

PACING: While you can use Honfleur as a base for this itinerary (except for visiting Mont St Michel) our preference is to spend two nights in Honfleur and a minimum of one night in Bayeux.

Follow the Seine north out of Paris (Porte d'Auteuil), travel the A13, and exit at Bonnières sur Seine. Travel a scenic route following the N15 north along the Seine to Vernon. As you cross the Seine you see the remains of a 12th-century bridge and an ancient timbered dungeon. Just a few kilometers upstream lies the village of **Giverny,** a name synonymous worldwide with artist Claude Monet who came to live in the village in April 1883.

Monet converted his barn into his studio, where he loved to paint, sit and smoke and reflect on his work. Now it's a visitors center and gift shop selling all things Monet from posters of his masterpieces to keyrings. The walls are hung with reproductions of some of his larger canvases and photos of the famous artist at work.

Monet's sunwashed peach stucco home with green shutters is decorated much as it was when he lived there—the walls hung with Japanese style paintings and family pictures. From the striking blue and yellow dining room with its matching china, through his bedroom to the cozy tiled kitchen, you get a feeling for the home life of this famous artist.

The highlight of the visit is the gardens, a multi-colored tapestry of flowers, meandering paths shaded by trellises of roses, and the enchanting oasis of the Water Garden, whose green waters are covered with lily pads and crossed by Japanese bridges hung with white and mauve wisteria. Monet loved to paint outdoors and it is memorable to search out just the spot where he stood and painted a masterpiece. Only one problem, you are not alone in your endeavors—Giverny attracts a multitude of pilgrims. However the influx of tourists also means that this tiny village has a surprising number of facilities, including cafés, restaurants and gift stores. (Open April to October, 10 am to 6 pm, closed Monday.)

Leaving Giverny, retrace your steps to Vernon and follow signposts for Rouen, then Caen along the A13. Exit the autoroute at Beuzeville and travel north on the D22 and then west on the D180 to Honfleur. **Honfleur** is a gem, its narrow, 17th-century harbor filled with colorful boats and lined with tall houses. Narrow cobbled streets lined with ancient timbered houses lead up from the harbor. Cafés and restaurants set up tables and umbrellas outside so that customers can enjoy the sun and the picturesque location. Small wonder that this pretty port has inspired artists, writers, and musicians. Markets are held every Saturday on St Catherine's Square with its unusual wooden belfry, a tall belltower and bellringer's home, standing apart from the nearby church. Just off the square, further up the hillside, on Rue de l'Homme de Bois, is the interesting **Eugène Boudin Museum** with its impressive collection of pre-Impressionist and contemporary paintings by Norman artists: Boudin, Dubourg, Monet Dufy, Friesz and Gernez. There are also displays of Norman costumes and paintings depicting life in 18th- and 19th-century Normandy. (Closed Tuesdays , and noon to 2 pm, tel: 31.89.23.30.)

Just by the harbor, in a former church, the **Musée Marine** traces the history of the port of Honfleur. Nearby the ancient timbered prison is now the **Musée d'Art Populaire** which consists of twelve rooms depicting the interiors of Norman houses including a weavers workshop and a manor house dining room. (Open 2:30 pm to 6 pm, closed January, tel: 31.89.23.30.) In addition to having quaint shops and inviting fish restaurants, Honfleur is a haven for artists and there are a number of galleries to visit.

We recommend three hotels, two in, and one on the outskirts of Honfleur. We advise that if you visit Honfleur you stay for the night because this will give you the opportunity to enjoy this scenic town without the hordes of daytime visitors.

By contrast to the quaintness of Honfleur you may choose to visit her two famous neighbors, Trouville and Deauville. **Trouville** has set the pace on the *Côte de Fleurie* since 1852. A stretch of water divides it from its very close neighbor, **Deauville**, a much ritzier resort where row upon row of beach cabanas line the sands and well-heeled folks parade the streets. The casinos are a hub of activity and if you visit in the late summer, you will experience the excitement and sophistication of a major summer playground for the rich and famous. For a few weeks each August there is the allure of the race tracks, polo fields, glamorous luncheons and black tie dinners. Celebrities and the wealthy international set come here to cheer on their prize thoroughbreds.

Honfleur

From Honfleur dip south into a region of Normandy referred to as the ***Pays d'Auge***, a lush region sandwiched between the Risle and Dives Rivers. Here quaint villages of timbered and some thatched houses cluster on rolling green hillsides grazed by cows or planted with apple orchards. It is a region to experience by driving its quiet country roads. The drive we suggest is a leisurely half-day outing beginning at **Lisieux**, the region's commercial center. If you are fortunate enough to arrive on Saturday, enjoy the town's colorful farmers market where stalls offer everything from live chickens, vegetables and cheese to underwear and shoes.

Leave Lisieux in the direction of Vimoutiers (D579) and travel for just a few kilometers and take a left turn down a country lane to **St Germain de Livet**, a hamlet at the bottom of the valley. Here you see a picture-postcard timbered farm, a couple of cottages, a church and the adorable 15th-century **Château St Germain de Livet**. This whimsical little château with pepperpot turrets and pretty pink and white checkerboard facade sits in geometric gardens behind a high wall. The interior contains some attractive furniture and some paintings and frescoes. (Closed Tuesdays, and noon to 2 pm, tel: 31.31.00.03.) Leaving the château follow signposts for Vimoutiers (D268) till you reach the D47 which you follow into **Fervaques**, a picturesque village in a green valley. Drive past its château, a vast 16th-century stone building, to the village with its timbered cottages set round a quiet square. Here you pick up signposts for *Route de Fromage*, a tourist route that guides you through this cheese producing region.

Follow the well-signposted *Route de Fromage* into **Les Moutier Hubert**, a hamlet of farms along the road, up to **Bellou** with its large brown timbered manor house, and on to **Lisores** with its little church, ivy-covered houses and farms in the valley. Regain the main road and turn towards Livarot (D579) and travel for a few kilometers before being directed right by the *Route de Fromage* onto a back road that brings you by a more scenic route into the heart of the attractive old town of **Livarot**, home of the cheese that bears the same name. Leave town in the direction of Caen to see the **Musée de Fromage** in the basement of one of the town's grand old homes. Here you watch a video on the production of Livarot, Pont l'Eveque and Camembert cheeses, and tour a replica of an old dairy farm with its traditional cheese making shop and old-fashioned dairy (tel: 31.63.43.13.)

Continuing on to Caen the countryside is pancake-flat (40 kilometers). **Caen**, one of Normandy's largest cities, is situated on the banks of the Orne, which lost nearly all of its ten thousand buildings in the Allied invasion of 1944. A large port, it is also the city that William the Conqueror made his seat of government. Your destination in Caen is the **Memorial** (Memorial to Peace). The museum is well signposted and has its own exit off the autoroute. Displays, films, tapes, and photos cover the events that led up to the outbreak of World War II, France's invasion, total war, D-Day, the Battle of Normandy and hope for lasting world peace. A "good look round" takes several hours, an "in depth visit" all day. (Open all year, 9 am to 7 pm, tel: 31.06.06.44.)

A 15-minute drive down the N13 brings you to **Bayeux**, a lovely old town where inviting shops and honey-colored stone houses line narrow streets. St Patrice square is filled with colorful market stalls on Saturday and Wednesday mornings (the **Hôtel d'Argouges** is found here). There has been a town on this site since Roman times: it was invaded by the Bretons, the Saxons and the Vikings, but thankfully escaped the allied bombers. It's an excellent place for shopping and serves as a convenient base for visiting the Normandy landing beaches.

Apart from the town itself your premier destination in Bayeux is the **Musée de Tapisserie,** which displays the famous tapestry that Odo, Bishop of Bayeux, had the English embroider following the conquest of England by his half-brother William the Conqueror in 1066. The color and richness of the tapestry looks as though the little stick figures were just stitched yesterday, not 900 years ago. With the aid of earphones the intricately embroidered scenes come alive and we found we needed to go past it twice—once quickly to appreciate its enormous proportions and second to hear the story it tells. (Open all year, closed 12:30 pm to 2 pm except in summer, tel: 31.92.05.48, fax: 31.92.06.41.)

Next to the cathedral, the **Musée Baron Gérard** has some lovely examples of porcelain and lace manufactured in Bayeux. (Open all year, closed 12:30 pm to 2 pm except in summer, tel: 31.92.14.21.) On the main ring-road around the old town is the **1944 Battle of Normandy Museum** with its exhibitions of the tanks, guns, and armored vehicles used in the Battle of Normandy. (Open all year, closed 12:30 pm to 2 pm except in summer, tel: 31.92.93.41.)

Bayeux Tapestry

A ten-minute drive north brings you to **Arromanches** and the D-Day beaches. Arromanches is a lively seaside town where the broad crescent of golden sand was one of the D-Day landing beaches. In June 1944 a huge floating harbor was erected in a gigantic U in the bay. Designed by British engineers, the harbor was comprised of massive concrete blocks, floating pier-heads and 10 kilometers of floating pier "roads." It was towed across the channel and erected here enabling the Allies to unload half-a-million tons of materials in a three-month period. After 50 years of Atlantic storms much of the harbor is still in place and you can get an up-close look at several enormous sections marooned on the beach. Beside the beach is the **D-Day Museum** with its displays of models, photographs and films of the military operations of June 1944. (Closed January, and 11:30 am to 2 pm except in summer, tel: 31.22.34.31.)

Follow the ***Route de Debarquement***, a route that weaves you through little gray-stone villages whose tall walled farmhouses and barns form their own little fortifications amongst the fields. **Longues sur Mer** is the only naval artillery battery on the Normandy coast that still has its guns. Further on is the section where the American troops landed, just west of the lovely **Omaha Beach**; the Pointe du Hoc was captured on June 6, 1944 by American Rangers. All along this stretch of coast are military cemeteries—the final resting place for the Americans, British, Canadian, Polish and Germans who died. Above Omaha Beach, set in manicured parklike grounds, are row upon row of white crosses, memorials to over 9,000 Americans.

This itinerary concludes at Mont St Michel, a 120 kilometer drive from Caen (about two hours). Straddling the border of Brittany and Normandy **Mont St Michel** is France's most visited tourist attraction. Joined to the mainland by a narrow strip of roadway Mont St Michel clings to a rock island and towers 150 meters above sea level. Depending on the tide, it is either almost surrounded by water or by marshes and quicksand. Wander up the narrow cobblestoned streets to the crowning 12th-century abbey and visit the remarkable Gothic and Romanesque complex, culminating in the glories of the *Merveille* (Marvel)—the group of buildings on the north side of the mount. St Michael, the militant archangel, is the saint for the beaches you have just seen. It became a place of pilgrimage, a fortress, and in the 19th century a prison. Now it attracts throngs of tourists. On the left as you enter under the city gates is **Hôtel Mère Poulard** with its famous and incredibly expensive omelette restaurant. The preparation of the omelette can be seen from the street and is an attraction in itself. The eggs are whisked at a tempo and beat set by the chef and then cooked in copper pans over an open fire. Staying overnight on the island enables you to experience the town without the crushing daytime crowds and tours, and the Hôtel Mère Poulard is one of a handful of hotels that offers simple accommodation at an inflated tourist price.

From Mont St Michel you can return to Paris, join the *Châteaux Country* itinerary, or continue on the following itinerary into *Brittany.*

Mont St Michel

Normandy

Brittany

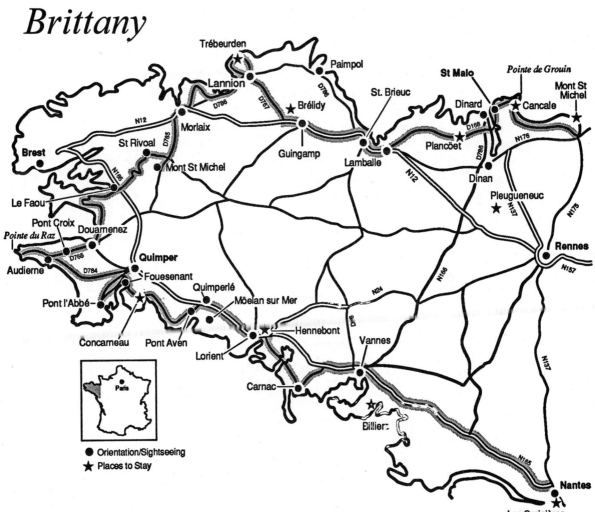

Trébeurden
Paimpol
Lannion
St Malo
Pointe de Grouin
D786
D767
Brélidy
St. Brieuc
Dinard
Cancale
Mont St Michel
N12
Morlaix
Lamballe
Plancöet
D168
D786
Brest
D785
Guingamp
N12
Dinan
N176
Mont St Michel
N165
N137
N175
Le Faou
Pleugueneuc
Pont Croix
Douarnenez
Pointe du Raz
D765
Quimper
Rennes
N166
N157
Audierne
D784
Fouesenant
Quimperlé
N24
Pont l'Abbé
Möelan sur Mer
Concarneau
Pont Aven
Hennebont
Vannes
Lorient
N137
Carnac
Billiers
N165
Nantes
Les Sorinières

Paris

● Orientation/Sightseeing
★ Places to Stay

27

Brittany

Brittany is a rugged region of beautiful forests bounded by nearly 1,000 kilometers of coastline. This peninsula, jutting out from the northwest side of France, was for many years isolated from the rest of the country and regarded by Bretons as a separate country. The regional language is Breton and you see signposting in both French and Breton. Most of the houses are fresh white stucco with angled blue-gray roofs. *Crêpes* filled with butter, sugar, chocolate or jam, or *gallettes* (wheat crêpes) enhanced with cheese, ham, onions or mushrooms, and cider are Brittany's culinary specialties. This itinerary begins on Brittany's border at Mont St Michel and explores the coast before it ventures into the forested interior, and culminates on her southern coast at Carnac with its mysterious fields of standing stones.

Mont St Michel

PACING: Select a location in northern Brittany for the northern portion of the itinerary and one on the southwestern coast for the southern portion. Two nights in each spot should give you ample time to explore the peninsula.

While **Mont St Michel** is technically in Normandy, it is geographically in Brittany. Mont St Michel is France's premier tourist attraction, and although it is wonderful, we thought it best to warn our readers that the effort of pushing your way uphill through teeming crowds, past souvenir shops, to reach the abbey at the summit is not enjoyable. The distinct appearance of the town is that of a child's sand castle, with narrow, cobblestoned streets winding up to the 12th-century abbey, crowned by the graceful church, dedicated to Archangel Michael. Depending on the tide the mount is either almost surrounded by water or by marshland and quicksand. Travel across the paved causeway that joins the mount to the mainland, park in the massive car park and explore on foot.

Leaving Mont St Michel take the D976 to Dol. Follow signposts for St Malo across the flat farmland to **Cancale** whose beachside port is full of lobsters, mussels, oysters, and clams, and whose attractive little town is nestled on the cliffs above.

Follow signposts for *St Malo par la Côte* to **Pointe du Grouin**, a windswept headland and promontory. Rounding the point you are rewarded by vistas of coastline stretching into the far distance.

St Malo corsairs were pirates with royal permission to take foreign ships and they handily menaced British seafarers during the 16th century. With its tall 13th- and 14th-century ramparts facing the sea and enormous harbor (the terminal of ferries from Portsmouth and the Channel Islands), the town is almost surrounded by water. Within the walls are narrow streets lined with interesting shops and small restaurants. Much was destroyed in battle between Germans and Americans in 1944 but it has all been magnificently restored. Walk round the walls (stairs by St Vincent's gate), visit the courtyard of the 14th-century castle (now the town hall) and sample *crêpes* or *gallettes*.

Follow the D168 cross the *barrière* (low pontoon bridge) over the bay to **Dinard**, a popular beach resort. Once a sleepy fishing village, a confusion of one-way streets and seafront hotels (blocking views) discourage you from leaving the main highway.

A 45-kilometer drive through Plancoët brings you to **Lamballe**. (Nearby at Pléven is **Manoir de Vaumadeuc**, a 15th-century manor house now a welcoming hotel.) At the heart of Lamballe's industrial sprawl are some fine old houses on the Place du Martrai, including the executioner's house that is now the tourist office. The traffic is congested.

Join the N12 bypassing St Brieuc and Guigamp (the town where gingham was first woven) and take the D767 northwest to Lannion. **Lannion** is an attractive town beside the fast flowing River Léguer with some fine medieval houses at its center, near the Place Général Leclerc. Follow signposts for Perros Guirac then **Trébeurden** which brings you to this attractive seaside resort. A small sheltered harbor is separated from a curve of sandy beach by a wooded peninsula, and overlooking the beach you find **Ti Al-Lannec,** one of our favorite hotels. Make your way back to Lannion along the beautiful stretch of coast and take the D786 towards Morlaix. At St Michel the road traces a vast sandy curve of beach and exposes vistas of succeeding headlands. Just as the road leaves the bay turn right following signposts for *Morlaix par la Côte,* which gives you the opportunity to sample another small stretch of very attractive coastline. At Locquirec turn inland through Guimaéc and Lanmeur to regain the D786 to Morlaix.

Morlaix is a central market town whose quays shelter boats that travel the passage inland from the sea. You do not have to deal with city traffic as you follow the N12 (signpost Brest) around the town for a short distance to the D785, signpost Pleyben Christ, which leads you into the ***Regional Parc D'Amorique***. After the very gray little towns of Pleyben Christ and Plounéour Ménez the scenery becomes more interesting as the road leads you up onto moorlands where rock escarpments jut out from atop the highest hill. A narrow road winds up to the little chapel high atop **Mont St Michel** (an isolated windswept spot very different from its famous namesake). Return to the D785 for a short distance taking the first right turn to **St Rivoal,** which has a *Maison Cornic,* a small park with an interesting collection of old Breton Houses.

Following signposts for Le Faou you travel up the escarpment to be rewarded by skywide views of the distant coast. Travel through **Forêt de Cranou** with its majestic oak trees to Le Faou where you continue straight (signpost Crozon). The route hugs the Aulne estuary and offers lovely vistas of houses dotting the far shore, then gives way to wooded fjords before crossing a high bridge and turning away from the coast. At Tar-ar-Groas make an almost 180-degree turn in the center of the village and continue the very pleasant drive following signposts for Douarnez, a large fishing port which you skirt on the D765 following signposts for Audierne. **Pont Croix** is built on terraces up from the River Goyen. Leading to the bridge, its photographic narrow streets are lined with old houses. **Audierne** is a pretty fishing port on the estuary of River Goyen where fishing boats bring in their harvest of lobsters, crayfish and tunny.

Your destination is **Pointe du Raz**, the Land's End of France. Thankfully it is less commercial than England's but it is certainly not isolated. Uniform sized white holiday cottages dot the landscape and a large café and grotesque museum lie at road's end. Ignoring the commercialism the views across the windswept headlands are spectacular. This journey is not recommended in the height of summer when the roads are congested.

An hours drive (60 kilometers D784) brings you to the large town of **Quimper,** set where the Odet and Steir rivers meet. Park by the river, wander the town's pleasant streets and visit the **Musée de Faience**, with its displays of attractive regional pottery (tel: 98.90.12.72).

This itinerary now explores Brittany's southern coast. The individual towns are very attractive but we were disappointed not to find more countryside between them. Your first stop is **Pont L'Abbé**, set deep in a sheltered estuary. The squat castle contains a museum of costume and furniture, with some fine examples of the tall white lace coiffes that women wear on their heads for festivals. (Open June to mid-September, closed noon to 3 pm, tel: 98.827.24.44.) A pleasant park borders the river and the town square has a large covered market.

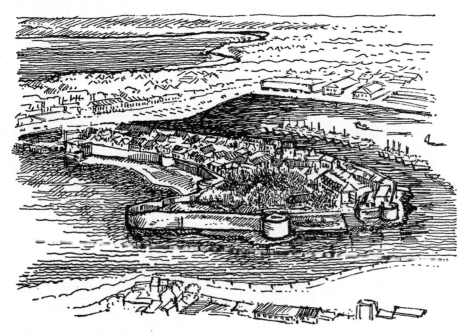

Concarneau, Ville Close

Cross the high bridge that spans the River Odet and catch a panoramic view of **Benodet.** If you go into its crowded streets follow signs for the port, which brings you to its yacht harbor—from here the coast road weaves past sandy bays and holiday hotels to the casino. In summer do not tackle the crowded streets, just admire the town from the bridge.

Ten kilometers away lies **Fouesnant,** a traditional center for cider production. Its pretty port **La Forét Fousenant,** with its harbor full of yachts and small arc of golden sand, lies just a few kilometers away. Leaving the village follow signs for *Concarneau par la Côte* which quickly takes you on a scenic back road into town.

Ignore **Concarneau's** bustling town, and park by the harbor as close as possible to *Ville Close,* the 14th-century walled town that sits amidst a vast harbor of colorful boats varying from sleek yachts to commercial fishing trawlers. The old town, with its narrow streets and old houses full of creperies and gift shops, is fun to explore. Visit the interesting **Musée de la Pêche** covering all things nautical inside and with three old fishing boats tied up outside of what was once the town's arsenal. (Open all year, closed 12:30 to 2:30 pm except July and August, tel: 98.97.10.20.) Climbing the walls gives you good views of the inner harbor where fishing boats unload their catch. (Open all year, closed 12:30 pm to 2:30 pm except July and August, tel: 98.50.38.38.)

The D783 brings you to **Pont Aven,** a pretty resort by the River Aven made famous by Gaugin and his school of artists who moved here in the 1890's. Gaugin with his bohemian ways was not popular with the locals and he soon moved on. There are a great many galleries and in summer it's a colorful and crowded spot.

Turning inland the D783 brings you to **Quimperlé** (20 kilometers) where the rivers Ellé and Isole converge to form the Lafta. One of the town's central streets is cobbled and lined with old houses. From here head through the large town of Hennebont for the 27 kilometer (D9 and D781) drive to the rather dull seaside town of **Carnac.** In the windswept fields on the edge of town are over 2,700 standing stones (*menhirs*) arranged in lines (*alignements*). The stones are believed to have been erected between 2,000 BC and 4,000 BC. They consist of three groups of stones each arranged in patterns of 10 to 13 rows. The area is somewhat divided by country roads but the site is large enough that you can meander around and enjoy the groupings unhindered by the milling crowds and ticket barriers that impede your enjoyment of the British counterpart, Stonehenge. The

Musée de Préhistoire will help you interpret the stones. (Closed Tuesdays, and noon to 2 pm, tel: 97.52.22.04.)

Leaving Carnac follow signposts to **Vannes**, the region's largest city, complete with all the traffic and navigation headaches that plague so many downtown areas. The old walled town grouped around **St Peter's Cathedral** is delightful. The cathedral was built between the 13th and 19th centuries and has a great mixture of styles. The nearby parliament building has been converted to a covered market for artists, leatherworkers, metalworkers, and crêperies. There is a maze of old streets with beautiful timbered and gabled houses. Market day is Wednesday and Saturday on the Place des Lices.

From Vannes the N165 whisks you around Nantes and onto the A11 which brings you to Angers, a convenient point to join our *Châteaux Country* itinerary.

Carnac

Châteaux Country

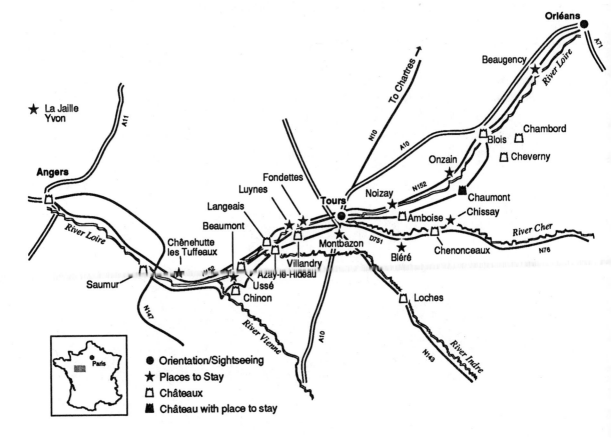

La Jaille Yvon

River Loire   A11

Angers

Orléans

A71

Beaugency

River Loire

To Chartres

N10   A10

Blois   Chambord

Cheverny

Onzain

Chaumont

Noizay   N152

Chissay

Fondettes   Tours

Luynes   Amboise   River Cher

Langeais

Beaumont   Montbazon   Bléré   Chenonceaux   N76

Chênehutte   Villandry

les Tuffeaux   Azay-le-Rideau   D751

Saumur   Ussé   Loches

N152   Chinon   River Vienne   A10

N147   River Indre

N143

Paris

● Orientation/Sightseeing

★ Places to Stay

🏰 Châteaux

🏰 Château with place to stay

Châteaux Country

A highlight of any holiday in France is a visit to the elegant châteaux of the Loire River Valley. This itinerary suggests a route for visiting the châteaux based on a logical sequence assuming Paris as a starting point. There are over 1,000 châteaux along the Loire River between Nantes and Orléans, and over 100 are open to the public. For the purposes of this itinerary *Châteaux Country* stretches from Angers to Orléans. Most of the châteaux were built for love not war and they range from traditional castles and grandiose homes, to romantic ruins. We try to paint a picture of what you will see when you tour each château. In our opinion the best are Azay le Rideau and Chenonceaux. Be forewarned that in July and August you will be caught up in a crush of visitors.

Chambord

PACING: Any hotel from Map 6B makes an ideal base for exploring the *Châteaux Country*. Please do not try to visit all our châteaux sightseeing selections, it would be just too many châteaux for one holiday. Rather, read our descriptions and choose those that appeal most to you. As we do not tell you how to get from château to château, we recommend Michelin map 64 with a scale of 1/200,000 (1 cm = 2 km) for outlining your route. Three nights in the region should give you all the time you need—one can only visit so many châteaux. Allow more if you are an avid fan of French furniture, or the like, and want to explore properties in depth.

Many visitors spend time in Paris before coming to *Châteaux Country*. An excellent sightseeing venue on the way to the Loire from Paris is **Chartres**, about an hour and a half southwest of Paris (97 kilometers). **Chartres Cathedral** towers high above the town. Inside, the three 13th-century stained glass windows dapple the church with color and light. It's a magnificent edifice and on most days you find the redoubtably British Malcolm Miller describing the history and design of this marvelous cathedral, his knowledge of Chartres giving an added dimension to any visit. If you would like to arrange a personal tour, you can write to him care of Chartres' Tourist Office, Place Cathédrale, 2800 Chartres, tel: 37.21.50.00. The old city, surrounding the cathedral, has been lovingly restored and it's delightful to explore its old winding streets.

From Chartres the N10 takes you to Tours (130 kilometers, about a 2-hour drive). Located at the junction of the Cher and Loire rivers, Tours is a convenient starting point for exploring *Châteaux Country*.

Begin your adventures in the Loire Valley by a visit to **Langeais**, one of the region's smaller châteaux. Remarkably it has not been altered since it was built between 1465 and 1471 for Louis XI as defense against Bretons. It is beautifully furnished and wax figurines commemorate the royal wedding of Charles VIII and Anne of Brittany that took place on a cold December morning in 1491. On a nearby ridge are the ruins of a 10th-century stone *donjon* or keep, one of Europe's first. It was a stronghold of the notorious Fulk Nerra the Black, Count of Anjou. (Open all year, closed Mondays and noon to 2 pm November to mid-March, tel: 47.96.72.60.)

Angers was the former capital of the Dukes of Anjou. Now it is a city full of factories with an old city and its 13th-century fortress at its heart. During the 16th century many of the seventeen massive towers were dismantled, on royal command, to the level of the wall-walk. The castle has some spectacular displays of tapestries, including the Apocalypse tapestry, the longest ever woven in France, displayed in a special gallery. It was originally 164 meters long but during the Revolution it was thrown over the walls into the street and citizens snipped bits off. In 1843 the Bishop managed to repiece two-thirds of it and about 100 meters are on display. (Open all year, closed noon to 2 pm except July and August, tel: 47.87.43.47.)

Saumur lies on the edge of the Loire River. Rising from the town are the walls of Saumur Castle, a 14th-century fortification built atop a sheer cliff. There are spectacular views from the walls and an interesting museum of ceramics and horses. Lovely tapestries hang in the church. In 1811 Laurence Ackerman, who hailed from Alsace, showed the locals how to put *mousseux* (sparkle) in their wines. It's an enjoyable local drink but no substitute for champagne. (Closed November to April, and 11:30 am to 2:30 pm except mid-June to mid-September, tel: 41.51.30.46.)

Chinon is a huge crumbling fortress set high above the River Vienne, with a medieval town and tree-lined boulevard at its feet. Henry II of England died here, his son Richard the Lionheart owned it, King John lost it to the French, and Joan of Arc came here to plead with Charles VII for an army. It is an interesting walk around the skeleton of this fortification, but be prepared to fill in large chunks of the interior with your imagination. There is an interesting museum celebrating Joan of Arc. (Open all year, closed noon to 2 pm October to March, tel: 47.93.13.45.)

Ussé overlooks the River Indre and is everything you expect a château to be with turrets, towers, chimneys, dormers and enchantment. The house is completely furnished in period style, illustrating the way things were in the 16th and 17th centuries complete with wax figurines dressed in period costume. Magnificent Flemish tapestries grace the Great Gallery and while you are waiting for your guided tour (narrated in French with English description sheets) you can climb the tower whose turret rooms are furnished with scenes from *Sleeping Beauty*. Conjecture has it that Ussé was the château that inspired Perault to write the famous fairytale. (Closed November to mid-March, and noon to 2 pm, tel: 47.95.54.05.)

Azay le Rideau

Azay Le Rideau and its elegant Renaissance château are not far from Ussé. Azay le Rideau's graceful facade is framed by wispy trees and is reflected in its lake and the River Indre, from whose banks it rises on one side. It was built by Gilles Berthelot, the treasurer to Francis I between 1518 and 1527. Francis accused Gilles of fiddling the nation's books and confiscated this ornate château. It was not until the 19th century that it was completed. You can accompany a knowledgeable guide on a detailed tour or explore on your own, walking from one showpiece room to the next admiring the fine furniture and tapestries. This is one of our favorite châteaux in the Loire Valley. (Open all year, closed 12:30 pm to 2 pm November to March, tel: 47.45.42.04.)

Villandry is known for its formal, geometric French gardens. Even the paths are raked into designs. While you can tour the house, the real reason for visiting Villandry is to spend time in the gardens wandering the little paths between the neatly clipped boxed hedges. Even the vegetable garden has been planted to produce geometric patterns. Be sure to capture the garden from the upper terrace which gives you a bird's-eye view of this colorful quilt. (Gardens open all year, house open mid-March to mid-November, tel: 47.50.02.09.)

Southeast of Montbazon is the town of **Loches**, found in the hills along the banks of the Indre, and referred to as the "City of Kings." The ancient castle is the "Acropolis of the Loire"; the buildings around it form what is called *Haute Ville*. It was a favorite retreat of King Charles VII and here you will find a copy of the proceedings of Joan of Arc's trial. The king's mistress, Agnes Sorel, is buried in the tower and her portrait is in one of the rooms. (Open all year, closed noon to 2 pm except July and August, tel: 47.59.07.86.)

Chenonceaux

Chenonceaux almost spans the River Cher and is without a doubt one of the loveliest of the Loire Valley's châteaux. This château owes a great deal to each of its six female occupants. Catherine Briconnet built Chenonceaux as a home, not a fortification. Sexy Diane de Poitiers, the mistress of Henry II, added a garden and the bridge between the house and the banks of the River Cher. When Henry died his jealous wife, Catherine de Medici, took it back and consigned Diane to Château Chaumont. Catherine had the gallery built on the bridge, laid out the park and held decadent parties. She bequeathed her home to Louise de Lorraine, her daughter-in-law. After her husband's death Louise retired here and went into mourning for the rest of her life. In 1733 it passed to Monsieur Dupin whose intellectual wife was so beloved by the locals that it escaped the Revolution unscathed. In 1864 it was bought by Madame Peolouze who made it her life's work to restore her home. The château is now the home of the Menier family. Chenonceaux merits a leisurely visit, you want to allocate at least two hours for wandering through the park, gardens and its elegant interior. The grounds also contain a wax museum with scenes from the château's history. (Open all year, 9 am to 5 pm tel: 47.23.90.07.)

Just a few kilometers north of Chenonceaux is the striking castle of **Amboise**. A tour of this large property will fill you with tales of grandeur, intrigue and gruesome goings on. Francis I loved to party, he reveled in grand balls, masquerades, festivals and tournaments. He invited Leonardo da Vinci here and the artist spent his last years at the neighboring manor **Clos Lucé**. You can see his bedroom, models of machines he invented and copies of his drawings. Catherine de Medici brought her young son, Francis II and his young bride Mary, later Queen of Scots, to Amboise when the Protestants rose up after the St Bartholomew massacre. The Amboise Conspiracy of 1560 involved a group of Protestant reformers who followed the royal court from Blois to Amboise under the pretense of asking the king for permission to practice their religion. However, their plot was betrayed to the powerful Duke of Guise (Scarface) and upon arrival they were tortured, hung from the battlements and left twisting in pain for days. The court and the royal family would come out to watch them. (Open all year, closed noon to 2 pm except July and August, tel: 47.57.00.98.)

From Amboise follow the Loire River to **Chaumont**, a château that has more appeal viewed from across the Loire River than up close. Catherine de Medici was supposedly living here when her husband Henry II was killed and she became Regent. She supposedly bought the château so that she could swap it with Diane de Poitiers (her husband's mistress) for Chenonceaux. Diane found it did not match up to Chenonceaux and left—you can understand why. Later Benjamin Franklin paid a visit to sit for an Italian Sculptor who had set up his headquarters in the stables. Approached across a drawbridge the château has three wings—the fourth side was pulled down in 1739 opening up to a fine view of the Loire Valley. You can tour the apartments and the stables. (Open all year, closed 11:45 am to 1:45 pm, tel: 54.20.98.03.)

Blois sits on the north bank of the Loire River. The Chamber of the States General and part of a tower are all that remains of the 13th-century fortification that occupied this site. Much of the magnificent edifice you see today is due to Francis I trying to keep his brother Gaston d'Orléans (who was always conspiring against him) out of trouble. In 1662 he banished him to Blois and gave him the project of restoring the château. Gaston hired the famous architect Mansart. The château has its stories of love, intrigue and politicking but its most famous is the murder of the Duke of Guise. In 1688 the powerful Henri de Guise called States General here with the intention of deposing Henry III and making himself king. Henry found out about the plot and murdered the Duke. Who did what and where is explained in great detail on the tour. The most interesting room on the tour is Catherine de Médici's bedchamber with its many secret wall panels, used in the true Médici tradition, to hide jewels, documents and poisons. (Open all year, closed noon to 2 pm October to mid-March, tel: 54.78.06.62.)

Ten kilometers from Blois lies **Cheverny**, a château that was built in 1634 for the Hurault family. It is smaller than Blois and Chambord and more interesting to tour because it still has its 17th-century decorations and furnishings. The Hurault family have carefully preserved their inheritance with its exquisite painted woodwork, tapestries and furniture. The kennels in the grounds are home to 70 hounds and watching them patiently line up for dinner is a popular event (April to mid-September except Sundays 5 pm, otherwise 3 pm except Tuesdays and weekends). In another outbuilding is a collection of 2,000 deer antlers—the family's hunting trophies. (Open all year, closed noon to 2:15 pm except June to mid-September, tel: 54.79.96.29.)

Cheverny

Standing on a grassy expanse amidst vast acres of forest, **Chambord** is enormous. Francis I built Chambord as a hunting lodge but he believed that bigger was better so the vast edifice has 440 rooms and 80 staircases. Francis only spent 40 days at his huge home that now has far less furniture than many other properties and is owned by the state. Apart from its impressive size and isolated location Chambord's most interesting feature is the double spiral staircase in the center of the building. (Open all year, closed 12:30 to 2 pm September to May, tel: 54.20.31.32.)

The last stretch along the Loire takes you to the lovely old town of **Beaugency** with its historic church, **Notre Dame**. A magnificent bridge with 22 arches spans the river. The French blew it apart in 1940 to delay the Germans. It has been completely restored (the central arches are original) and provides an ideal viewpoint for looking at the river and this delightful little town with its narrow medieval streets.

Orléans is a modern town rebuilt after World War II destruction. Here was the scene of Joan of Arc's greatest triumph, when she successfully drove the English from France in 1429. There is little left for Joan of Arc fans to visit except her statue in Place Martoi.

From Orléans it is a 120-kilometer drive on the autoroute A10 back to Paris.

Dordogne & Lot River Valleys

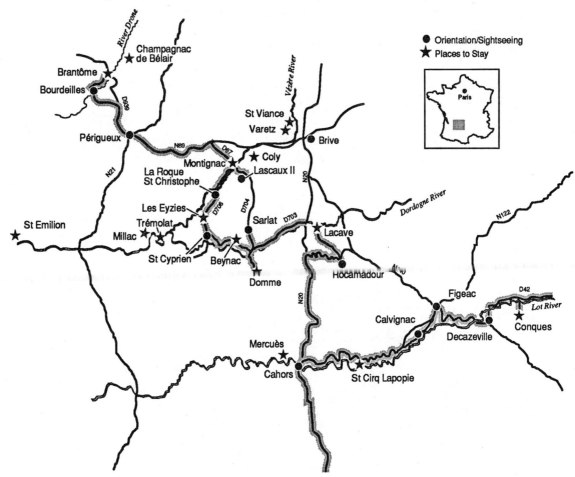

● Orientation/Sightseeing
★ Places to Stay

River Drône

Champagnac
de Bélair

Brantôme

Bourdeilles

Périgueux

N89

D939

N21

St Viance
Varetz

Brive

Coly

Montignac
La Roque
St Christophe
Lascaux II

D67

D704

D706

Les Eyzies

Trémolat

Millac

St Cyprien

Sarlat

D703

Beynac

Domme

Lacave

Rocamadour

St Emilion

Vézère River

Dordogne River

N122

N20

N20

Figeac

Calvignac

Decazeville

D42

Lot River

Conques

Mercuès

Cahors

St Cirq Lapopie

Paris

Dordogne & Lot River Valleys

The lazy Dordogne and Lot Rivers wind gracefully through some of France's most picturesque countryside past villages dressed with grand castles, through peaceful meadows dotted with farms, beneath towering cliffs and into pretty woodlands. But this itinerary is more than just traveling along river valleys for the Dordogne region is France's prehistoric capital: the cro-magnon skull was discovered at Les Eyzies; colorful 15,000-year-old paintings decorate the Lascaux, Font de Gaum and Les Combarelles caves; and man occupied the terraces on the cliffside of La Roque St Christophe as long ago as 70,000 BC. Visit Rocamadour, an ancient village that tumbles down a rocky canyon, and Conques, a medieval village on a dramatic hillside site.

Dordogne River from Domme

PACING: You could happily spend a week in the Dordogne, venturing along the river valley then adding unscheduled meanderings up little side roads to country villages. For the purposes of this itinerary base a night or two in the northern region, two to three nights close to the river itself (more if you make reservations at several of the caves), and then at least one night along the Lot River (optional) and a night at the hillside village of Conques.

In the northern region of the Dordogne, **Brantôme** is a delightful little town on the banks of the River Dronne with narrow winding streets, and a riverside park which leads you across the famous 16th-century elbow bridge to the old abbey, nestled at the foot of a rocky cliff. Founded by Charlemagne in 769, the abbey was reconstructed in the 11th century after it was ransacked by the Normans. The church and adjoining buildings were constructed and modified between the 14th and 18th centuries. Also beside the ancient bridge is the delightful **Le Moulin de l'Abbaye**. If you love to stay in historic mills, **Le Moulin du Roc** is found just a short distance from Brantôme, tucked away on a small country road on the outskirts of Champagnac de Bélair.

Follow the River Dronne for 10 kilometers on the D78 into the very pretty village of Bourdeilles. A little bridge takes you across the river to its 12th-century castle that the English and French squabbled about for years. From Bourdeilles country roads direct you to the D939 that takes you into Périgueux.

Périgueux changed sides twice in the 100 Years War, eventually opting for France. It's a pleasant large town with an interesting domed cathedral resplendent with little turrets. From Périgueux follow signposts towards Brive (D47) and at Thenon take the D67 to Montignac (40 kilometers).

Montignac is a popular tourist town because on its outskirts are the wondrous Lascaux caves with their magnificent 15,000-year-old paintings. In 1963 these caves were closed to the public because the paintings were being damaged by the rise and fall in temperature as hordes of visitors came and went. It took ten years to construct an exact replica—**Lascaux II**. Except for the even non-slip floor you will not know that you are not in the real Lascaux. The bulls, bison and stags appear to be moving around the cave—so skillfully did the artists utilize every feature of the rocks so that bumps appear as humps, cheekbones and haunches. In July and August the quota of 2,000 tickets a day go on sale at 9 am at the *Syndicat d'Initiative* (Tourist Office) in Montignac. Tickets are not available in advance. For the rest of the year tickets are sold at the site on a first come, first served basis, so you may arrive at 11 am and find that you are offered a 4 pm tour. Tours are offered in English and French.

Leaving Lascaux II watch for signs that will direct you to Le Thot along the D65. The admission ticket for Lascaux includes admission to **Le Thot** where you can see a film of the building of Lascaux II and displays of large photos of the many prehistoric paintings found in caves in the valley. The grounds also have a park and a recreation of a prehistoric village.

Leaving Le Thot follow signposts for **La Roque St Christophe**. As the road winds by the river a sheer cliff rises to a deep natural terrace before continuing upwards. As long ago as 70,000 BC man took advantage of this natural terrace for shelter and by medieval times it was home to over 1,000 people. The thousands of niches that you see today were used to hold up supporting beams for the houses and the rings you see carved into the rock were used to hang lamps and to tether animals. (Open mid-June to September 25th, closed noon to 2 pm, tel: 53.50.70.45.)

Following the winding River Vézère the D706 brings you into **Les Eyzies**. The caves in the cliff that towers above the town were home to prehistoric man who took shelter here during the second Ice Age. People lived here for tens of thousands of years. Archaeologists have uncovered flints, pottery, jewelry, and the skeletons that have been identified as those of the cro-magnon man found in the cave behind the hotel of the same name. Visit the **Musée National de Préhistoire** in the 11th-century castle set high on the cliff beneath the overhanging rock, guarded by the gigantic sculpture of Neanderthal Man. (Open mid-June to September 25th, closed noon to 2 pm, tel: 53.50.70.45.)

Nearby the **Font de Gaum** cave has prehistoric wall paintings of horses, bison, mammoths and reindeer with colors still so rich that it is hard to comprehend the actual passage of time. The caves are a bit damp and dark and entail a steep 400 meters climb to reach the entrance. The grotto is deep, winding and narrow in parts. There are some 230 drawings, of which about 30 are presented and discussed. Displayed in three tiers, some drawings are marred by graffiti, others are not clearly visible as the walls tower above the floor of the cave. The tour highlights about 30 friezes. Entrance is limited to 200 people per day but you can make reservations in advance by calling Les Eyzies, tel: 53.06.90.80. There is a small additional charge for advance booking. The caves are open all year (10 am to noon, 2 pm to 5 pm—later in September) but closed every Tuesday. With the closure of more caves each year we cannot be certain how much longer this opportunity will continue.

A short distance from Font de Guam is **Les Combarelles**, a cave discovered in 1901. The entrance is about a 100 meter (level) walk from the carpark. The cave is a winding passage with engravings of mammoth, ibex, bears, reindeer, bison and horses, and man in the last 70 meters. Entrance is limited to 100 visitors per day and it's closed every Wednesday. Advance booking and hours of opening are identical to Font de Gaum.

From Les Eyzies follow the scenic D706 to **Campagne** with its abandoned château sitting behind padlocked gates. From Campagne take the scenic D35 to **St Cyprien**, an attractive town just a short distance from the Dordogne River. It has more shops and cafés than most small towns in the valley, making it an attractive place to break your journey.

Through pretty countryside follow the Dordogne River Valley, just out of sight of the river. As you approach **Beynac** you are presented with a lovely picture of a small village huddled beneath a cliff crowned by a 12th-century fortress before a broad sweep of the

Dordogne River. The castle is being restored and while its furnishings are sparse it is well worth visiting for the spectacular views. (Open March to October.) On the water's

edge is **Hôtel Bonnet**, run for generations by the Bonnet family. It's an excellent choice for lunch under vine-covered trellises or a stay in the hotel's simple, reasonably priced bedrooms.

Have your cameras ready as you approach **La Roque Gageac**. The town, clinging to the hillside above the Dordogne River and framed by lacy trees, is a photographer's dream. There's a grassy area on the river bank with a few picnic tables and an inviting path, following the curves of the river, tempts you further.

Beynac

Just upstream cross the bridge and climb the hill to **Domme**, a medieval walled village that has for centuries stood guard high above the river and commanded a magnificent panorama. The town itself is enchanting, with ramparts that date from the 13th century, and narrow streets that wind through its old quarter and past a lovely 14th-century **Hôtel de Ville**. At the town center under the old market place, you find access to some interesting stalactite and stalagmite grottos. But most visitors come to Domme for its spectacular views—the best vantage point is from the *Terrasse de la Barre*. Very near to *la Barre*, facing the church, is **Hôtel de l'Esplanade**, an ideal place to stay if you want to enjoy the village after the crowds have departed.

Because it is more scenic on the north side of the river, retrace your steps across the bridge and continue down river on the D703 to **Château de Montfort**, a majestic castle shadowing a wide loop in the river. Built by one of the region's most powerful barons, this intimate, restored castle, furnished like a private residence, rises out of a rocky ledge. The ***Cingle de Montfort*** offers some delightful views of the river.

When the D703 intersects with the D704, take a short detour north to the city of **Sarlat**. Sarlat has a delightful old quarter with narrow cobbled streets that wind through a maze of magnificent gourmet shops. The church and the Episcopal palace create a roomy space along the narrow bustling streets.

After visiting Sarlat return to the banks of the Dordogne and continue east once again along its shore, this time in the direction of Souillac. When the D703 comes to an end, travel south (right) in the direction of Cahors. As you leave houses behind you turn left on the D43 (rather than crossing the river) and begin a very picturesque stretch of the valley. As you cross a single lane wooden bridge that spans the Dordogne take note of the picture-postcard **Château de la Treyne** perched above the riverbank. **Lacave** is also known for some spectacular geological formations in its caves that you can tour on a diminutive train.

Climbing out of Lacave towards Rocamadour the fields are filled with bustling geese being fattened for *foie gras* and you are offered a picturesque viewpoint of a castle sitting high above the distant Dordogne River. A scenic country road winds to where the ground disappears into an abyss and the village of **Rocamadour** tumbles down the narrow canyon. Our preference is to park in the large car park adjacent to the castle, but if it is full, head for the valley floor and park in one of the grassy car parks. A stairway leads down from beside the castle to the chapels, houses and narrow streets that cling precipitously to the rock face. From the 12th century onwards Rocamadour was a popular pilgrimage site. The stairs lead you to her little chapels and large basilica that incorporates the cliff face as one wall of the building. Of course there are lots of tourist shops and, thankfully, cafés offering a spot to sit and rest after climbing up and down the staircases. If steep climbs are not for you, buy a ticket on the elevator that goes up and down the hillside.

St Cirq Lapopie

From Rocamadour, travel a rocky valley (D673) west to Payrac (21 kilometers) where you join the N20 for the scenic 50 kilometers drive to Cahors where you join the Lot River Valley. Arriving at the outskirts of Cahors turn left following signposts for Figeac along the north bank of the river.

This portion of the **Lot Valley** can be driven in half a day on roads that wind along a riverbank that is narrower and quieter than that of the Dordogne. It winds along the curves of the wide, calm river, cutting into the chalky canyon walls. At some stretches the route follows the level of the river and at others it straddles the cliff tops. Vistas are dramatic at every turn although the restricting narrow roads will frustrate the eye of any photographer because there is rarely a place to stop.

Cross the river at **Bouzies** and take a moment to look back across the bridge and see the medieval buildings constructed into the walls of the canyon above the small tunnel. Just outside Bouzies, the road (D40) climbs and winds precipitously to the top of the cliff and rounding a bend, **St Cirq Lapopie** clings precipitously to the sheer canyon walls and cascades back down towards the river. Drive around the village to one of the carparks and walk back up the hill to explore. Many of the buildings have been restored and only a few of the houses are lived in. It's most enjoyable to wander the quiet streets without being overwhelmed by tourist shops. You can spend the night here at **Hôtel de la Pélissaria**, an engaging inn with idyllic views of this village perched high above a wide band of the meandering Lot River.

Travel down to the Lot River and cross to its northernmost bank. As the river guides you further, it presents a number of lovely towns and with each turn reveals another angle and view of the valley. **La Toulzanie** is a small, pretty village nestled into a bend of the river, interesting because of its houses built into the limestone cliffs. **Calvignac** is an ancient village clinging to the top of the cliff on the opposite bank. At Cajarc be careful to keep to the river road (D662). A short drive brings you to the village of **Montbrun**, a village that rises in tiers on jutting rock by steep cliffs. It looks down on the Lot, up at its ruined castle and across the river to *Saut de la Mounine* (Jump of the Monkey). It seems that to punish his daughter for falling in love with the son of a rival baron, father ordered daughter to be thrown from the cliffs. A monkey was dressed in her clothes and thrown to its death instead. Father, regretting his harsh judgment, was overcome with joy when he discovered the substitution. Set on a plateau, the **Château de Larroque Toirac** is open to visitors and makes an impressive silhouette against the chalky cliffs and the village of **St Pierre Toirac**.

Continue on to Conques, a bonus to this itinerary that requires that you journey further along the winding Lot River (N140 signpost Decazeville and then D963 and D42 signpost Entraygues). The route weaves through some beautiful farmland and attractive little villages. At La Vinzelle leave the Lot River Valley and climb up the D901 to **Conques**, a tiny medieval town on a dramatic hillside site. Tucked a considerable distance off the beaten track, it is a delightful, unspoiled village that was once an important pilgrimage stop on the way to Santiago de Compostela in Spain. Conques' pride is its 11th-century **Abbaye Ste Foy** whose simple rounded arches give it the look of a Gothic cathedral. The carving of the Last Judgment in a semi-circle over the central door shows Christ presiding over the Last Judgment. Of the 124 characters the grimacing devils and tortured souls are far more amusing than the somber few who are selected to go to heaven. Its treasure is the 10th-century Ste Foy reliquary, a statue sheathed in gold leaf and decorated with precious stones. Directly across from the abbey is the **Hôtel Ste Foy** and on a nearby cobblestoned street lies **Hôstellerie de l'Abbaye**.

Conques

Gorges du Tarn

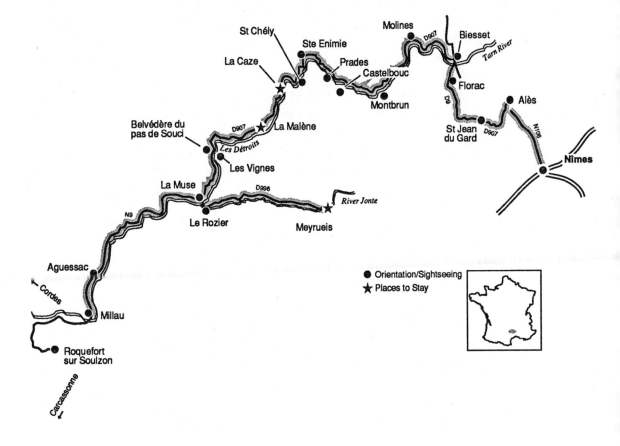

Molines
Biesset
D907
Tarn River
St Chély
Ste Enimie
La Caze
Prades
Castelbouc
Florac
Montbrun
D907
La Malène
D9
Belvédère du
pas de Souci
Les Détroits
Alès
St Jean
du Gard
D907
N106
Les Vignes
La Muse
Nîmes
D996
River Jonte
Le Rozier
Meyrueis
N9
Aguessac
Cordes
Millau
Roquefort
sur Soulzon
Carcassonne

● Orientation/Sightseeing
★ Places to Stay

Gorges du Tarn

This itinerary follows the truly spectacular River Tarn as it winds back and forth along the Tarn Canyon or *Gorges du Tarn*. With each turn the drive becomes more beautiful, never monotonous. The road cuts through the canyon, hugging its walls, always in sight of the peaceful waters of the Tarn and the picturesque village clusters of warm stone buildings that nestle above its shore. Encased in deep limestone cliffs, the river canyon is at its most glorious in early autumn—a perfect time to visit. In the fall the traffic has subsided and nature's colors contrast beautifully with the canyon walls: grass carpeting the mountains and hillsides are lush, all shades of green, and the trees blaze gold, red and orange in the sunlight. But whatever time of year, the Gorges du Tarn is lovely.

Gorges du Tarn

PACING: This itinerary covers approximately 220 kilometers and can be driven in about 4 hours. The stretch along the canyon from Florac to Millau covers approximately 75 kilometers, is sometimes crowded, often narrows to two lanes, and there are no short cuts once you're following the river. If you plan to cover the distance in a day's journey, get an early start. We suggest that you overnight in proximity to the river and give yourself two full days to drive, walk, picnic, and even float your way through the Tarn Canyon.

With either **Avignon** or **Nîmes** on the western edge of Provence as a point of reference, travel northwest in the direction of Alès. Using a good map to plan the best route depending on your origin, travel southwest of Alès to the D907, traveling north in the direction of St Jean du Gard. **St Jean du Gard** is a very scenic village, located just before the **Corniche des Cevennes**. Just outside of St Jean du Gard you are faced with the option of traveling the Corniche along the canyon's south or north rim. This itinerary travels the D9 which follows the north rim and is the more scenic and better of the two roads. The drive is lovely, traveling through and above the forests of the region. At the northern tip of the corniche the road number changes from D9 to D983 and travels 6 kilometers to the junction of D907. Follow the D907 north just over 5 kilometers to **Florac** and then join the N106 continuing north in the direction of Mende, but at the tiny village of Biesset veer off and head west on the D907 bis. It is here that your true journey of the Tarn Canyon begins. To appreciate the region you need to simply travel it: each turn affords a lovely vista or breathtakingly beautiful portrait of a hillside village. Opportunities to stop along the roadside are limited and will frustrate most photographers, but drive it leisurely and stop when possible to explore the little hamlets. The following is an overview of the river and its path, and some of its most picturesque highlights. With a good map in hand, enjoy its scenic journey.

The Ispagnac Basin, located at the entrance to the canyon, is filled with fruit trees, vineyards and strawberries. Here towns are scattered artistically about; châteaux and ruins appear often enough to add enchantment. A lovely wide bridge spans the river at **Ispagnac** and further along at **Molines**, set in the bend of the river, the canyon boasts a picturesque mill and castle. As the road hugs the hillside, the picturesque town of **Montbrun** blends into the hillside on the opposite side of the river. The road then narrows and winds along the base of the canyon, looking up to rugged canyon walls and down to stretches of green along the river's edge. **Castelbouc,** on the other side of the river, is idyllically nestled on the hillside and is spectacular when illuminated on summer evenings. Just a short distance further past Castelbouc the road carves a path to the north and another scenic overlook is afforded of the neighboring castle of **Prades.** One of the larger towns in the region, **Ste Énimie,** is a pretty village caught in the bend of the canyon. An old attractive bridge arches across the river and a church wedged into the mountainside piques the curiosity. From Ste Énimie the road cuts into the canyon walls and tunnels through nature's wall colored in orange, gold and green. **St Chély du Tarn** is nestled on the sides of the canyon wall above the river, and is illuminated in a spectacle of sound and light. A short distance south of St Chély, majestically positioned above the Tarn, is a fairytale castle offering accommodation, the **Château de la Caze.**

From the spectacular setting of La Caze, the road follows the river as it bends past the **Château Hauterlves** and then passes through the lovely and probably most active village on the river bank, the village of **La Malène.** Many companies offer raft, kayak and canoe trips that depart from La Malène. You have a better view of some of the old medieval towns and a section of the Tarn referred to as **Les Détroits,** the Straits, not visible from the road. Here the river is only a few meters wide, towered by canyon cliffs rising more than 300 meters straight above. From La Malène, the road winds through the canyon rock and a cluster of buildings appear huddled on the other bank, just at the entrance to Les Détroits. Further on, numerous buses stop at **Belvédère du Pas de Souci** and you can join the crowds for a 2F admission fee to climb the steep metal stairway to views of the water pools below. From Pas de Souci, the river widens and the canyon walls turn to gentle slopes at the town of **Les Vignes.** From the little village of Les Vignes it is worth a short detour following signs to the **Point Sublime.** It is a steep climb up to one of the most impressive viewpoints of the canyon 400 meters above the river.

Carcassonne

Cross the river at La Muse to the village of **Le Rozier,** which enjoys a pretty setting at the junction of the Tarn and Jonte Rivers. From Le Rozier you have a couple of options to extend your visit in this lovely region before continuing along the D907 the last 20 kilometers along the Tarn River to Millau. You can venture east along the D996, a narrow, often roughly paved road following the dramatic **Gorges de la Jonte** to Meyrueis. Overpowered by the towering Jonte Canyon walls, the picturesque village buildings of **Meyrueis** lie approximately 21 kilometers east of Le Rozier and huddle together along the banks of the Jonte. A farm road's distance from this quaint village is the enchanting **Château d'Ayres.** Tucked away on its own expanse of rich grounds, this enchanting hotel offers a lovely peaceful escape. From Le Rozier you can also follow a narrow winding road a long, twisting, 10 kilometers south to **Montpellier Le Vieux** where there is an admission charge for driving through this intriguing rock formation and then another winding stretch of almost 20 kilometers on to Millau. **Millau** is a lovely city located at the junction of two rivers, the Tarn and the Dourbie, known for its leather goods, particularly gloves. Millau marks the end of the canyon.

However, from Millau we suggest that you journey southeast to Carcassonne stopping enroute to visit Roquefort sur Solzon, Albi and a short detour to the hilltown of Cordes. **Roquefort sur Solzon** is home to the distinctive Roquefort cheese. If this regional specialty appeals, you might enjoy a tour of one of the cheese cellars. **Albi**, a large city, is about a two-hour drive through farmland from Roquefort. With its cathedral dominating the entire city, Albi, mostly built of brick, is also referred to as "Albi the red." The **Musée Toulouse Lautrec** is one of its more interesting attractions.

From Albi it is another half-hour drive to the medieval town of Cordes above the Cerou Valley, **Cordes** has been given the poetic title of "Cordes in the Heavens". It is an enchanting hilltop village, a treasure that will prove a highlight of any itinerary. Known for its leather goods and hand-woven fabrics, Cordes offers many *ateliers* (craft shops) along its cobblestoned streets. At the heart of Cordes is **Hôtel du Grand Écuyer**.

Retracing your path back to Albi, it is an undemanding drive south along the N112 and the D118 to Carcassonne. Europe's largest medieval fortress, **Carcassonne** is a highlight of any visit to France and a wonderful grand finale to this itinerary, Carcassonne rises above the vineyards at the foot of the Cevennes and Pyrénées. The massive protecting walls were first raised by the Romans in the first century BC. Though never conquered in battle, the mighty city was lost to nature's weathering elements and has since been restored. It looks as it did when constructed centuries ago. Stroll through the powerful gates along its winding cobbled streets and wander back into history. The walled city boasts numerous shops, delightful restaurants and wonderful hotels should you wish to stay overnight. We recommend the **Hôtel de la Cité** in the city walls.

From Carcassonne you can take the autoroute back to Provence or northwest to Toulouse and on to connect up with the *Dordogne & Lot River Valleys* itinerary.

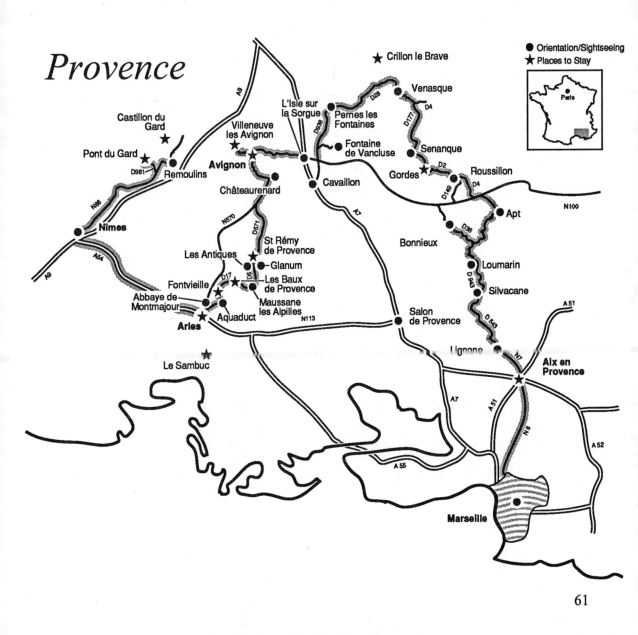

Provence

Orientation/Sightseeing
Places to Stay

Paris

★ Crillon le Brave

Castillon du Gard
Pont du Gard
Remoulins
D981
N86
A9
Nîmes
A54
A9

Villeneuve les Avignon
Avignon
Châteaurenard
N570
D571

L'Isle sur la Sorgue
D938
Pernes les Fontaines
Fontaine de Vancluse
Cavaillon
A7

Venasque
D28
D177
D4
Senanque
Gordes
D2
Roussillon
D4
D149
D36
Apt
N100

Les Antiques
St Rémy de Provence
Glanum
D5
Les Baux de Provence
Fontvieille
D17
Abbaye de Montmajour
Aquaduct
Maussane les Alpilles
N113
Arles

Bonnieux
Loumarin
D943
Silvacane
D543

Salon de Provence

Lignane
N7
A51
Aix en Provence
A52

Le Sambuc

A7
A51
A55
N8

Marseille

61

Provence

Provence, settled by the Romans around 120 BC, is a region of contrasts and colors. This delightful region of the French *Midi* (the South) is associated with warm breezes, a mild climate and rolling hillsides covered in the gray washes of olive trees and lavender. Its rich soil in the bath of the warm southern sun produces a bounty of produce that is incorporated into its regional cuisine. Also some of the world's most popular wines are produced here and complement the offerings of the restaurant. The romance and beauty of Provence has inspired artists and writers for generations.

Pont du Gard

PACING: This itinerary assumes the large port city of Marseille as a starting point, winds north to the beautiful university city of Aix en Provence, into the hilltowns of Haute Provence, and then circles back to the heart of the region and the lovely towns set in its valley. It is possible to see Provence in just a few days, but the countryside calls for you to linger, to settle and absorb the climate, the beauty and the landscape. Our ideal would be a night in Aix en Provence, one to two nights in one of the hilltowns of Haut Provence and at least three nights at the heart of Provence.

Marseille is the second largest city in France. Settled as a Phoenician colony, this major Mediterranean port with twenty-five centuries of history is where our Provence itinerary begins. Apart from the Roman docks and fortified church of St Victor, there are few monuments within the city to its past. However, you must see La Canebière, a major boulevard which captures the activity, gaiety and pace of Marseille. The old port has a number of museums to draw your interest; the **Musée Grobet-Labadie** has a beautiful collection of tapestries, furniture, paintings, musical instruments, pottery and sculpture. (Open daily 10 am to 5 pm, Sundays noon to 7 pm.)

From Marseille drive north either following the N8 or the Autoroute 51 to the southern periphery of **Aix en Provence**, an elegant city that deserves an overnight stay. Aix achieved fame when the "Good King René," count of Provence, and his wife chose it as their preferred residence. Upon his death Aix fell under the rule of the French crown and was made the seat of parliament. The city flourished in the 17th and 18th centuries and became one of the most prosperous metropolises of the region. Much of Aix's elegant architecture is attributed to this period of affluence. Today it is predominately a university town, home to some 40,000 students who represent almost a third of the population. Numerous fountains adorn the elegant tree-lined Cours Mirabeau, edged by aristocratic residences and numerous cafés. The Cours Mirabeau separates the Quartier Mazarin to the south from the Quartier Ancien on the north. The Quartier Mazarin attracted dignitaries and many lovely parliamentary homes still prevail within this quarter. By contrast, the Quartier Ancien is the heart beat of the city, a bustle of activity along its charming little back streets lined with numerous cafés and restaurants. Aix is an enchanting city to explore. The beckoning cobblestone streets of its old quarter are intriguing to wander at night and the illuminated tree-lined Boulevard Mirabeau is enchanting—a bit reminiscent of Paris with its many sidewalk cafés.

Nineteen 17th-century tapestries from Beauvois are on display in the **Museum of Tapestries**. Another fifteen Flemish tapestries can be found in the Cathedral St Sauveur. (Closed Tuesdays and daily noon to 2:30 pm.) Aix is also the birthplace of Paul Cézanne who was born here in 1839 but left the city to join his colleagues and the impressionistic fever that prevailed in Paris. He returned to his hometown in 1870 and settled here until his death in 1906. You can visit the studio he built, **Atelier Paul Cézanne**, set behind a little wooden gate just north of the old quarter. Paul Cézanne studied in Aix with Émile Zola and the distant Mont St Victoire, which inspired much of his work can be seen from various vantage points in the city. (Closed Tuesdays and daily noon to 2 pm except in summer: noon to 2:30 pm.)

Should you decide to use Aix en Provence as a base from which to explore Provence, or simply want to spend more than just an afternoon in a beautiful, aristocratic city, we recommend two hotels: At the heart of the old quarter is the **Hôtel des Augustins** and from the city fountain it is just a 15-minute walk to the attractive **Hôtel le Pigonnet**.

From Aix en Provence travel north on country roads through groves of olive trees and acres of vineyards to the hill towns of *Haute Provence*. Less traveled, the medieval hillside-perched villages of this region are intriguing to explore. From Aix follow the N7 northwest in the direction of St Cannat. Turn north 6 kilometers out of Aix at Lignane following the D543 north across the Chaîne de la Tréversse to Silvacane on the waters of the River Durance and the Canal de Marseille. Cross the River and the D543 becomes the D943, traveling first to Cadenet and then on to **Loumarin**, the capital of this region of Luberon. Loumarin is a small city surrounded by the bounty of the region: fruit trees, flowers and produce. The château on the outskirts of town is a school that attracts artists.

Gordes

From Loumarin, the D943 enjoys the beautiful path of the Aigue Brun for 6 kilometers and then the D36 travels just a few kilometers further west to the hillside village of **Bonnieux**. From Bonnieux you can wind a course northeast to the thriving city of **Apt**, known for its crystallized fruits and preserves, truffles, lavender perfume and its Ancienne Cathedrale Ste Anne that is still the site of an annual pilgrimage. From Apt travel first the N100 west for 4½ kilometers to the D4 north to the turnoff west to Roussillon.

Another option is to navigate a course directly north to Roussillon, an exploration along countryside roads. Whichever the route, **Roussillon** is worth the effort to find. This lovely village is a maze of narrow streets, small shops and restaurants that climb to the town's summit. In various shades of ochres, Roussillon is an enchanting village, especially on a clear day when the sun warms and intensifies the colors.

From Roussillon travel first north on the D105 and then west on the D2 to the neighboring village of **Gordes** perched at one end of the Vaucluse Plateau and dominating the Imergue Valley. Dressed in tones of gray this is a wonderful town to visit and explore. It is also known for the ancient village of twenty restored *bories* or drystone huts that lie in its shadow. Unusual in their round or rectangular shapes, these intriguing buildings (many of which accommodate 20th-century conveniences) are thought to date from the 17th century.

Just 4 kilometers to the north of Gordes lies the village of **Senanque** whose 12th-century Cistercian abbey stands at the edge of the mountainside surrounded by lavender and oak trees. Vacated by the monks in 1869, and accessible by a 2-kilometer path up from the car park, the abbey is now a religious cultural center and hosts concerts in the summer months.

From Senanque follow the small country road (D177) north to connect with the D4 and then travel west through the **Forest of Vénasque** to the beautiful and striking hilltop village of **Vénasque**. Charmingly untouched by civilization, this village holds a position tucked between a dense forest and cupped between two steep hills. Notable for its **Eglise de Notre Dame**, a structure built in the 6th century, and the 17th-century **Chapelle Notre Dame de Vie**, constructed on the site of a 6th-century edifice. The town comes to life during the early summer when it is the market center for the regions crop of cherries.

From Vénasque weave a course south in the direction of the market town of **Cavaillon**. Known for its melon fields Cavaillon is another village to include should your schedule permit. On the outskirts of Cavaillon, detour east to the amazing **Fontaine de Vaucluse**. In the late afternoon as the sun begins its descent, walk around the celebrated natural fountain: at certain times of the year the shooting water is so powerful that it becomes dangerous and the fountain is closed to observers. Fed by rainwater that seeps through the Vaucluse Plateau, the most dramatic seasons to visit the spewing fountain are either winter or spring. Over a million tourists travel to Vaucluse each year to see the fountain, but few venture the 4 kilometers further on to the idyllic perched village of **Saumane de Vaucluse**. The hillside location affords magnificent views of the countryside—an idyllic spot from which to watch the sun bathe the countryside in the soft hues so characteristic of Provence.

Retrace a path back in the direction of Cavaillon from Fontaine de Vaucluse and take the N100 23 kilometers south to Avignon.

Avignon, Palais des Papes

Considered a gateway to Provence **Avignon** is one of France's most interesting and beautiful cities. Easy to navigate, it is encircled by one main boulevard and various ports allow entry into the walled city. The Porte de l'Oulle on the northwestern perimeter has parking just outside the wall, a small tourist booth with maps and information, and provides convenient access into the heart of the old city. The Porte de la Republique on the south side is opposite the train station and opens onto the Cours Jean Jaures, the location for the main tourist office. The Cour Jean Jaures becomes the Rue de la République and leads straight to the Place du Palais on the city's northern border. You might want to inquire at the tourist office about the miniature train that travels the city, highlighting the key points of interest and the excellent guide service that conducts either full or half-day walking tours of the city. Avignon is a fun city to explore. A wonderful selection of shops line its streets, a festive air prevails with numerous street performers, and the historical attractions are monumental.

Avignon was the papal residency from 1309 to 1377 and the **Palais des Papes** is a highlight of a visit to this lovely city—if only to stand on the main square and look up at the long, soft yellow stone structure that dominates the city skyline, stretching the length of the square and towering against the blue skies of Provence. If time permits enter through the Porte des Chapeaux into the Grande Cour. A little shop just off the entrance provides maps, information and admission into the Palace. Just off the entry, the impressive inner courtyard and beginning point for a tour of the Palace is often a stage for the open air theater performances of the popular summer festival. Allow approximately an hour to effectively explore the Palace, noting the distinction between the old palace, built by Pope Benedict XII from 1334 to 1342, and the new palace that was commissioned by his successor, Pope Clement VI and finished in 1348. The tour will take you down the Hall of the Consistory (*Aile du Consistoire*), hung with portraits of popes who resided in Avignon, to the upstairs banqueting hall (*Grand Tinel*), to the impressive Deer Room (*Chambre du Cerf*), whose walls display a beautifully painted fresco by Giovanetti depicting the decadent life of leisure afforded the papal court in the

14th century, on to the Audience Hall (*Aile de Grande Audience*), elaborate with its star-studded ceiling and the magnificent St Martial Chapel. (Open all day July through September, Closed 11:15 am to 2:15 pm October through June. Guided English tours daily at 3 pm.)

Devote the majority of your time to visiting this feudal structure, but don't miss the two lovely churches, **Cathedral de Notre Dame des Doms** and the **Eglise St Didier**.

Just off the Rue Joseph Vernet is the **Musée Calvet**. The museum is named for a doctor who upon his death left his personal collection of art and funds responsible for its start. The museum displays a rich collection of work from artists of the French and Avignon schools of painting and sculpture: Delacrois, Corot and Manet are some of the impressive masters represented. (Closed Tuesdays and daily noon to 2 pm.)

Although only four of its original twenty-two arches still stand, the **Pont St Bénezet** is an impressive site. A small chapel still stands on one of its piers and shadows the waters of the encircling Rhône River. This is the bridge referred to in the song familiar to all French children, *"Sur le pont d'Avignon, on y dance, on y dance."* Even if all the arches still stood, passage would be difficult by modern day transportation as the bridge was constructed at the end of the 12th century with pedestrians and horses in mind.

We recommend two elegant hotels within the city walls: the **Hôtel d'Europe** easily located just off the Porte de l'Oulle facing the Place Crillon, and the truly luxurious **La Mirande** which backs onto the Palace and once accommodated guests of the Pope.

Villeneuve les Avignon is separated from Avignon by the Rhône River. (Cross the river by following the N100 west of the city and then turn immediately on D900 in the direction of Villeneuve.) It is a stronghold that once guarded the frontier of France when Avignon was allied to the Holy Roman Empire. Towering on the city skyline is the **Fort St André** whose vantage point commands a magnificent view across the Rhône to Avignon and the Popes' Palace. Another military structure still standing is the **Philippe le Bel Tower** and the curator is always on hand to provide all the historical facts.

Villeneuve flourished when the Pope held residence in Avignon. A number of cardinals chose Villeneuve for their magnificent estates. Today it affords a lovely setting on the river, enjoys magnificent views of its neighbor and yet benefits from a quieter setting and pace. Another attraction is its Saturday morning antique and flea market. Highly recommended as a place to stay in Villeneuve les Avignon is **Le Prieuré** which is housed in a 13th-century priory.

From Avignon it is a very pleasant drive south along a lazy, tree-lined road, the D571, to **St Rémy de Provence,** a pretty, sleepy town, nestled in the shade of its plane trees. On the outskirts of town is the **Château des Alpilles,** a lovely hotel that offers a quiet setting and lovely base from which to explore the heart of Provence. Of interest in the town is a Romanesque church, Renaissance houses and a busy public square.

Les Baux

On the outskirts of St Rémy, following the D5 south in the direction of Les Baux de Provence, you can visit: the **Clinique de St Paul** where Van Gogh was nursed back to health after slicing off his earlobe; **Les Antiques**, an impressive arch and mausoleum commissioned by Augustus; and **Glanum**, a thriving point of commerce during the Gallo-Greek years that was virtually destroyed in the 3rd century.

It is a beautiful drive along the D5 as it winds through the chalky gray hills referred to as *Les Alpilles* and then turns off to cover the short distance across the valley to the charming Provençal village of **Les Baux de Provence**. (The mineral bauxite was discovered here and derives its name from the town.) The village appears to be a continuation of the rocky spur from which it rises. This site has been occupied for the past 5,000 years, and is now visited by more than a million visitors every year. A number of craft shops, inviting crêperies and ice cream vendors are tucked away along the village streets. From Les Baux you not only have splendid views of the area, but also two marvelous hotels nestled in its shadow: **L'Auberge de la Benvengudo** and **Mas de l'Oulivie**.

Enroute to the lovely Roman city of Arles from Les Baux, the D17 travels first to the small roadside town of **Fontvieille**. Fontvieille is home to a wonderful hotel and restaurant, **La Régalido**, and is also worth a stop to visit the **Moulin de Daudet**, an abandoned mill set on the hillside above town, reputedly where Daudet wrote *Letters from My Windmill*. Continuing on the back road from Fontvieille, the D33, as it travels beyond the mill, passes the ruins of an old **Roman Aqueduct** that stand unceremoniously in a field just off the road at the intersection of the D82. Head west from the aqueduct along the D82 to connect with the D17 and travel once again in the direction of Arles. On the approach to the city, surrounded by fields, stands the ruins of **Abbaye de Montmajour**, which was built in the 10th century by Benedictine monks.

The skyline of **Arles** can be seen as you approach the city. Abounding in character, this is a truly lovely city whose growth is governed by the banks and curves of the Rhône

River. It has fierce ties to its Roman past when it thrived as a strong port city and gateway. Arles is glorified because of its magnificent Gallo-Roman arenas and theaters that remain and are found at the heart of the old city. This is a city to explore on foot. The narrow maze of winding streets weave through the old section and are fun to wander. Bullfights and festivals are still staged in the magnificent **Amphithéâtre** or arena, able to accommodate in its prime a surplus of some 20,000 spectators. (Open all day June to September, closed noon to 2 pm October to May.) The **Théâtre Antique**, although apparently in ruin by day, becomes a lovely stage on summer nights under the soft lights of the Festival d'Arles. (Same hours as the Amphithéâtre.) The Place du Forum is bordered by cafés and is a social spot to settle in the afternoons and into the balmy evenings of Provence. Just a block from the Place du Forum, the **Muséon Arlaten**, was conceived and funded by the town's poet, Frédéric Mistral, from the monies he received for winning the Nobel Prize in literature, to honor all that is Provençal. The museum is rich in its portrayal of the culture and fierce traditions of Provence. (Closed Mondays in winter and daily noon to 2 pm.) At the gateway to the Camargue and nestled at the heart of Provence, Arles is a wonderful base from which to experience the region. The **Hôtel d'Arlatan** is in the old quarter, while the more elegant **Hôtel Jules César** is found on a main road that bands the ramparts.

Nîmes lies approximately 35 kilometers west of Arles. A Gallic capital, it was also popular with the Romans who built its monuments. Without fail see the **Amphitheater** that once held 21,000 spectators, the **Arénas**, **Maison Carrée**, the best preserved Roman temple in the world, and the magnificent fountain gardens.

As a final destination journey just another 20 kilometers or so north of Nîmes (N86 Remoulins, D981) to the spectacular **Pont du Gard**, an aqueduct that impressively bridges the River Gard. Still intact, three tiers of stone arches tower more than 36 meters across the valley. Built by Roman engineers about 20 BC as part of a 50-kilometer-long system bringing water from Uzès to Nîmes, the aqueduct remains one of the world's marvels. Park in the carpark amidst the tourist shops and food stands and walk a pedestrian road to the span which thankfully lies uncluttered, dominated only by the impact and shadow of the towering structure.

From Pont du Gard you can easily return to Nîmes or complete the circle back to Avignon. If you want to spend a night nearby we recommend the **Hôtel du Vieux Moulin,** which overlooks the aqueduct, or the luxurious **Le Vieux Castillon** in the neighboring village, **Castillon du Gard.**

Grand Gorges du Verdon

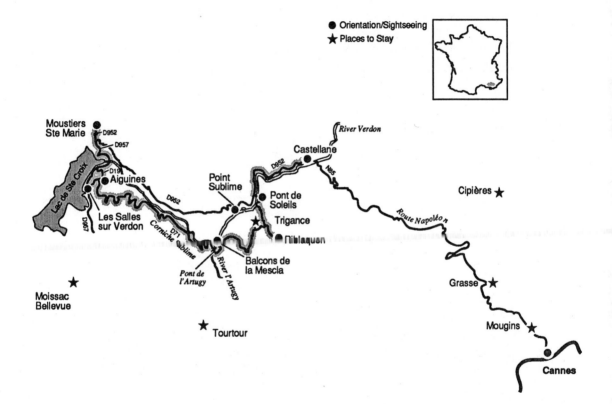

● Orientation/Sightseeing
★ Places to Stay

Moustiers
Ste Marie ●
D952
D957
D19
Aiguines ●
Lac de Ste Croix
Les Salles
sur Verdon
D957
Corniche Sublime
D71
D952
Point
Sublime ●
Pont de
Soleils ●
Trigance ★
Niblaquon ●
Balcons de
la Mescla
Pont de
l'Artugy
River l'Artugy
River Verdon
Castellane ●
D952
N85
Cipières ★
Route Napoléon
Grasse ★
Mougins ★
Cannes ●
Moissac
Bellevue ★
Tourtour ★

Grand Gorges du Verdon

The Grand Gorges du Verdon is the French equivalent of the Grand Canyon. The striking blue-green water of the Verdon is dramatic in its intensity as it carves and contrasts through the magnificent limestone plateau. The river then plunges into the spectacular trench-like Grand Gorges du Verdon and is enclosed within its steep jagged walls. When traveling between the Riviera and central Provence the Grand Gorges du Verdon makes for a wonderful detour and a few days spent in this region will prove memorable.

Grand Gorges du Verdon

Grand Gorges du Verdon

PACING: The core of this itinerary extends from Castellane to Lac de Ste Croix and just to the north of the lake—the delightful village of Moustiers Ste Marie. The total distance that this itinerary covers is only approximately 40 kilometers which includes the dramatic 20-kilometer span of the canyon from the Pont de Soleils to the town of Aiguines. The most logical access from the Riviera is to follow the N85, a lovely forested road that winds from Grasse northwest along the Route Napoléon to Castellane, a town set on the banks of the Verdon. You can include a visit to the canyon and cover the distance between the Riviera and Provence in a day's time but it would require a very early start and make for an exceptionally long day. We recommend an overnight on the edge of the canyon at the Château de Trigance in the small hillside village of Trigance. Breaking the journey here affords time to enjoy an unhurried drive along the dramatic canyon rim and an afternoon to explore Moustiers Ste Marie before continuing on to Provence.

Castellane is a natural starting point for an exploration of the canyon. It enjoys a lovely setting on the banks of the Verdon River and is famous for its crowning rock that towers above the town, crested by the **Notre Dame du Roc Chapel**. Traveling the D952 west following the path of the Verdon, at Pont de Soleils you can either choose to follow the south bank or the north bank of the canyon. (If time and enthusiasm allows, it is also possible to make one grand circle journey traveling both sides of the canyon.) For the purposes of this itinerary, the suggested routing follows the south bank of the canyon, the *Corniche Sublime*, as it is spectacular in the vistas that it affords of the canyon and it also conveniently routes past the enchanting medieval village of Trigance whose thick stone walls guard a wonderful hotel and restaurant, the Château de Trigance. To reach Trigance from Pont de Soleils, travel first south 16 kilometers on the D955 and just before the village of Riblaquon cross over the Jabron River to Trigance on the opposite hillside. **Trigance** is a sleepy little town whose population seems to double with the occupancy of its château-hotel, the **Château de Trigance**.

Following the road round the back side of Trigance, the D90 travels a short distance (6 kilometers) before it ends at the D71. Turn north on the D71 and you will soon be rewarded with a spectacular vista of the dramatic Verdon at the **Balcons de la Mescla.** You can pull off and there are terraced points from which you can look down at the dramatic loop in the path of the river some 760 meters below. (There is also a small café where you can purchase snacks and postcards.) From Mescla the road winds through sparse vegetation of box-wood, and then crosses over a dramatic span, the **Pont de l'Artugy,** a concrete, one arch bridge that rises precariously high above the waters below. From the bridge, the drive is constantly spectacular in its drama and scenery. It rises and falls above the canyon walls, winding in and out of tunnels impressively cut into its rock face. From Artuby the road climbs on the fringe of the ravine to the **Fayet Pass.** Here a tunnel carves through the rock, and square openings through the thick tunnel walls create windows which afford glimpses of the river's dramatic passage. Every second of the drive is spectacular following the jagged mouth of the Verdon Canyon. The canyon is almost overpowering: its sides plunge down to depths far below where the river forges a path through narrow stretches and then slows and calms in wider sections, pausing to create glistening, dark green pools.

The road periodically veers away from the edge of the canyon and rolls past beautiful green meadows dotted by a few mountain cabins and hamlets. In Spring wildflowers bloom everywhere. As the ruggedness and fierceness of the canyon wanes, the road gradually returns to the valley, opening up to vistas of the brilliant blue waters of **Lac de Ste Croix**. **Aiguines** is a village of a rosy hue that silhouettes against the backdrop of the lake. The numerous docks hint at what a paradise the lake is for sportsmen in summer months. At the water's edge, the road, now numbered D957, travels in the direction of Moustiers Ste Marie, crossing over the Verdon as it flows into the lake. Be sure to take a moment and park just before the bridge as it is a beautiful site looking back up the narrow canyon and if fortunate, you might see the passage of kayakers as they conclude their journey.

Moustiers Ste Marie is a grand finale to this itinerary. Famous for its pottery it is a wonderful village whose cluster of buildings with their patchwork of red-tile roofs, hugs the hillside and crawls back into the protection of a sheltered mountain alcove. Monks came here in 433, took shelter in caves dug into the mountainside, and founded the monastery **Notre Dame de Beauvoir** which towers over the village. The church was rebuilt during the 12th century and enlarged in the 16th century. You can reach the sanctuary by a winding footpath paved with round stones that leads up from the heart of the village.

This is a beautiful, Provençal hilltown whose narrow streets wind through the village and offer a wealth of stores displaying the famous Moustiers pottery. As early as 1678, the first master potter created a pattern that originated the style associated with the village and its name. Today, some fifteen master potters offer high quality hand-made and hand-decorated products and it is the principal industry in the area. You can actually come to Moustiers and commission a personalized pattern with one of the workshops.

Considering the size of the village and its seemingly remote location, it is hard to believe that the workshops of Moustiers Ste Marie fulfill requests from all over the world for their hand-painted *faience*. Located at the heart of the village overlooking the river is one of France's most charming restaurants, **Les Santons de Moustiers** (Place de l'Eglise, tel: 92.74.66.48, closed Tuesdays). I was drawn to the restaurant because of its bountiful array of window boxes hung heavy with overflowing red geraniums. Inside, beautiful antiques decorate a number of individual dining rooms, each intimate and cozy in size. Michelin has awarded this restaurant, named for the regional dolls that you will see throughout the region, a coveted star.

From Moustiers Ste Marie it is a 1½ hour drive to Aix en Provence where you can join our *Provence* itinerary.

Hilltowns of the French Riviera

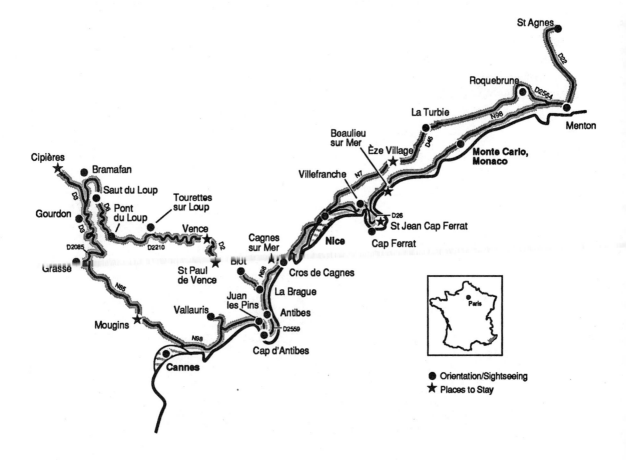

St Agnes

Roquebrune

La Turbie

Menton

Beaulieu
sur Mer

Monte Carlo,
Monaco

Èze Village

Villefranche

St Jean Cap Ferrat

Cipières

Bramafan

Cap Ferrat

Saut du Loup

Tourettes
sur Loup

Nice

Gourdon

Pont
du Loup

Cagnes
sur Mer

Vence

Grasse

Biot

Cros de Cagnes

St Paul
de Vence

La Brague

Juan
les Pins

Vallauris

Antibes

Mougins

Cap d'Antibes

Cannes

Paris

● Orientation/Sightseeing
★ Places to Stay

Hilltowns of the French Riviera

People in the hundreds of thousands flock to the Riviera for its sun and dazzling blue waters. When planning your trip, know that most of these sun-worshippers congregate during the spring and summer with the coastal towns as their base and during this time the coastside is a constant hub of activity and excitement. The Riviera attracts an international group, jet setters here to see and be seen. In the mountains overlooking the Mediterranean are a number of smaller, "hillside-perched" towns, removed from the continuous activity of the Riviera and offering a beautiful setting and escape.

View from Èze Village

PACING: We recommend at least three full days to explore the coastal and hilltowns of the French Riviera. Assuming your time is going to be devoted to the Riviera, this itinerary suggests a routing that both begins and ends in Nice. Keep in perspective that distances between destinations are short, (the entire distance between Nice and Menton is just 23 kilometers) and although you can make a circle trip staying at one or two places, it would also be feasible to select one hotel from which to base and explore the entire region. Also, remember that during peak summer months the Riviera is crowded with tourists. It is difficult to find places to stay and dine, negotiate the roads, find parking, visit museums, and thus you must incorporate more time into your itinerary to do so. Our suggestion would be to avoid summer on the Riviera and, if nothing else, escape up into the hills above the coastal towns.

The French Riviera or the Côte d'Azur is actually the area between Menton and Nice. Even the French say the "Niçoise" are not typically French—warmed and subdued by the climate they are more gentle and agreeable. We recommend that you begin your explorations at its capital, Nice, "Queen of the Riviera." France's wonderful express trains service the Nice train station and convenient connections can be made from many cities within Europe into the Nice Airport (the second busiest in France). Equally appealing, both the train station and airport are small and easy to get around and car rental agencies are represented at both.

Nice is a large city whose population of 400,000 has carpeted the land with apartments and condominiums bounded only by the ocean and the surrounding hills. Along the waterfront, the Promenade des Anglais takes a grand sweep from the city's western edge along the Baie des Anges and the new city to the edge of the picturesque old quarter. The new district of Nice is a mecca for tourists with the Promenade along the seashore lined with elegant hotels and casinos. Lighted at night, the promenade is a romantic place to stroll. Just off this majestic promenade is the **Musée International d'Art Naïf** (Avenue Val Marie) that boasts an inventory of over 6,000 paintings from all over the world. (Closed Tuesdays, November and daily noon to 2 pm.) The **Musée Chérit des Beaux**

Arts (33, Avenue des Baumettes) focuses on a wealth of paintings of the 19th century. (Closed Mondays, November and daily noon to 2 pm except in summer, closed noon to 3 pm.) A landmark of the Promenade is the stately Hôtel Negresco whose terrace is a wonderful place to settle and enjoy a café or glacé, a tradition to be equated with tea at Harrods. Just a little further on, the Jardin Albert 1 is dressed with fountains and a bandstand that hosts numerous rock concerts. From the Jardin a mini-train departs every twenty minutes to tour the old town, the flower market and castle gardens. The lovely Place Masséna stands proud on the promenade with its dramatic fountains and fronts the area's principal shopping district along the Avenue Jean Médecin. Also stemming off the Place Masséna, the Rue Masséna and the Rue de France are charmingly restricted to pedestrian traffic, banked by cafés, boutiques and restaurants.

On the other side of the Paillon River is the old quarter of Nice, **La Vieille Ville**, full of character and ambiance. Narrow alleys wind through this district of cobbled streets, shaded by towering buildings. The district is colored with flower boxes and upward glimpses of sky are criss-crossed by banners of laundry. Very picturesque is the flower market—a display of color all day and every day on the Cours Saleya, except on Mondays when a flea market of antiques and collectibles invades its space. A bountiful fish market is set out every morning (except Mondays) on the Place St François. From the Cours Saleya it is possible to climb the hill, referred to as the Château, (by stairs, a lift or by strolling up the Rue Ségurane), to some spectacular views of the Baie des Anges. The term Château is reminiscent of the château that last stood between the harbor and the old town some three hundred years ago. The harbor is fun to explore with its colorful melange of fishing boats and neighboring yachts. The territory mapped out and referred to as Cimiez, is where the Romans constructed Cemenelum, a town to rival the then existing Greek town of Nikaia (Nice) in the first century BC. The renovated Roman amphitheater hosts one of the most accredited jazz festivals that takes place every July. Cimiez also flourishes in March during the Festival des Cougourdons, and in May, Sundays are an offering of dances, picnics and folklore presentations during the Fêtes des Mais. Cimiez is also worth the journey to visit the **Musée d'Archéologie** (160 Avenue des Arènes) (Closed Sunday mornings, Mondays and daily noon to 2 pm.), the **Musée Chagall** (at the corner of Blvd de Cimiez and Ave Dr Ménard) (Closed October through June: 12:30 pm to 2 pm, July through September: 12:30 pm to 1 pm.) and the **Musée Matisse** (in the Villa des Arènes). (Closed Sunday mornings, Mondays and October to April noon to 2 pm and May to September from noon to 3:30 pm.) The Musée Chagall houses the largest single collection of the master's work. The Musée Matisse honors its namesake, a man who made Nice his home for a period of twenty years, through the artist's paintings, drawings, and figurines.

Leaving Nice in the direction of Menton, you have a choice of three roads. The roads all run somewhat parallel to each other following the contours of the coast. The *Grand Corniche* or "high" road was built by Napoleon and passes through picturesque *villages perchées*. The *Moyenne Corniche* or "middle" road is a lovely, wide, modern road. The *Corniche Inferieure* or "low" road was built in the 18th century by the Prince of Monaco and enables you to visit the wealthy coastal communities and the principality of Monaco. Each road offers a uniquely appealing route. A suggestion would be to loop one direction on the *Corniche Inferieure* to enjoy the water and the coastal towns (this is the busiest road during the summer months), and return via a combination of both the *Grande* and *Moyenne Corniche.*

St Jean Cap Ferrat

From Nice the *Corniche Inferieure*, the N98, hugs the contours of the coast and the lovely inlet of **Villefranche sur Mer** whose gentle waters are home to numerous yachts and fishing boats. Round the bay from Villefranche and follow the D26 through the exclusive residential district and peninsula of **Cap Ferrat**. Sometimes only glimpses are possible of the million dollar mansions, home to many celebrities, which stand proud behind towering hedges and security gates along this 10 kilometers drive. It is possible to visit the former residence of the Baroness Ephrussi de Rothschild, who commissioned the Italian style palace to house her personal art collection. It is now owned by the state and open to the public as a museum. The gardens and setting alone merit the visit.

Traveling further along the peninsula, climb the steps of the lighthouse for a wonderful view, and further out on the tip is a tower which housed prisoners in the 18th century. **St Jean Cap Ferrat** is nestled on the other side of the peninsula from Villefranche. It enjoys a picturesque setting and a quiet ambiance, as it is just a few homes, restaurants and hotels tucked into the hillside enjoying views across the towering masts of yachts that grace its waters. **La Voile d'Or** is a lovely, elegant hotel overlooking the water should you decide to settle in at St Jean Cap Ferrat.

Continuing on from St Jean Cap Ferrat, the road winds back to the N98 through another wealthy enclave of homes and luxurious hotels enjoying the protected climate of the neighboring town of **Beaulieu sur Mer**. In Beaulieu, another hotel that we recommend that savors a position right on the water's edge is the lovely **Hôtel la Réserve**. As the N98 leaves Beaulieu sur Mer the road hugs the mountain and tunnels through the cliff-face just above the Mediterranean, through Cap d'Ail and into the principality of **Monaco**. First class hotels and excellent restaurants are numerous in **Monte Carlo**, catering to the millions of annual visitors who come to play in its casino and hope to catch a glimpse of the royal family or resident international celebrities. Monaco is independent of French rule, and an exclusive tax haven for a privileged few. If you have time, step inside the **Palais du Casino**, fronted by beautifully manicured gardens. To really experience the fever of the gambling enter the private salons in the afternoon where high stakes are an everyday agenda.

Beyond Monaco the N98 merges with the N7 and continues on to the graceful city of **Menton**, on the Italian border. Menton boasts streets shaded by fruit trees, stretches of sandy beach in addition to a colorful harbor, casino and an endless array of shops. At the heart of the old town, Rue St Michel is a charming shopping street restricted to foot traffic. Nearby the Place aux Herbes and the Place du Marché are picturesque with their covered stalls and flower displays. Menton is also known for its gardens, the most famous being the **Jardin des Colombières** (Rue, Ferdinand Bac) located on the hill above the town, enjoying lovely views through pines and cypress trees to the waters of the Riviera.

From Menton, a 10-kilometer detour into the hills brings you to the picturesque walled town of **St Agnes**. The D22, often just a single lane, winds precariously up into the hills to this attractive mountain village of cobbled streets, a few restaurants, shops and unsurpassed views of the coastline. (Although the hillside town of **Gorbio** is often recommended in connection with St Agnes, the drive is even more demanding, and the time and energy expended is not worth the journey—St Agnes is a little larger and very similar with better views.)

Returning in the direction of Nice with Menton and the Italian border at your back, follow signs to Roquebrune Cap Martin and you find yourself traveling on the D2564 and the *Grande Corniche*. **Roquebrune** is divided into two districts: the new town on the water and a medieval village on the hillside dating from the dynasty of Charlemagne. Very picturesque on the approach, Roquebrune is well worth a detour and some time for exploration. Park on the main square and follow its maze of narrow, cobbled streets to the 13th century keep, protected at the core of this medieval village. From Roquebrune the *Grande Corniche* continues along a very scenic stretch affording beautiful views of the principality of Monaco stretched out below. Just past the charming hillside town of **La Turbie**, watch for the D45, a short connector to the *Moyenne Corniche* and the idyllic village of Èze. Like Roquebrune, there are two divisions of Èze, **Èze Village**, the medieval village perched on the hillside above the Riviera and **Èze Bord de La Mer**, a modern town on the water's edge. Of all the perched villages along the Riviera, Èze Village remains a favorite. It is a quaint medieval enclave with cobblestoned streets overlooking the sea. Park your car below the village and explore this enchanting medieval village on foot. If you decide to use Èze as a base, you will discover two fabulous hotels protected within its walls: the **Château de la Chèvre d'Or** and the **Château Eza**—both residences that for more than a thousand years have soaked up the sun and looked down upon the beautiful blue water associated with the Côte d'Azur.

Èze Village

From Èze the *Moyenne Corniche* enjoys a beautiful route, the N7, that winds back into Nice. Once back in Nice you can either follow the Promenade des Anglais once again along its waterfront, the N98, in the direction of Cannes, or circumvent the city and traffic by taking the Autoroute, the A8, where you will want to exit at Cagnes Est and follow signs to Haut de Cagnes. (If you opt for the N98, take the D18 at Cros de Cagnes and follow signs away from the coast in the direction of Haut de Cagnes.) **Cagnes sur Mer** is on the waterfront, a port town struggling to resemble the other coastal centers. **Haut de Cagnes**, however, is an old section located on the hill, with an abundance of charm and character. Follow narrow, steep, cobbled streets to the heart of the old village.

Opt for the underground parking just on the approach to the village crest. You might find space on the street but it takes a brave soul to negotiate a spot, and unless you find a generous section, the streets are so narrow, it's never certain that there is enough room left for passing vehicles—the roads weren't designed for cars. Originally built as a fortress in 1309, the **Château Grimaldi** was commissioned by Raynier Grimaldi, Lord of Monaco and Admiral of France. A citadel was built a year later and then in the 17th century, Henri Grimaldi had the citadel refurbished into very spacious accommodations. His descendent, Gaspard Grimaldi, was forced to abandon the castle at the time of the French Revolution. During the reign of the Grimaldis, the residents who resided within the walls of this medieval enclave prospered by cultivating wheat, wine and olives. (Closed Tuesdays in winter from noon to 2 pm and in summer from noon to 2:30 pm.) Mules were used to haul the bounty of produce from the neighboring hillsides and a wealth of seafood from the coast to the village. **Le Cagnard**, a marvelous, hotel-restaurant, is tucked away in the old village.

On the other side of Cagnes Sur Mer from Haut de Cagnes and definitely worth the hassle of its congested streets is the absolutely wonderful **Musée de Renoir**. Advised to move to a warmer climate because of ill health, Renoir relocated to the coast and lived his last years in this sun-washed villa above the town. Surrounded by a sprawling, peaceful garden graced with olive trees, rhododendron, iris, geraniums, and stretches of lawn, you can almost sense the peace and quiet that he must have been rewarded and the environment that inspired him to paint—artists today frequent the gardens seeking inspiration from the setting and its sentiment. The town of Cagnes purchased the home and have displayed many of Renoir's works, photos and personal and family memoirs. Especially moving is the sentimental staging in his studio: Renoir's wheelchair is parked in front of the easel, dried flowers rest on the easel's side, and a day bed is set up nearby which enabled Renoir to rest between his efforts. When you study the photo of Renoir during his later years, he appears so old and yet determined to give the world his last ounce of creativity. (Closed October 15 to November 15, Tuesdays, daily noon to 2 pm except summer months: 12:30 pm to 2 pm.)

Return to the water from Haut de Cagnes and follow the N7 or the N98 along the Baie des Anges in the direction of Antibes. At La Brague detour just a few kilometers off the coastal road following the D4 to the hillside village of **Biot**. Biot, where glassware has been made for just under three decades, has already won high acclaim. A visit to a glass factory to see the assortment of styles and types of glassware available is quite interesting. They vary from the usual types to the Provençal *caleres* or *ponons-bouteilles* that have two long necks and are used for drinking. The medieval village of small narrow streets, lovely little squares and a maze of galleries and shops is a gem.

After retracing your path back to the coastside, continue to **Antibes**. **Fort Carré**, not to be confused with the Château de Grimaldi, is closed to the public and located on the south entrance of town. The Fort guards the waters of Antibes which is home to thousands of yachts, berthed in the modern Port Vauban Yacht Harbor. The rectangular towers and battlements of the **Château de Grimaldi** can be seen beyond the Fort, within the ramparts of the medieval village. At the heart of the village the château commands some of the town's best views and now houses some of Picasso's work in the **Musée Picasso**. Picasso resided at the château just after the war in 1946 and in appreciation of his stay, left much of his work to the town. Spacious and uncluttered, open bright rooms of the château admirably display his work, photographs of the master when he resided here in addition to contemporary works by Léger, Magnelli and Max Ernst. Entry to the museum also affords some of Antibes' most beautiful views of the water framed through the thick medieval walls. (Closed November, Tuesdays and daily noon to 3 pm.) The town itself is charming and its cobbled streets are fun to wander. Allow at least half a day if not more for exploring the waterfront fortress of Antibes.

From Antibes a scenic drive follows the D2559 around the peninsula to its point, **Cap d'Antibes**, another exclusive residential community which boasts gorgeous homes, exclusive hotels and lovely sand beaches. The dramatic **Hôtel du Cap** enjoys acres of lawn that stretch down to its waters and afford privacy for a long list of celebrities who sequester away here. On the other side of the peninsula from Antibes is the pretty resort town of **Juan les Pins** which is popular for its lovely stretch of white sand beach and whose sparkling harbor shelters many attractive boats.

As the N98 hugs the bay of Golfe Juan and before it stretches to **Pointe de la Croissette** in Cannes, you can detour into the hills just up from the town of Golfe Juan to **Vallauris**. Picasso settled in Vallauris after his time in Antibes and tested his skill at the potter's wheel. He produced thousands of pieces of pottery using the Madoura pottery shop as his *atelier*. He restored the craft and brought fame to the village and in gratitude the town made him an honorary citizen. He, in turn, showed his appreciation by crafting a life-size bronze statue which stands on Place Paul Isnard outside the church. A museum, **Musée de Vallauris**, displaying Picasso's work is housed in the château, originally a 13th-century priory that was rebuilt in the 16th century. Now considered the ceramic capital of France, there are numerous workshops—the Galerie Madoura remains one of the best, and stores sell a vast assortment of styles and qualities. (Closed Tuesdays and daily noon to 2 pm.) Over two hundred craftsmen reside in Vallauris, creating original designs and copying patterns made famous by Picasso.

From Vallauris, return to the coast and continue on to the cosmopolitan city of Cannes. Located on the Golfe de Napoule, **Cannes** is the center for many festivals, the most famous being the Cannes Film Festival held annually in May. The **Boulevard de la Croissette** is a wide street bordered by palm trees separating the beach from the elaborate grand hotels and apartment buildings. La Croissette is congested with stop and go traffic in the summer, and the lovely beaches that it borders are dotted with parasols and covered with tanning bodies. The old port (Vieux Port) is a melange of fishing boats and sleek luxury craft. The flower market, Forville, takes place along the Allées de la Liberté and the bounty displayed at the covered market is set up every morning except Mondays. The picturesque pedestrian street of Rue Meynadier is worth seeking out as it is also the best place to purchase delicious picnic supplies such as cheeses, bread and paté. Rising above the port at the western end of the popular Boulevard de la Croissette is **Le Suquet**, the old quarter of Cannes. Le Suquet appears as if from the past and has a superior view of the colorful port.

It is easy to escape the bustle of the cosmopolitan fever of Cannes by traveling just a few short miles directly north out of the city along the N85 to the hilltown village of **Mougins**. This charming village achieved gastronomique fame when Roger Vergé converted a 16th-century olive mill into an internationally famous restaurant. Other notable chefs have been attracted to the village and Michelin has awarded the village and its restaurants five gourmet stars. **Les Muscadins**, located at the entrance to the old village, is a delightful inn that we recommend and which boasts one of the coveted stars. The fortified town of Mougins is characteristic of many of the medieval towns that are accessible only to pedestrian traffic which luckily preserves the atmosphere that horns and traffic congestion all too often obliterate. Located in the center of Mougins is a small courtyard decorated with a fountain and flowers and shaded by trees. Here you will discover a few small cafés where locals meet to gossip about society, life and politics.

Continuing further into the coastal hills is a region of lavender, roses, carnations, violets, jasmine, olives and oranges. Approximately 12 kilometers north of Mougins in the heart of this region is **Grasse**. Grasse's initial industry was the tanning of imported sheep skins from Provence and Italy. It was Catherine de Médici who introduced the concept of perfume when she commissioned scented gloves from the town in a trade agreement with Tuscany. When gloves fell out of fashion and their sales dwindled, the town refocused on the perfume industry. The town is constantly growing, but the old section is fun to wander through. Interesting tours of perfume factories are given in English by: **Fragonard** (at 20 Boulevard Fragonard and at Les 4 Chemins), **Molinard** (60 Boulevard Victor-Hugo), and **Gallimard** (73 route de Cannes).

Cipières

Leave Grasse to the northeast on the D2085 and travel for 6 kilometers to the D3 which travels north and winds back and forth along a steep ascent to the beautiful village of **Gourdon**. Endeared as one of France's most beautiful villages, Gourdon is an unspoiled gem that commands an absolutely spectacular setting as it hugs and clings to the walls of the steep hillside. Vistas from the village look north down the Loup Canyon or southeast over the countryside dotted with villages of sun-washed stucco and tile roofs to the glistening water of the distant Riviera. On clear days you can see from Nice to the Italian border. The village's cobbled streets are lined with delightful untouristy shops, and a handful of restaurants. **Le Nid d'Aigle**, Place Victoria, 06620 Gourdon, tel: 93.09.68.52 is a restaurant whose terraces step daringly down the hillside.

From Gourdon the D3 hugs the hillside and affords glimpses of the twisting Loup River far below. As the road winds down to a lower altitude you are faced with the option of driving north on the D603 to the medieval village **Cipières** (where we recommend the

Château de Cipières) and crossing the river at a more northerly point or continuing on the D3 and crossing the Loup River on the Pont de Bramafan. After crossing the river, just before Bramafan, follow the D8 south in the direction of Pont du Loup. This 6-kilometer stretch of road winds through the **Gorges du Loup**. The canyon's beauty and the intensity of its high granite walls beckon you into the ever narrowing gorge. The Loup River flows far below, only visible to the passenger who might chance a peak over the edge. The road passes through some jaggedly carved tunnels—pathways blasted through sheer rock that open to glorious vistas of the canyon, trees and rock. Pull off the road at **Saut du Loup**. The stop requires no more than 15 minutes and for an entrance fee of 1,50F you can walk down a short, steep flight of steps to a terrace that overlooks magnificent water falls and pools. The small riverside village of **Pont du Loup** is situated at the mouth of the canyon, on a bend in the river shadowed by the ruins of a towering bridge. It is a pretty town and a lovely end to the Loup Canyon.

Beyond Pont du Loup, traveling east along the D2210 in the direction of Vence you pass through a few more towns, each consisting of a cluster of medieval buildings and winding, narrow streets that, without exception, encircle a towering church and its steeple. **Tourrettes sur Loup** is an especially lovely town whose medieval core of clustered rosy golden stone houses enjoy a backdrop of the three small towers that give the town its name. Every March the hillsides of Tourrettes sur Loup are a mass of violets and the village is dressed with fragrant bouquets for the *Fête de Violettes*. After World War II the town revived its long-abandoned textile production and is one of the world's top *tissage a main* (hand weaving) centers. The workshops are open to the public.

The D2210 continues from Tourrettes sur Loup and approaches the wonderful old town of **Vence** from the west. Located just 10 kilometers above the coast and Riviera, the hillsides surrounding Vence afford a lovely coastal panorama and are dotted with palatial homes and villas. Entering through the gates into the old village you find dozens of tiny streets with interesting shops to investigate and little cafés where you can enjoy scrumptious pastries. The Place du Peyra was once the Roman forum and it's now the colorful town marketplace. In 1941 Matisse moved here and, in gratitude for being nursed back to health by the Dominican Sisters, he constructed and decorated the simple **Chapelle du Rosaire**. (Follow the Avenue des Poilus to the Route de St Jeannet La Gaude. Open Tuesdays and Thursdays, 10 am to 11:30 am and 2:30 pm to 5:30 pm.) Vence makes a wonderful base from which to explore the coast and the hilltowns. A favorite inn, **L'Auberge des Seigneurs et du Lion d'Or**, is set off one of the old town squares and on the outskirts of Vence we recommend the luxurious **Château St Martin**.

Just a few kilometers beyond Vence (D2 in the direction of Cagnes sur Mer) is the picturesque mountain stronghold of **St Paul de Vence** which once guarded the ancient Var Frontier. Cars are forbidden inside the old town walls whose cobbled streets are lined with galleries and tourist shops. From the walls there are panoramic views of the hilltowns of the Riviera. Located outside the walled town in the woods along the Cagnes road, the **Foundation Maeght**, a private museum that sponsors and hosts numerous collections of works of some of the world's finest contemporary artists, is one of the principal attractions of St Paul de Vence. (Open all year, 10 am to 12:30 pm and 2:30 pm to 6 pm.) St Paul de Vence is also a convenient base from which to explore the Riviera. We recommend a number of hotels, both within the fortified walls and on the outskirts.

From St Paul de Vence it is a short drive back to Nice. From Nice you can join our *Provence* itinerary by taking the scenic autoroute through the mountains, bridging the distance with our *Gorges du Verdon* itinerary or enjoy the following coastal route.

The coastline between La Napoule and St Raphaël is called the *Corniche d'Or*. The road offers spectacular views: fire-red mountains contrast dramatically with the dark blue sea. St Raphaël is a small commercial port with a pleasant tourist-thronged beach. Continuing on St Tropez is easily the most enchanting of the dozens of small ports and beaches that you'll pass. If you choose to continue along the coastal road, the *Corniche des Maures* hugs the waterfront at the base of the *Massif des Maures*. At Hyères, the scenery wanes, and we suggest you take the A50 to the A8-E80 that travels west to Aix en Provence.

Wine Country—Burgundy

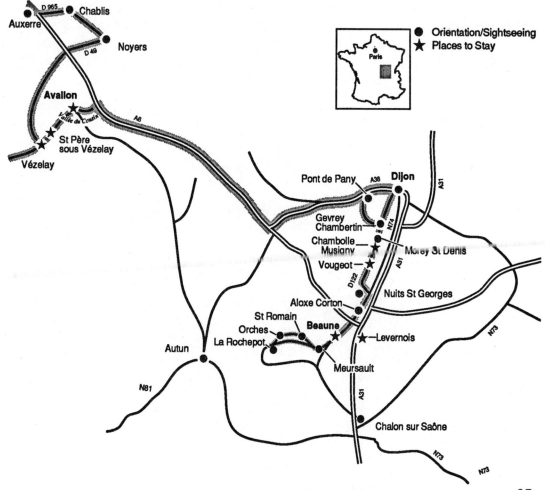

Wine Country—Burgundy

Burgundy lies in the heart of France and we introduce you to its charms at Vézelay, an idyllic medieval village sitting high atop a hill. We briefly explore Chablis and then travel the backbone of its wine district *Côte d'Or* which is divided into *Côte de Nuits* from Dijon to beyond Nuits St Georges and *Côte de Beaune* that continues south from Aloxe Corton to Chagny. Exploring the area is like traveling through a wine list, for the region supports half the famous names in French wine.

Vézelay

PACING: It would be a shame not to spend time in or around Vézelay because it is such a lovely spot. While it is possible to cover all that we propose using Vézelay as a base, we recommend two nights in Vézelay, and two nights at a hotel in or around Beaune.

Leave Paris to the southeast and take the A6 autoroute for the 1½-hour drive to the *Auxerre Sud* exit where you take the D965 for the 12-kilometer drive into **Chablis**, a busy little town synonymous with the dry white wine of Burgundy. Chablis wine roads extend like spokes of a wheel into the surrounding hills. The finest vineyards are found just northeast of the town. Cross the River Serein and turn left on the D91, a small road that leads you to the region's seven grand crus which lie side by side: Bougros, Les Preuses, Vaudésir, Les Clos, Grenouilles, Valmur, Blanchot. Returning to Chablis follow the River Serein upstream to **Noyers**, a charming little walled town of timbered houses.

Crossing the A6 just beyond Nitry a 30-kilometer drive brings you into **Vézelay** sitting high on its hilltop above the surrounding countryside. For many this is the highpoint of their visit to Burgundy for this little town is full of narrow streets lined with old houses with sculptured doorways and mullioned windows that lead up to the 12th-century **Basilica St Madeleine**—the enormous building that sits above the village. This extraordinarily long church is beautiful in its simplicity with its soaring columns and paved floor and when religious pilgrimages were the fashion, it was an important stop on the pilgrimage route to Santiago de Compostela in Spain. In amongst the winding streets you find the **Résidence Hôtel le Pontot**, and on the main square the larger more utilitarian **Hôtel Poste et Lion d'Or**.

Nestled at the foot of Vézelay is the tiny village of **St Père sous Vézelay** where Marc Meneau's famous restaurant, **L'Espérance**, is a modern day pilgrimage site for gourmands.

Arriving in **Pontaubert** cross the river and turn immediately right, signpost *Vallée du Cousin*, a country road that follows the picturesque narrow wooded valley of the rushing River Cousin (past **Le Moulin des Templiers**) and up the hill into the narrow cobbled streets of **Avallon,** a larger town with cozy old houses and narrow streets at its center. From Avallon follow signposts for the autoroute A6 which you follow to the A38 in the direction of Dijon.

If you like bustling cities, follow the A38 all the way to **Dijon** where sprawling suburbs hide a historic core. Rue des Forges is the most outstanding of the old streets. Even if you are not a museum lover you will enjoy the **Musée des Beaux Arts** in the palace of Charles de Valois. It is one of France's most popular museums with some wonderful old wood carvings and paintings. (Closed Tuesdays, and 12:45 pm to 2:20 pm, tel: 80.30.35.39.) The aperitif Kir (cassis and white wine) was named after Canon Kir, the city's mayor and wartime resistance leader. There are plenty of opportunities to purchase Dijon mustard. If you visit in November you can attend the superb Gastronomic Fair.

If the countryside holds more appeal, leave the autoroute after Sombernon at the village of Pont de Pany, pass the large hotel on your right, cross the canal and turn right on the D35, signpost Urcy and Nuits St Georges. This scenic little country road winds steeply up a rocky limestone escarpment past the **Château Montclust** and through rolling farmland to **Urcy,** a tight cluster of cottages set around the church. After passing through Quemigny Poisot turn left for Chamboef and left again in the village for Gevrey Chambertin. Down the limestone escarpment you go through a rocky tunnel around a couple of precipitous bends and you're in the vineyards.

Turn right and follow the D122 into **Gevrey Chambertin** where you join the great wine route (***Route des Grands Cru***), a tourist route that winds you through the villages that produce the premier Burgundian wines. As you drive around look for the Flemish-style colored tiles, arranged in patterns, that decorate the roofs of the region—a reminder of the time when the Dukes of Burgundy's duchy stretched into the Low Countries. There are very few large estates in this region; most of the land belongs to small farmers who live and make wine in the villages and go out to work amongst their vines. Fields are called *climats* and every *climat* has a name. Some *climats* produce better wines which are identified by their own name; others are identified by the name of the village. This is fine for the larger centers such as Beaune and Pommard, but the little villages—searching for an identity—incorporate the name of their best known vineyard into the village name. Thus Gevrey became Gevrey Chambertin, St Georges became Nuits St George, and Vougeot became Clos de Vougeot. Gevrey Chambertin is one of the region's most delightful villages and like so many others has joined the name of its village Gevrey to the name of its premier *climat*, Chambertin. Its narrow streets are lined with gray stone houses and vintners' signs inviting you in to sample their wares.

Village on the Burgundy wine road

Arriving at **Morey St Denis** park in the large car park before the village and walk its narrow streets.

The vineyards of **Chambolle Musigny** produce some spectacular wines and you can learn about them at the wine museum housed in the cellars of the **Château André Ziltener** (also a hotel). This informative tour (given in English, French or German) includes a tasting of the four grades of wine produced in the area.

The hillsides of **Clos de Vougeot** were first planted by Cistercian monks in the 14th century and a stone wall was built to encircle the vineyards and protect them from raiders in the One Hundred Years' War. Now recognized worldwide, an organization called *Chevaliers du Tastevin* chose the 16th-century **Château de Vougeot** in 1944 as a base from which to publicize Burgundy wines. You can see the courtyard, the great pillared hall where banquets take place, and the impressive cellars and 12th-century wine presses of Beaune. If you want to stay nearby you can cross back over the N74 and drive up over one arm of the moat to **Château de Gilly**, a lovely hotel.

Nuits St Georges is somewhat larger than the other towns along the route. A great deal of wine is blended here under the town's name. After Nuits St Georges the *Route des Grands Cru* continues along the N74 to end at Corgoloin. The *Côte de Beaune* begins virtually where the *Côte de Nuits* ends.

After the *Route des Grands Cru* the first great commune is **Aloxe Corton**. The vineyards of Aloxe Corton were once owned by Charlemagne. Legend states that Aloxe Corton is known for both its red and white wines because during the time that Charlemagne owned the vineyards, his wife claimed that red wine stained his white beard and so he ordered the production of white wine too. He is commemorated by the white wine Corton-Charlemagne.

Arriving in **Beaune** do not follow signs for *Centre Ville* but stay on the ring-road that circles the city's walls in a counter-clockwise direction. Park in one of the car parks adjacent to the ring-road and walk into the narrow old streets of the wine capital of

Burgundy. Today the most important landowner in the region is the Hospices de Beaune, a charitable organization that over the years has had valuable plots of land donated to it. Every year they hold a wine auction at the Hôtel Dieu—it is one of the wine trades' most important events. Built as a hospital the **Hôtel Dieu** is so elegantly decorated that it seems more like a palace. You will want to take a guided tour of this lovely building. (Open all year, closed 11:30 am to 2 pm except May to September, tel: 80.24.45.00.) You can also visit the **Musée du Vin de Bourgogne** in the Hôtel des Ducs de Bourgogne. (Closed Tuesdays December to February, and noon to 2 pm, tel: 80.22.08.19.) There are delightful shops, restaurants and cafés aplenty and wine lovers may want to visit one of the *négotiant-éleveurs* who buy wines of the same *appellation* from growers and blend and nurture them to produce an "elevated" superior wine.

Hôtel Dieu

Leave Beaune on the A74 in the direction of Chagny. After a short distance take the D973 to **Pommard** where tasting is offered at the château on the outskirts as well as at vintners in the crowded confines of the village. Detour into **Meursault**, a larger village that offers tasting at small vintners as well as the larger Domaine du Château de Meursault.

The D973 brings you into Auxley Duresses. At the far end of village turn right following the brown signs indicating *Haute Côte de Beaune*. This wine route takes you on a narrow country lane up the slopes through the steeply sloping village of **St Romain**, high above the vineyards and back down to vineyards in **Orches,** a village clinging to the limestone cliffs, through **Baubigny** and into the wine center of **La Rochepot.** A short drive brings you to the N74 which will quickly bring you back to Beaune.

From Beaune a 250-kilometer drive (3 hours) on the autoroute will bring you to Alsace where you can join the *Alsace* wine route, or a 330-kilometer drive (4 hours) on the autoroute will bring you to Reims where you can join the *Champagne* wine route.

Wine Country—Alsace

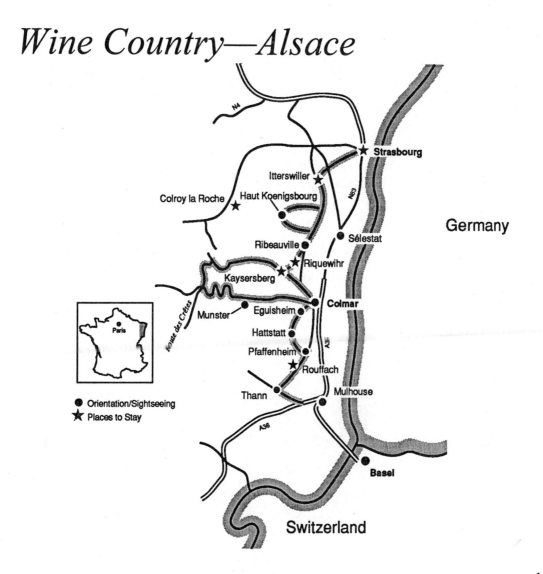

Itterswiller

Strasbourg

Colroy la Roche   Haut Koenigsbourg

Germany

Sélestat

Ribeauville

Riquewihr

Kaysersberg

Colmar

Paris

Route des Crêtes

Munster   Eguisheim

Hattstatt

Pfaffenheim

Rouffach

Thann

Mulhouse

Basel

● Orientation/Sightseeing
★ Places to Stay

N4

N63

A35

A36

Switzerland

Wine Country—Alsace

Alsace borders Germany, in fact from the Franco-Prussian war to the end of World War I Alsace was part of Germany. After World War II the district began to market its white wines sold in long, distinctive, thin, green or brown bottles. The vineyards are at the foot of the Vosges mountains on east facing hills set back from the broad Rhine River Valley. The hills are never particularly steep or spectacular but are laced by narrow roads that wind amongst the vines from one picturesque village to the next. Villages such as Riquewihr and Kaysersberg are picturebook perfect with their painted eaves and gables, narrow cobbled streets, archways and windowboxes brimming with colorful geraniums.

Riquewihr

PACING: Select a hotel in the wine region and use it as a base for your explorations of the area—two nights minimum. Finish your itinerary with a night or more in Strasbourg, you will be glad you did—it is a beautiful city.

In Alsace the wines are known by the names of the vineyards or villages and are identified by the type of grape from which they are made: Riesling, Gewürtztraminer, Muscat or Pinot Gris, and sometimes by the phrase *Réserve Exceptionelle* which indicates a higher price and premier wine. The grapes are similar to those used for German wines but the majority are used to make dry wines, not dessert wines.

Just before reaching Mulhouse (a sprawling industrial city) leave the autoroute (exit 6). Take the N83 (follow signposts for Thann) around the outskirts of Cernay (signpost Colmar) to Pfaffenheim, a tiny wine village just to the north of the larger wine town of Rouffach where the **Château d'Isenbourg** sits above the town amidst the vineyards.

At **Pfaffenheim** you leave the busy N83 to weave through the narrow village streets and into the vineyards to join the *Route du Vin*, a signposted routing that follows a winding itinerary through the vineyards. You soon arrive at **Gueberschiwiler** a cluster of gaily painted houses where as you reach the village square intricate painted signs advertise wine tasting in cobbled courtyards.

From the square turn right and drive 2 kilometers to **Hattstat**, and on to **Obermorschwir** where the narrow road climbs steeply to **Hussern en les Châteaux**, a cluster of homes with its castle perched high above the village.

Plan on spending some time in **Eguisheim**, a trim little town with lovely old timbered houses, shops and restaurants set along narrow cobbled lanes. From Eguisheim the road drops down to the busy N83 that quickly brings you into Colmar.

Colmar is the largest town along the wine road and an important center for wine trade. Beyond the suburbs lies a pedestrian zone—an interesting mix of French and German culture and architecture. Short streets wind round old buildings between the plazas and lead you to the town's old quarter with its intricately carved and leaning houses known as *Petite Venise* because a shallow canal weaves its way through the narrow streets. The Dominican monastery is now the **Unterlinden Museum** with its excellent collection of portraits, and an exhibition of crafts and customs. One room is a recreated Alsatian vintner's cellar complete with wine presses. (Closed Tuesdays November to March, and noon to 2 pm, tel: 89.41.89.23.)

From Colmar make a deviation off the *Route du Vin* up the D417. As the vineyards wane the valley narrows and pine trees decorate the heights as you drive the 15 kilometers to **Munster,** situated at the foot of the Vosges. Muster is famous for being the home of the celebrated cheese, rather than for its picturesque streets.

From Munster the D417 climbs and twists through green alpine fields dotted with farms. Climbing higher you enter a vast pine and oak forest to emerge at the summit, **Col de la Schlucht,** which offers spectacular views across the wild slopes of the Vosges mountains. Turn right on **Route des Crêtes** (D61), a skyline road constructed by the French during World War I to ensure communications between the different valleys. Now the route winds a scenic trip and signposts several beauty spots that you can walk to before coming to **Col de Calvair,** a tiny ski resort. At **Col du Bonhomme** join the D415 that travels down the ever widening valley to Kaysersberg.

Kaysersberg rivals its neighbors as being one of the most appealing towns in Alsace. Vineyards tumble down to the town from its ancient keep and 16th-century houses line narrow roads along the rushing River Weiss. **Albert Schweitzer** was born here and his house is open as a small museum. (Open May to October, closed noon to 2 pm.)

Leave Kaysersberg on the narrow D28 in the direction of Ribeauvillé and pass **Kinzheim** a picture perfect little village encircled by a high wall and surrounded by vineyards. Riquewihr, the finest walled town and a gem of Alsace lies just a few kilometers further north.

Riquewihr is completely enclosed by tall protective walls and encircled by vineyards. This picturebook village is a pedestrian area, its narrow streets lined with half timbered houses. Signs beckon you into cobbled courtyards to sample the vintners produce, and cafés and restaurants spill onto the street. It is easy to understand why this picturebook spot is a magnet for visitors. The local museum is housed in the tall, square stone and timber tower **Dolder Gate** and **Tour des Voleurs** (Thieves Tower) which exhibits grisly instruments of torture. (Dolder Gate: open July and August, closed October to Easter, open weekends rest of year, closed noon to 2 pm, tel: 89.47.80.80.)

Nearby **Hunawihr** boasts a much photographed fortified church sitting on a little hill amongst the vineyards beside the village and the *Centre de Reintroduction des Cigones* (Center for the Reintroduction of Storks). Just a few years ago the roofs of the picturebook villages of Alsace were topped with shaggy stork's nests. Alas in recent years fewer and fewer storks have returned from their winter migration to Africa and the center is dedicated to their reintroduction into the area. (Open all year, closed noon to 1:30 pm.)

Rising behind the attractive town of **Ribeauvillé** are the three castles of Ribeaupierre, a much photographed landmark of the region. Cars continually climb the main street while the shady side streets with their beamed houses are quieter and contain some lovely buildings. **Bergheim**, protected by its walls, lies just off the main road and is a much quieter village.

Haut Koenigsbourg

Alsace

Make a sharp left in the medieval village of **St Hippolite** and climb steeply up from the vineyards to **Haut Koenigsbourg**, the mighty fortress which sits high above the town. This massive castle was rather over-zealously restored by Kaiser Wilhelm II in the early part of this century to reflect his concept of what a medieval fortress should look like, complete with massive walls, towering gates, a drawbridge, a keep, a bear pit, towers, a baronial great hall and an armory. The view from the walls of vineyards tumbling to a skywide patchwork of fields that stretches to the Rhine River Valley is superb. On especially clear days you can see the very distant outline of the Black Forest. (Open all year, closed noon to 2 pm.)

Leave the castle in the direction of Kintzheim and turn left on the D35 for **Chatenois**. Take the narrow entry into the town square and continue straight across the busy N59 on the D35 through **Schwiler**, dominated by the ruined castles of Ortenbourg and Ramstein high on the hill above, through the vineyards to **Dieffenthal** and **Dambach la Ville**. A bear clutching a flagon of wine between its paws decorates the fountain in front of the Renaissance town hall. **Itterswiller** has its attractive houses strung along the ridge facing south to the vineyards. Here you find the **Hôtel Arnold** and the Arnold family's other enterprises including a most attractive gift shop and restaurant.

From Itterswiller the *Route du Vin* wanes and you may prefer to follow the well-signposted route to Strasbourg rather than continuing to the larger towns of Molsheim and Obernai before taking the A352 into Strasbourg.

Strasbourg, on the border with Germany, is one of France's largest cities and also one of its most beautiful. Set on the banks of the River Rhine where it meets the Ill, the city center is full of charm. Around its lacy, pink sandstone **Notre Dame Cathedral** the old quarter is filled with interesting little streets of shops, restaurants and hotels and leads to the footbridges which span the River Ill. The nearby *Petite France* quarter, where craftsmen plied their trades in the 16th and 17th centuries, is full of old timbered houses, most notably the fine **Maison des Tanneurs** with its intricate wooden galleries. Many of the craftsmen's old workshops are now delightful restaurants.

From Strasbourg you can cross into Germany's Black Forest, journey on into Switzerland, or a 350-kilometer drive (4 hours) on the autoroute will bring you to Reims where you can join the *Champagne* wine route. It is also an approximate 300-kilometer drive (3½ hours) from Strasbourg to the heart of the *Burgundy* region and its capital city, Beaune.

Wine Country—Champagne

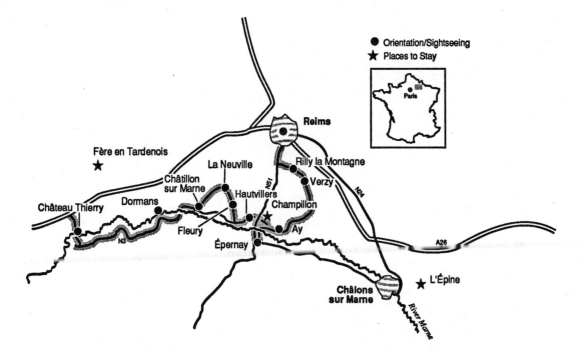

Wine Country—Champagne

Champagne is a small wine district dedicated to the production of the effervescent liquid that we associate with happy occasions and celebrations. The name champagne can only be used for the wines produced by this region's vineyards. Its capital is Reims, a not very attractive city due to being almost razed in World War I, but, many of its buildings and its fine old gothic cathedral have been restored. Below the city is a honeycomb of champagne cellars. The most important town for champagne, Épernay, lies nearby, where the mighty mansions of the producers alternate with their *maisons*, (the term for their offices, warehouses, cellars and factories). The vineyards are south of Reims, along the valley of the Marne. It is not particularly beautiful countryside, just gentle slopes that face towards the sun, interspersed with workaday villages that offer opportunities for sampling but few tourist facilities such as cafés, restaurants and shops.

Épernay, Mercier champagne cellars

PACING: Our Champagne itinerary covers a very small geographic area. Two or three nights at one location should afford all the time you need for exploring this region and sampling its bounty.

Unlike Burgundy, the quality of champagne is not derived solely from the area but also from the manufacturing process. It is the dose of sugar or "bead" that makes the bubbles, and the smaller the bead, the better the champagne. The essence of champagne is the blending of several different grapes; a branded wine, it is known by the maker and not by the vineyard. There are three distinct zones for the fifty-five thousand acres in Champagne: the *Montagne de Reims*, the *Vallée de la Marne* and *Côte des Blancs*. This itinerary visits the champagne houses in Reims and Épernay and drives round the Mountain of Reims and along the Valley of the Marne before returning you to Paris.

This journey begins in **Reims**, once the capital of France (4th to 9th centuries) and now one of the capitals of the Champagne district. The **Notre Dame Cathedral** dates from the 12th century and is where the kings of France used to be crowned (follow signs for *Centre Ville*). It is one of the oldest examples of Gothic architecture in France. It was begun in 1211 and while it suffered heavy damage in World War I, it was beautifully restored in 1938. Traffic around the cathedral is terribly congested.

You may want to save your cellar tours until Épernay but if you like to visit a house in each city, several invite you to come by without appointment. While the basic procedures and methods used to produce champagne are similar, the grand names for champagne all have their own history and interesting stories to tell. Tours are available in English and take about an hour. Except in July and August the houses are usually closed between 11:30 am and 2 pm.

Mumm, 34 rue de Champ de Mar, offers a film, guided tour of the cellars, and tasting. (Open all year, closed weekends in winter, tel: 26.49.59.70, fax: 26.40.46.13.)

At **Piper-Hiedsieck**, 51 Blvd Henry Vasnier, visitors tour the galleries in 6-passenger cars that take you on a Disney-like tour of the cellars with giant dioramas of grapes and interesting explanations on the production of champagne from harvest to disgorging. (Open all year, closed midweek in winter, tel: 26.84.43.00, fax: 26.84.43.49.)

Pommery, 5 Place du Général Gourard, offers a film, guided tour of the cellars, and tasting. (Open all year, closed weekends in winter, tel: 26.61.62.63, fax: 26.61.63.98.)

Tattinger, 9 Place Saint-Nicaise, offers a film, guided tour of the cellars, and tasting. (Open all year, closed weekends in winter, tel: 26.85.45.35, fax: 26.85.17.46.)

Leave Reims in the direction of Épernay (N51). After leaving the suburbs and light industrial areas behind, when you're amongst the fields and vineyards take the first left turn signpost *Route du Champagne* that charts a very pleasant horseshoe-shaped drive around the **Montagne de Reims** to Épernay. Above, the vineyards end in woodlands and, below, they cascade to the vast plain, the scene of so much fighting during World War I.

The first small village you come to on the D26 is **Villers Allerand**, which leads you to **Rilly la Montagne**, a larger village that offers the opportunity for a stroll and a drink in a café as well as the chance to sip champagne. As you drive along look for the peculiar looking tractors with their high bodies and wheels set at a width that enables them to pass through the rows of vines and meander down the little lanes.

Faux de Verzy

As the route nears **Mailly Champagne** and **Verzy** you pass some of the most superior vineyards for the production of champagne grapes. The picturesque windmill, found between the two villages, was used as an observation post during World War I.

The wine route rounds the mountain at **Verzy** where a short detour up into the woodlands brings you to **Faux de Verzy,** an unusual forest of gnarled, stunted and twisted beech trees hundreds of years old. Return to Verzy and continue along the D26 turning south through **Villers Marmery, Trépail** and **Ambonnay** to **Bouzy,** a community famous not only for its champagne grapes but also for its red wine. At Bouzy the wine route splits and our route follows signposts into nearby Épernay.

Traffic is much less of a problem in **Épernay** than Reims. While much of the damage has been repaired, there are still several scars from the severe bombing that Épernay suffered in World War II. Follow signposts for *Centre Ville* and particularly *Office de Tourisme,* which brings you to your destination in this sprawling town, the Rue de Champagne, a long street lined with the *maisons* (offices, warehouses, factories, cellars) and mansions of the premier champagne producers Möet et Chandon, Perrier Jouët, Charbaut, De Venoge Pol Roger and Mercier.

Try to allow time to take both the Möet et Chandon and Mercier cellar tours. **Möet et Chandon,** founded in 1743, is across the street from the tourist office. They offer a very sophisticated tour of their visitors center (where Napoleon's hat is displayed), a walk through one of the largest champagne cellars in the world, and an excellent explanation on how champagne is made. (Open all year, closed weekends in winter, closed 12:30 to 2 pm, tel: 26.54.71.11, fax: 26.54.84.23.)

Just as the Rue de Champagne leaves behind its grand mansions you come to **Mercier's** modern visitors center where the world's largest wine cask sits center stage. Holding 200,000 bottles of champagne it was made to advertise Mercier at the World Trade Fair in Paris in 1889 and proved as great an attraction as the Eiffel Tower. Houses that interrupted its progress to Paris had to be razed. Mercier's tour gives you an upbeat movie history of Mercier champagne, then whisks you in a glass-sided elevator past a diorama of the founders ballooning over their estate, as you descend to the galleries. An electric train weaves you through the vast cellars past some interesting carvings and boundless bottles of bubbly. (Open all year, closed Tuesday and Wednesday, December to March, closed 11:30 am to 2 pm, tel: 26.54.75.26, fax: 26.55.12.63.)

Set in the imposing 19th-century Château Perrier behind tall wrought-iron gates, **Musée du Champagne et de Préhistoire**, 13 Rue de Champagne, has interesting exhibits of maps, tools, wine labels and bottles. (Closed December to March, closed noon to 2 pm.)

Leaving Épernay follow signposts for Reims until you see the *Route de Champagne* signpost to both the left and right. Turn left to **Ay** and follow the route along the *Vallée de la Marne* to **Hautvillers**, the prettiest of Champagne's villages with its spic-and-span homes and broad swatch of cobbles decorating the center of its streets. It was in the village basilica that Dom Perignon performed his miracle and discovered how to make still wine sparkling by the *méthode champenoise*. He also introduced the use of cork stoppers (tied down to stop them from popping out as pressure built up in the bottles) and he blended different wines from around the region to form a wine with a superior character than that produced by a single vineyard. The abbey is now owned by Möet et Chandon and contains a private museum. However you can enjoy the lovely view of the valley from the abbey terrace.

From Hautvillers descend through the vineyards to **Cumièrs**, a workaday village known for its red wine, and on to **Damery** with its pretty 12th- and 16th- century church. Climbing through vineyards you have lovely views across the River Marne to the villages and vineyards strung along the opposite bank. Pass through **Venteul** and **Arty** and on to the more attractive village of **Fleury** that offers tasting in the large building decorated with the murals. As you climb through pretty countryside to **Belval**, vineyards give way to fields. Passing through woodland you come to **La Neuville aux Larris** with its enormous champagne bottle sitting next to the church, and return to the River Marne

Hautvillers

at **Chatillon-sur-Marne**. A huge statue overlooking the river proclaims this village as the birthplace of Pope Urban II.

At **Verneuil** cross the river and continue on the N3 into **Dormans** which saw fierce fighting in World War I and was badly damaged. Set in a large green park, the **Chapelle de la Reconaissance** (Chapel of Gratitude) commemorates those killed in the battles of the Marne in 1914 and 1918 and offers splendid views over the valley. You can quickly return to Épernay on the N3 or continue to Paris via **Château Thierry** set on the River Marne against a lovely wooded backdrop. The English claimed the town as theirs in 1421, then Joan of Arc recaptured it for France. The gates through which she entered the city still stand—**Porte St Pierre**. Napoleon defended the city against Russian and Prussian troops in 1814.

Map Key

SIGHTS & LANDMARKS

A Trocadéro
B Palais de Chaillot
C Arc de Triomphe
D Grand Palais
E Petit Palais
F Place de la Concorde
G Ste Marie Madeleine
H Gare St Lazare
I Opéra
J Place Vendôme
K Jardin des Tuileries
L Palais du Louvre
M Palais Royal
N Forum
O Centre George Pompidou
P Hôtel de Ville
Q Île de la Cité—Notre Dame
R Musée Picasso
T Gare du Nord
U Gare de l'Est
V Place des Vosges
W Gare du Lyon
X Gare d'Austerlitz
Y Panthéon
Z Palais du Luxembourg
AA Musée d'Orsay
BB Hôtel des Invalides
CC École Militaire
DD Tour Eiffel

HOTELS

First Arrondissement
1 Hôtel Mayfair
2 Hôtel Vendôme

Third Arrondissement
3 Pavillon de la Reine

Fourth Arrondissement
4 Hôtel de la Bretonnerie
5 Hôtel du Jeu de Paume

Fifth Arrondissement
6 Hôtel Colbert
7 Hôtel des Grands Hommes
8 Hôtel du Panthéon

Sixth Arrondissement
9 St Germain Left Bank Hôtel
10 Relais Christine
11 Hôtel le Relais Médicis
12 Relais St Germain

Eighth Arrondissement
13 Hôtel Beau Manoir
14 Hôtel Lido
15 Hôtel San Regis
16 Hôtel Vigny

Paris

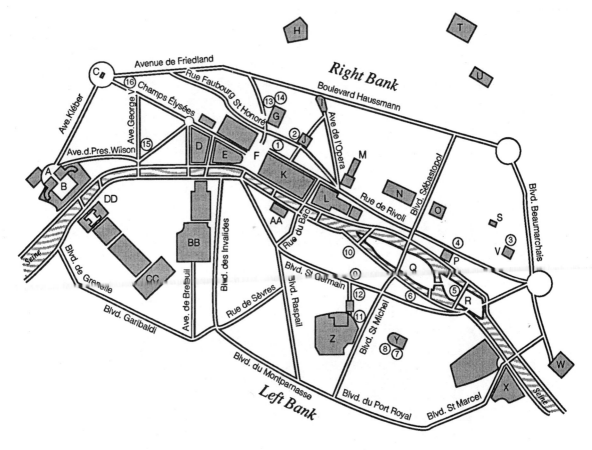

Avenue de Friedland

Right Bank

Rue Faubourg St Honoré

Boulevard Haussmann

Ave. Kléber

Ave. George V

Champs Élysées

Ave.d.Pres.Wilson

Ave. de l'Opera

Rue de Rivoli

Blvd. Sébastopol

Blvd. Beaumarchais

Seine

Blvd. de Grenelle

Blvd. des Invalides

Ave. de Breteuil

Rue de Sèvres

Rue du Bac

Blvd. Raspail

Blvd. St Germain

Blvd. St Michel

Blvd. Garibaldi

Blvd. du Montparnasse

Left Bank

Blvd. du Port Royal

Blvd. St Marcel

Seine

121

Paris

Paris, beautiful and sophisticated, lives up to her reputation. Sectioned off by "arrondissements," there is not just one interesting area to visit, but many. Each arrondissement has its own character, flavor and style. It is almost as if "Paris" were a name given to a group of clustering villages. Depending on the reason for your trip or the number of times you've been to Paris, each arrondissement will have its own appeal and attraction. We include descriptions of selected arrondissements and a few small hotels found within each. The arrondissements chosen are especially interesting and have some charming, hotels to offer. Avoid disappointment and make hotel reservations as far in advance as possible.

Paris Hotels

First Arrondissement

The First Arrondissement is an ideal location for "first-timers" in Paris. At the heart of the city, many of the major tourist attractions are situated here: the Place de la Concorde, Rue de Rivoli, the Madeleine, elegant and expensive shops along the well-known Rue du Faubourg Saint Honoré, the Tuileries and the Louvre. Find a hotel here and you will never have to deal with the Métro or taxi drivers. You can take romantic walks along the Seine or in the Tuileries Gardens. Excitement was born on the Champs Élysées, a wide boulevard that runs from the Place de la Concorde to the Arc de Triomphe at the Place de L'Étoile, officially known as the Place Charles de Gaulle.

HÔTEL MAYFAIR   First Arrondissement   Map: 1

On a small street just off the Rue de Rivoli is a well-located hotel combining modern comforts with style. The rooms are pleasing in their decor and service is attentive. The bedrooms are not all the same size, but all have private bath, direct dial phones and mini-bar. The newly-renovated rooms have air-conditioning. The Mayfair does not have a restaurant, which might prove to be more fortunate than not, for Paris already has numerous restaurants from which to choose. The hotel does have a comfortable salon-bar.

HÔTEL MAYFAIR
Directeur: Charles Keyan, 3, rue Rouget de Lisle, 75001 Paris
Tel: (1) 42.60.38.14, Fax: (1) 40.15.04.78, Open all year
53 Rooms, Double from 1490F to 1790F, Credit cards: all major
No restaurant, Located off the Rue de Rivoli, Métro: Concorde

The Hôtel Vendôme is a small distinguished hotel, located on the Place Vendôme, a neighbor of the famous Ritz Hôtel, designer shops and prestigious financial offices. The varying sizes of the bedrooms are reflected in their prices, but all are attractive and comfortable. On the first floor are a bar and simple restaurant, modern in their decor. The foyer of the hotel is small but is the base for the receptionist and accommodating concierge. Although not overly luxurious and polished in its offerings, the hotel has a great location, and rates at the Vendôme are reasonable compared to neighboring deluxe hotels.

HÔTEL VENDÔME
Directeur: Catherine Gigoux, 1, Place Vendôme, 75001 Paris
Tel: (1) 42.60.32.84, Fax: (1) 49.27.97.89, Open all year
51 Rooms, Double from 1150F to 2690F, Credit cards: all major
Restaurant, Located 3 blocks off the Rue de Rivoli, Métro: Tuileries

Third and Fourth Arrondissements

The highlight of the Third Arrondissement is the picturesque Place des Vosges and the focus of the Fourth Arrondissement are Paris' two picturesque and charming islands, the Île St Louis and the Île de la Cité. The Place des Vosges is a tranquil park, shaded by trees and echoing with the sound of children at play. The Île St Louis is a charming island with many enticing antique, craft shops and neighborhood restaurants. The larger Île de la Cité is home to Paris' "Grande Dame"—the spectacular Notre Dame and the intricate and delicate Sainte Chapelle with its stunning display of stained glass. Crossing bridges in either direction, it is a short walk along the "quai" to the Latin Quarter or a pleasant stroll to the Louvre.

PAVILLON DE LA REINE   Third Arrondissement   Map: 3

This charming hotel offers visitors to Paris a wonderful location on the beautiful square and park, the Place des Vosges. The Pavillon de la Reine, owned and operated by the same management as the very popular Relais Christine, benefits from the same trademarks of tasteful furnishings and, most importantly, the same pride and excellence of service. Set back off the Place, fronted by its own flowered courtyard, the Pavillon de la Reine was built on the site of an old monastery. With every modern convenience the hotel offers luxurious comfort and a warm decor of beamed ceilings, antiques, handsome reproductions, beautiful art and paintings. Accommodations are offered as standard double rooms, two level duplexes and two bedroom suites. The hotel has a lovely salon, and breakfast is served under the vaulted ceilings of the old cellar.

PAVILLON DE LA REINE
Hôtelier: Serge Sudre, 28, Place des Vosges, 75003 Paris
Tel: (1) 42.77.96.40, Fax: (1) 42.77.63.06, Open all year
55 Rooms, Double from 1300F to 2500F, Credit cards: all major
No restaurant, Located on the Place des Vosges, Métro: St Paul

This is a lovingly cared-for hotel whose owners believe in offering good value and quality instead of competitive prices. Walk the streets of Paris looking at other hotels and you will realize that the Sagots are an excellent buy and offer charming accommodation. In the basement under vaulted beams, heavy wood tables are matched with high backed chairs and stage a medieval atmosphere for breakfast. The reception is on the first floor and sits opposite an inviting sitting area. The rooms are found tucked along a maze of corridors, all attractive in their furnishings with lovely modern bathrooms. Many of the rooms are set under heavy wooden beams, some cozy under low ceilings, ours was quite spacious with 13-foot-high ceilings at the back. Madame Sagot has done a lovely job selecting complementary fabrics, drapes and furnishings for each room. A few rooms are two level and offer a loft bedroom and sitting room below. The hotel has a great location within walking distance of the Place de Vosges, the Picasso Museum, the Pompidou Center and Les Halles. The hotel is set on a quiet street and offers a comfortable and peaceful night's sleep.

HÔTEL DE LA BRETONNERIE
Hôtelier: Valerie Sagot, 22, rue Sainte-Croix-de-la-Bretonnerie, 75004 Paris
Tel: (1) 48.87.77.63, Fax: (1) 42.77.26.78, Closed in August
31 Rooms, Double from 620F to 800F, Credit cards: MC, VS
No restaurant, Located across the river from Notre Dame, Métro: Hôtel de Ville

HÔTEL DU JEU DE PAUME Fourth Arrondissement Map: 5

To find the Hôtel du Jeu de Paume it is easier to locate the imposing deep blue door than the small identifying brass plaque. Behind the large door, a long outdoor corridor with stone tile floor and heavy wooden timbers buffers the hotel from any street noise. Inside the Jeu de Paume is an architectural wonder, whose walls and vaulted ceilings are striped with beams. Dramatic in its furnishing, the decor is an artistic blend of tapestries, chrome, glass and leather set against a backdrop of wood and plaster. The core of the hotel, converted from a 17th century Jeu de Paume, is one large room divided up into a series of rooms: the entry, the living room warmed by a lovely fire and the dining room whose tables are overpowered by the stunning end beams and soaring rafters. A few of the guest rooms open on to the central room, while the majority of rooms are located in a side annex and open onto a courtyard and garden. The guestrooms, some boasting a tiered duplex layout, are small and minimal in their furnishings.

HÔTEL DU JEU DE PAUME
Hôtelier: Elyane Prache, 54, rue St-Louis-en-l'Île, 75004 Paris
Tel: (1) 43.26.14.18, Fax: (1) 40.46.02.76, Open all year
32 Rooms, Double from 880F to 1190F, Credit cards: all major
No restaurant, Located on the Île St Louis, Métro: Pont-Marie

Fifth, Sixth and Seventh Arrondissements

All three, the Fifth, Sixth and Seventh, are the Arrondissements which comprise the ever-popular Latin Quarter. Here you will find activity and companionship abounding. There are crêperies, sidewalk cafés, food stands, the Sorbonne and its students, antique shops and art galleries, and so many restaurants—all promising "favorites" to be discovered. At night many of the small streets are blocked off and the Latin Quarter takes on a very special ambiance. The Left Bank of the Latin Quarter is separated from the Right Bank by the Seine and the Île de la Cité. The grandeur of Notre Dame is overpowering when illuminated at night. Along the "quai" are many secondhand book stalls. Housed in the grand old train station, the recently opened Musée d'Orsay houses an exhibition of Paris' greatest collection of Impressionist art. With the Left Bank as a base, you can also conveniently tour the Luxembourg Gardens and Les Invalides, and view Paris from the Eiffel Tower. The Left Bank and Latin Quarter offer an endless wave of activity, and several charming hotels.

HÔTEL COLBERT	Fifth Arrondissement	Map: 6

Hôtel Colbert is a quiet hotel at the hub of the Latin Quarter. Located on a small side street of the same name, Rue de l'Hôtel Colbert, it enjoys a secluded location. A private courtyard leads to the entrance and adds to the hotel's peaceful setting. Recent renovation has left the bedrooms with a much more spacious feeling and modernized all the baths while retaining character. The top floor now houses two apartments, one a luxurious two-bedroom, two-bath suite connected by a sitting area and the second a two-bedroom, one-bath suite, both of which afford spectacular views of Notre Dame. Of the thirty-six bedrooms, ten enjoy glimpses of Notre Dame, and many of the others enjoy the quiet tranquillity of the courtyard view. A brightly painted bar just to the left of the reception area is a welcome spot to relax after long Parisian walks.

HÔTEL COLBERT
Hôtelier: M J. Canteloup, 7, rue de l'Hôtel Colbert, 75005 Paris
Tel: (1) 43.25.85.65, Fax: (1) 43.25.80.19, Open all year
36 Rooms, Double from 995F to 1900F, Credit cards: all major
No restaurant, Located off Quai de Montebello, Métro: Maubert Mutualite

HÔTEL DES GRANDS HOMMES   Fifth Arrondissement   Map: 7

Facing onto the Place du Panthéon, the Hôtel des Grands Hommes is a haven in Paris. Small and quiet, the lobby has an interior court garden and inviting leather couches and chairs adorning its marble floors. A delicious *café complet* can be savored at small wooden tables paired with tapestry chairs all set under the light stone arches of the house's original cellar. The bedrooms are found up a spiral staircase (or elevator) and are beautiful in their decor of warm colors, fabrics, antiques and exposed beams. The beds are firm and the bathrooms lovely and modern. This is a delightful hotel, a bargain for its price, owned and managed by a very gracious and attentive Madame Brethous. She and her staff are friendly and speak wonderful English, yet they are courteous if you would like to practice your French.

HÔTEL DES GRANDS HOMMES
Hôtelier: Corinne Brethous, 17, Place du Panthéon, 75005 Paris
Tel: (1) 46.34.19.60, Fax: (1) 43.26.67.32, Open all year
32 Rooms, Double from 800F to 850F, Credit cards: all major
No restaurant, Located on Place du Panthéon, near Luxembourg Gardens, Métro: Luxembourg

HÔTEL DU PANTHÉON   Fifth Arrondissement   Map: 8

This hotel is located next door to the Hôtel des Grands Hommes and is also owned and managed by Madame Brethous. Identical in feeling and decor, both 18th-century houses have been attractively converted and the Panthéon's thirty-four bedrooms all profit from Madame's excellent taste and are furnished in period style. Although there is no restaurant, the vaulted basement cellar is a breakfast room or you can enjoy morning coffee and croissants in the privacy of your room.

HÔTEL DU PANTHÉON
Hôtelier: Corinne Brethous, 19, Place du Panthéon, 75005 Paris
Tel: (1) 43.54.32.95, Fax: (1) 43.26.64.65, Open all year
34 Rooms, Double from 800F to 850F, Credit cards: all major
No restaurant, Located on Place du Panthéon near Luxembourg Gardens, Métro: Luxembourg

ST GERMAIN LEFT BANK HÔTEL   Sixth Arrondissement   Map: 9

The St Germain Left Bank Hôtel is one of Paris's best offerings for travelers. It has a fabulous location on a quiet street just off the Boulevard St Germain within comfortable walking distance of the Île de la Cité and the colorful heart of the district with its narrow cobbled streets, many restaurants and shops. The St Germain Left Bank Hôtel also offers charming accommodation and very professional service. The entry is warm and inviting with its handsome wood paneling, tapestries, paintings and attractive furnishings. Set with tables, a small room tucked off the entry serves as an appealing spot for a breakfast of croissants, rolls, juice and coffee which can also be enjoyed in the privacy of your room. A small elevator conveniently accesses the thirty-two rooms evenly distributed on five levels. Windows of rooms at the back open up to views of the distant Notre Dame and the vantage improves with each floor. Attractive in their decor, often set under exposed beams, the rooms are small, but comfortable with a writing desk, built in armoire, direct dial phones and modern bathrooms.

ST GERMAIN LEFT BANK HÔTEL
Hôtelier: The Teil Family, 9, rue de l'Ancienne Comédie, 75006 Paris
Tel: (1) 43.54.01.70, Fax: (1) 43.26.17.14, Open all year
32 Rooms, Double from 895F to 1500F, Credit cards: all major
No restaurant, Located off the Blvd St Germain, Métro: Odéon

RELAIS CHRISTINE   Sixth Arrondissement   Map: 10

The Relais Christine achieves a countryside ambiance at the heart of Paris' Latin Quarter. A large, flowering courtyard buffers the hotel from any noise and a beautiful wood-paneled lobby ornamented with antiques, Oriental rugs and distinguished portraits is your introduction to this delightful hotel. A converted monastery, the hotel underwent complete restoration and modernization in 1979. Fully air conditioned, there are thirty-five double rooms whose beds easily convert to twin beds. There are two-level and single-level accommodations, all individual in their decor—ranging from attractive contemporary to a dramatic Louis XIII. A few of the bedrooms overlook a small back street, but the majority open onto the garden or front courtyard. The Relais also has sixteen beautiful suites, of which four on the ground floor open directly onto a sheltered garden. The Relais Christine is an outstanding hotel and the only property on the Left Bank to offer secure, underground parking.

RELAIS CHRISTINE
Hôtelier: Jean-Jacques Regnault, 3, rue Christine, 75006 Paris
Tel: (1) 43.26.71.80, Fax: (1) 43.26.89.38, Open all year
51 Rooms, Double from 1430F to 2600F, Credit cards: all major
No restaurant, Located a few blocks up from the Pont Neuf, Métro: Odéon

HÔTEL LE RELAIS MÉDICIS   Sixth Arrondissement   Map: 11

The Relais Médicis is a family run hotel located just off the Place Odéon at the heart of the Left Bank. Gypsy, a lovable shepherd, the inn's mascot, guards the front door with toys close by and tail always a-wag. A beautiful central courtyard, enclosed by white paned windows sets an attractive mood, and lovely sitting rooms are found just off the reception area. An elevator transports you up to the guestrooms, and at each level the hallways are noticeably attractive with handsome wallpapers and paintings on the walls. The bedrooms overlook quiet streets or the central courtyard. They enjoy the coziness of exposed wood beams against warm-colored walls, a melange of Provençal fabrics and lovely furnishings, snug bathrooms tucked into a niche, and air-conditioning. Breakfast is served either in the dining room or your bedroom. This is the sister hotel of the equally lovely Relais St Germain.

HÔTEL LE RELAIS MÉDICIS
Hôtelier: Alex Laipsker, 23, rue Racine, 75006 Paris
Tel: (1) 43.26.00.60, Fax: (1) 40.46.83.39, Open all year
16 Rooms, Double from 1190F to 1480F, Credit cards: all major
No restaurant, Located just off Place de l'Odéon, Metro: Odéon

Look for the rich green door standing proud under windows hung with geraniums and you will discover an enchanting Left Bank hotel. Recently converted to a hotel, the walls between two adjoining buildings were knocked down to accommodate ten guest rooms. There are just two rooms that share the landing of each floor, all facing onto the Carrefour de l'Odéon, a quiet plaza. The rooms are narrow, intimate and set under heavy beams. The prints chosen for the furnishings, spreads and drapes coordinate beautifully and are individual to each room. Accommodations, although not spacious, are roomy with excellent lighting, modern bathrooms, direct dial phones, mini-bar and television. Of the rooms, one is an apartment that is accessed by its own private stairway. Prices are at the top end but then so are the style and accommodation. On a recent visit I was informed that the Laipsker family has plans to merge rooms and offer more spacious accommodation in the main building and convert the neighboring building to offer additional guestrooms.

RELAIS SAINT GERMAIN
Hôtelier: Gilbert Laipsker, 9, Carrefour de l'Odéon, 75006 Paris
Tel: (1) 43.26.00.60, Fax· (1) 46.33.15.30, Open all year
10 Rooms, Double from 1430F to 1850F, Credit cards: all major
No restaurant, Located off the Blvd Saint Germain, Métro: Odéon

Eighth Arrondissement

The Eighth Arrondissement crowned by the Arc de Triomphe and graced by the Champs Élysées is a bustle of activity. There are shops, sidewalk cafés, nightclubs, cinemas and opportunities for endless people-watching. It makes for a wonderful evening's enjoyment to stroll the wide boulevard, people are always about and it is safe and well-lit.

HÔTEL BEAU MANOIR	Eighth Arrondissement	Map: 13

Just around the corner from its sister hotel, the Hôtel Lido, The Hôtel Beau Manoir is found on a side street just off the Place Madeleine. The Hôtel Beau Manoir resembles the decor in the Teil's other hotels with beautiful rich woods from the Auvergne enhancing the walls, rough hewn beams, exposed stone walls, handsome tapestries and rich, Provençal fabrics used to decorate the rooms—all ingredients married together to achieve a cozy and intimate atmosphere. Guestrooms are comfortable in size and appointments: all with marbled bath, air-conditioning, cable TV, mini bar, and direct dial phone. Three top floor suites are tucked under the eaves and each has an intimate sitting room and views out through dormer windows. A buffet breakfast is included in your rates. The Teil's do a wonderful job in terms of accommodation and service and offer well-priced rooms. If your first choice of their hotels is not available, try a second.

HÔTEL BEAU MANOIR
Hôtelier: The Teil Family, 6, rue de l'Arcade, 75008 Paris
Tel: (1) 42.66.03.07, Fax: (1) 42.68.03.00, Open all year
32 Rooms, Double from 1155F to 1465F, Credit cards: all major
No restaurant, Located on Place Madeleine; Metro: Madeleine

Bright, overflowing windowboxes hung heavy with red geraniums caught my eye and tempted me down a small side street just off the Place de Madeleine to the Hôtel Lido. My small detour was greatly rewarded. The Hôtel Lido is a gem. Tapestries warm the heavy stone walls and Oriental rugs adorn the tile floors. Copper pieces are set about and wooden antiques dominate the furnishings in the entry lobby, an intimate sitting area and cozy bar. Downstairs breakfast is served under the cellar's stone arches. Comfortable but not large, the bedrooms are charmingly decorated with reproduction antiques, handsome fabrics and set under heavy beams. An excellent value for Paris, the Lido has two equally lovely sister hotels, the St Germain Left Bank Hôtel and the Hôtel Beau Manoir.

HÔTEL LIDO
Hôtelier: The Teil Family, 4, Passage de la Madeleine, 75008 Paris
Tel: (1) 42.66.27.37, Fax: (1) 42.66.61.23, Open all year
32 Rooms, Double from 770F to 900F, Credit cards: all major
No restaurant, Located off the Place de Madeleine, Métro: Madeleine

Small, traditional and intimate, the San Regis was once a fashionable townhouse. With exclusive boutiques and embassies as its sophisticated neighbors, the hotel maintains an air of simple yet authentic elegance. It is easy to pass this marvelous hotel by: a small sign is the only thing that advertises its presence. Beyond the small foyer is a comfortable lounge area and small dining room, where you can enjoy a quiet drink and/or dinner. The bedrooms are large and handsomely furnished, and the bathrooms are very modern and thoughtfully stocked. Huge double doors buffer sounds from other rooms. The rooms that front the Rue Jean Goujon are favored with a view across to the tip of the imposing Eiffel Tower, but rooms on the courtyard are sheltered from any street noise and quieter.

HÔTEL SAN REGIS
Hôtelier: M Maurice Georges, 12, rue Jean-Goujon, 75008 Paris
Tel: (1) 43.59.41.90, Fax: (1) 45.61.05.48, Open all year
54 Rooms, Double from 2000F to 5000F, Credit cards: AX, VS
Restaurant, Located between the Seine and the Champs Élysées, Métro: Franklin Roosevelt

HÔTEL DE VIGNY   Eighth Arrondissement   Map: 16

For those who appreciate discretely elegant small hotels, the Hôtel de Vigny is appealing. The lounge has the understated, yet expensive look of a private club with comfortable chairs, the finest fabrics, paneled walls, handsome oil paintings, and a fireplace. A small writing desk where guests register is the only subtle indication that this is not a private home. Not just the decor, but the location is also excellent: just a couple of blocks north of the Champs Élysées.

HÔTEL DE VIGNY
Hôtelier: Christian Falcucci, 9-11 rue Balzac, 75008 Paris
Tel: (1) 40.75.04.39, Fax: (1) 40.75.05.81, Open all year
37 Rooms, Double from 2000F to 5000F, Credit cards: all major
Restaurant, pool, Located near the Champs Élysées, Métro: George V/Etoile

Hotel Descriptions

Located on a small side street just off the Cours Mirabeau (the Champs Élysées of Aix en Provence), the Hôtel des Augustins was once a convent of the Augustins. Its towering, vaulted stone walls and tile floors are handsome and dramatic. Beautiful trunks and heavy wood pieces are set on a large Oriental rug that warms the entry, the reception is set behind a wall of the arched entry, and a stairway with wrought iron rails winds up to the guestrooms. All twenty-nine rooms have recently been redecorated and are fresh, clean and simply appointed. One of the most attractive rooms has a terrace and a fine view over the rooftops of Aix en Provence. The hotel also has four suites. If you are on a budget ask for one of the smaller rooms. While this is not a luxury hotel, it is extremely clean, well kept, and centrally located—perfect for exploring the old winding pedestrian streets of this town. It also employs a gracious staff and offers the convenience of a parking garage. *Directions:* Rue de la Masse is located just off the Cours Mirabeau on its north side, just a block east of the Place Charles de Gaulle.

HÔTEL DES AUGUSTINS
Hôtelier: Valerie & Thiery Ducatel
3, Rue de la Masse
13100 Aix en Provence
Tel: 42.27.28.59, Fax: 42.26.74.87
29 Rooms, 4 Suites
Double from 600F to 1200F, Suite from 1300F
Open all year
Credit cards: all major
Restaurant
Region: Provence; Michelin Map: 245, 246

Aix is an intriguing city to explore. The cobbled streets of the old quarter are lovely to wander and at night the illuminated tree-lined Cours Mirabeau is enchanting—reminiscent of Paris with its many sidewalk cafés. It is just a fifteen-minute walk from the old quarter to the very professionally, family run and attractive Hôtel le Pigonnet. A tree-lined road leads you away from the noise and traffic of the city center to this hotel. Set in its own two-and-a-half-acre garden, the Hôtel le Pigonnet is surrounded by an abundance of flowers and towering ancient chestnut trees. It was from this garden that Paul Cezanne painted the Mountain of Sainte Victoire. Most inviting on a hot summer day in Provence, the hotel also has a lovely large pool. Inside are cozy sitting rooms and a large airy restaurant whose tables are set on the back patio on balmy evenings to overlook the lush expanse of garden. The hotel's bedrooms, all with private bathroom, vary dramatically from elegant suites to attractive, but standard hotel rooms. Le Pigonnet is not a country inn, but a lovely hotel with first class accommodation and service that maintains a country ambiance and setting within the city of Aix en Provence. *Directions:* Take the *Pont de l' Arc* exit off the autoroute and turn north in the direction of the center of town. At the third light turn left. Le Pigonnet is 50 meters on the left.

HÔTEL LE PIGONNET
Hôtelier: Swellen family
5, Avenue du Pigonnet
13090 Aix en Provence
Tel: 42.59.02.90, Fax: 42.59.47.77
52 Rooms
Double from 600F to 1200F
Open all year
Credit cards: all major
Restaurant, pool
Region: Provence: Michelin Map: 245, 246

With the River Rhône running through it, Arles is a beautiful city, rich with Roman and medieval monuments. Just 50 kilometers from the sea, Arles has long guarded a strategic location. It is also convenient to all of Provence and an ideal base for exploring the region. The Hôtel d'Arlatan is tucked away on a small street in the center of town near the Place du Forum, within easy walking distance of all the city's major sights. In the 12th, 15th and, 17th centuries the Hôtel d'Arlatan belonged to the Counts of Arlatan de Beaumont and served as their private home. It is now the pride of Monsieur and Madame Yves Desjardin who offer an ideal retreat with charming accommodation and service. This is a quaint hotel, ornamented with antiques and pretty fabrics. Many of the bedrooms overlook a quiet, inner courtyard or garden. Although there is no restaurant, a delightful breakfast can be enjoyed in the inviting salon or on the patio. For those traveling by car it is also noteworthy that the hotel has secure parking in their private garage. *Directions:* Arles is located 36 kilometers south of Avignon traveling on the N570. At Place Lamartin enter through the ramparts on Rue Septembre which becomes the Rue du Sauvage.

HÔTEL D'ARLATAN
Hôtelier: Mme & M Yves Desjardin
26, Rue du Sauvage
13631 Arles
Tel: 90.93.56.66, Fax: 90.49.68.45
46 Rooms
Double from 385F to 780F
Open all year
Credit cards: all major
No restaurant
Region: Provence; Michelin Map: 245

In the middle of the 17th century a Carmelite convent was erected in Arles by Mother Madeleine St Joseph. It was a residence for nuns until 1770 when the order was expelled in the midst of the French Revolution. The convent then became State property until it was purchased and transformed into a hotel in 1929. In this beautiful old convent, the Hôtel Jules César has earned a rating of four stars under the directorship of Monsieur Michel Albagnac. The hotel is situated next to and shares a courtyard with the Chapelle de la Charité, which belongs to the hotel and dates from the 17th century. The restaurant, Lou Marquès, is air conditioned and lovely, known for its classic and Provençal cooking. Little tables and chairs are set in the cloister, and here breakfast and light and quick lunches are served. Most bedrooms are air-conditioned and spacious; room 72, with windows opening onto the garden, is an elegant large room with two double beds. The pool is a welcome addition for those hot summer days in Provence. *Directions:* Arles is located 36 kilometers south of Avignon traveling on the N570. The Jules César is located on the Blvd des Lices, a main artery that borders the ramparts on the south.

HÔTEL JULES CÉSAR
Hôtelier: Michel Albagnac
Blvd des Lices, BP 116
13631 Arles Cedex
Tel: 90.93.43.20, Fax: 90.93.33.47
55 Rooms
Double from 820F to 1800F
Open Christmas to November
Credit cards: all major
Restaurant, pool
Region: Provence; Michelin Map: 245, 246

The Château d'Audrieu affords the countryside traveler luxurious Relais & Châteaux accommodation within the walls of a beautiful 18th-century château. This large, somewhat austere, gray stone manor dominates its vast expanse of graveled driveway with lawns beyond. The inside is far cozier than the exterior where the drawing room and dining rooms have the feel of being a grand family home. Many special grand pieces are found in the richly appointed salons which bridge the two wings of the château. All thirty bedrooms, nine of which are spacious suites, are furnished with elegant antiques and have private bathrooms. Although a château demands constant upkeep, the accommodations are beautifully maintained and the family takes pride in refurbishing one or two rooms each year. There are three intimate dining rooms where service is elegant and formal. On the grounds a lovely pool proves a welcome treat on warm summer days. *Directions:* Turn off N13, the road that travels between Caen and Bayeux, onto D158B, and head south on a small country road, in the direction of Tilly sur Seulles. Travel 3 kilometers to the château.

CHÂTEAU D'AUDRIEU
Hôtelier: Mme & M Livry-Level
Audrieu
14250 Tilly sur Seulles
Tel: 31.80.21.52, Fax: 31.80.24.73
21 Rooms, 9 Suites
Double from 1000F to 1250F, Suite from 1900F
Open March to November
Credit cards: MC, VS
Restaurant closed Wednesday, pool
Region: Normandy; Michelin Map: 231

I wanted to abort my travels, unpack bags and settle in at the beautiful Château de Vault de Lugny. I arrived on a warm spring afternoon and the obvious contentment of guests who were lounging at tables on the front lawn was enviable. Voices were subdued and did not break the lovely quiet of the setting—perhaps because the individual desires of each guest were well tended to. It was early afternoon, yet I noticed one guest lounging over a late breakfast, a few guests sleeping with books neglected on their laps and a foursome playing a game of cards under the shade of a large central tree. The Château de Vault de Lugny is a handsome cream stone building with white shuttered windows and weathered tile roof and secluded by a high wall, moat and tall gates. There are eleven rooms in the château, all with lovely modern bathrooms. Lavish and regal in their decor, the larger rooms are very popular. The smaller standard rooms are also charming and a better value. Meals are available at any hour, although *table d'hôte* fashioned dinners are served at a handsome trestle table set before a massive open fireplace. *Directions:* Traveling the A6 between Paris and Beaune, take the Avallon exit and follow the direction of Vézelay west to Pontaubert, turn right after the church. The château is on the right, 550 meters from the village.

CHÂTEAU DE VAULT DE LUGNY
Hôtelier: Elisabeth Matherat-Audan
Pontaubert, 89200 Avallon
Tel: 86.34.07.86, Fax: 86.34.16.36
11 Rooms
Double from 850F to 2200F
Open end March to mid-November
Credit cards: all major
Restaurant, tennis
Region: Burgundy; Michelin Map: 238

Nestled along the river's edge in the lovely Cousin river valley, Le Moulin des Templiers offers a peaceful night's rest at an inexpensive price. The rooms are all extremely small and very simply decorated. Only a few rooms have miniscule ensuite shower or bathrooms. But, everything is fresh, clean and carefully tended to by Madame Hilmoine. You can hear the soothing sounds of the cascading river from each of the bedrooms, which open up to either a flower-filled courtyard or the garden. If you are blessed with warm sunshine, enjoy either afternoon drinks or breakfast of fresh bread, jam and hot coffee at white wrought-iron tables set along the water's edge. There is not a restaurant at the hotel, but Madam recommends Les Chenêts 3 kilometers away, and there are other restaurants nearby to suit every taste. This is a quaint little hotel, quite inexpensive and convenient for exploring Vézelay and venturing into the heart of the Burgundy wine region. *Directions:* Located between Avallon and Vézelay on the Route de la Vallée du Cousin. At Avallon take the direction Vézelay (N957). At the first village, Pontaubert, turn left on the Route de la Vallée du Cousin. Le Moulin des Templiers is the third hotel that you come to in the valley.

LE MOULIN DES TEMPLIERS
Hôtelier: Francoise Hilmoine
Vallée du Cousin,
Pontaubert, 89200 Avallon
Tel: 86.34.10.80
14 Rooms
Double from 304F to 410F
Open mid- March to October
Credit cards: none
No restaurant
Region: Burgundy; Michelin Map: 238

Hôtel d'Europe is a classically beautiful 16th-century mansion, formerly the home of the Marquis of Gravezon. Just inside the Porte de l'Oulle, on the Place Crillon, the mansion was converted into a hotel in 1799 as it is within walking distance of the River Rhône, a prime location to attract travelers who in that period voyaged predominantly by boat. The present owner, René Daire, has completely modernized the hotel using handsome furnishings that suit the mood and complement this grand home. The walls of the marble entry hall, once an open courtyard, and the walls of the upper levels are now hung with magnificent tapestries. The bedrooms of the hotel are all different in character and size and furnished in traditional pieces and antiques. Many of the rooms are quite spacious and extremely comfortable for extended stays. Although within the city walls of Avignon, many of the rooms overlook the hotel's courtyard and afford a quiet night's rest. The hotel has a fine restaurant, La Vieille Fontaine. You can dine in its elegant formality or under the trees in the courtyard on balmy Provençal nights. *Directions:* On the A7 from the south take the Avignon *Sud* (south) exit direction Avignon. Follow the ramparts around to the left to the entrance of L'Oulle in front of the bridge. Turn inside the ramparts. Place Crillon is on the left.

HÔTEL D'EUROPE
Hôtelier: René Daire
12, Place Crillon
84000 Avignon
Tel: 90.82.66.92, Fax: 90.85.43.66
44 Rooms, 3 Suites
Double from 650F to 1500F, Suite from 2200F
Open all year
Credit cards: all major
Restaurant closed off season
Region: Provence; Michelin Map: 245, 246

La Mirande was built in the 13th and 14th century as a residence for Cardinals visiting the Pope. When the Pope moved his headquarters, the complex became a private residence. The Stein family came from Germany, fell in love with the property and converted it to a luxury hotel with a desire to improve upon the four-star hotels they had experienced in their travels. They have exceeded their goals and created a superlative property. Every luxurious detail has been well thought out and implemented, seemingly without consideration of cost—only consideration of the guests and their comfort. A multitude of public rooms and the guestrooms are beautifully appointed with rich fabrics and gorgeous antiques. The dining room has an absolutely stunning 17th-century French ceiling and Oriental carpet, an Aubusson tapestry draping an entire wall, and is warmed by a large open fireplace in winter months. Dinner is served on the terrace patio on balmy summer nights. Overlooking the Palace walls, La Mirande is spacious and luxurious, an oasis for its guests. It has even been said that, "Had the Pope ended up at La Mirande instead of across the street he might never have returned to Rome." *Directions:* Exit off A7 at Avignon Nord, take the gate *Porte de la Ligne* into the walled city, and follow signs to La Mirande.

LA MIRANDE
Hôtelier: Stein Family
4, Place de la Mirande
84000 Avignon
Tel: 90.85.93.93, Fax: 90.86.26.85
18 Rooms, 1 Suite
Double from 1300F to 1900F, Suite from 2600F
Open all year
Credit cards: all major
Restaurant, sauna
Region: Provence; Michelin Map: 245, 246

The cobblestoned town of Barbizon has attracted artists for many years, and the 19th-century timbered Hôstellerie du Bas-Bréau has had its share of famous guests. Robert Louis Stevenson wrote in *Forest Notes* about this hotel and it is often called "Stevenson's House." Famous painters who treasured this corner of the Forest of Fontainebleau include Millet, Corot, Sisley and Monet. Some accommodations are in the main timbered house, but most are in a two-story building in the back garden. Each room is different in decor and has a bath. The restaurant is superb, drawing dinner guests from as far away as Paris. With unusually attractive flower arrangements on each table, the atmosphere of the dining room is elegant and romantic. Political leaders from Italy, Germany, Great Britain, Ireland, Greece, Luxembourg, Denmark and the Netherlands recently selected the hotel as a conference location—you will understand their choice when you dine at Hôstellerie du Bas-Bréau where the menu features homegrown vegetables and herbs and specialties such as wild boar. The house wine list is incredible. *Directions:* From Paris take A6 south in the direction of Fontainebleau. Exit at Barbizon. From the south on A6 exit at Fontainebleau. At the Obélisque in Fontainebleau take the N7 in the direction of Paris and travel 8 kilometers to Barbizon.

HÔSTELLERIE DU BAS-BRÉAU
Hôtelier: Mme & M Fava
Directeur: M Nalchiodi
22, Rue Grande, 77630 Barbizon
Tel: (1) 60.66.40.05, Fax: (1) 60.69.22.89
12 Rooms, 8 Suites
Double from 950F to 1500F, Suite from 1800F
Open all year
Credit cards: all major
Restaurant, pool, tennis
Region: Île de France; Michelin Map: 237

L'Auberge de la Benvengudo is tucked away along the road as it winds through the valley traveling from the hillside town of Les Baux de Provence. L'Auberge de la Benvengudo began as a family home offering rooms to friends and overnight guests. In response to the number of returning guests as well as those who were guided here by their praise, L'Auberge de la Benvengudo has expanded from a private home into a proper hotel. Sheltered behind a vast garden, the hotel extends out from, and beautifully copies the design of the original home. Ivy has now covered the newer stucco walls as it does on the main home, and the Provençal sun has already warmed and mellowed the red tile roofs. Green shuttered windows open onto the surrounding rocky hillsides, low green shrubbery and the large swimming pool, tennis court and gardens. Heavy, dark colors (very Mediterranean in flavor) are used to decorate the bedrooms. Accommodations are comfortable, basic, some quite spacious, all with modern bathrooms. For those on a longer stay, you might want to reserve a room equipped with a kitchenette. The restaurant is lovely and the menu is tempting in its selection. *Directions:* From St Rémy de Provence, travel south on the D5 to Les Baux de Provence. Turn off the D5 onto the D27. L'Auberge is located off the D27 below the village.

L'AUBERGE DE LA BENVENGUDO
Hôtelier: Jocelyne & Jean Pierre Rossi
Vallon de l'Accoule
13520 Les Baux de Provence
Tel: 90.54.32.54, Fax: 90.54.42.58
17 Rooms, 3 Suites
Double from 500F to 650F, Suite from 750F
Open: 5 February to 10 November
Credit cards: MC, VS
Restaurant closed Sunday, pool, tennis
Region: Provence; Michelin Map: 245, 246

Opened just a few years ago, this newly built inn is nestled at the base of the village of Les Baux de Provence. It offers a quiet setting among the olive trees surrounded by the chalky white rock hillsides dotted with the green shrubbery of Provence. The soft sandstone color of its exterior, dressed with soft green shutters, white trim and a rust tile roof, was beautifully selected to blend, rather than contrast, with the warmth of its setting. The entry of the hotel is light and spacious, decorated with a mix of modern pieces and contemporary fabrics. Beams contrast with white washed walls and the floor is of terra-cotta tile. The lovely bedrooms are all similar in their decor with rustic oak furniture and dressed with Provençal prints and light colors. Bathrooms are spotless and modern and each room is equipped with color TV, safe, minibar and air conditioning. A few guestrooms open onto garden terraces with their own garden entry. The pool is a peaceful oasis, surrounded by a lush green lawn. After a day of sightseeing, you can relax on a comfortable lounge, looking out to the hills of Provence. *Directions:* Mas de l'Oulivie is located in the shadow of Les Baux, its entrance is just off the D27.

MAS DE L'OULIVIE
Hôtelier: Mme & M Achard
13520 Les Baux de Provence
Tel: 90.54.35.78, Fax: 90.54.44.31
20 Rooms
Double from 560F to 930F
Open 15 March - 30 October
and 20 December - 3 January
Credit cards: all major
Pool, tennis court
Region: Provence; Michelin Map: 245, 246

Bayeux is renowned for being the home of the Bayeux tapestry. It is also one of France's most picturesque towns. The delightful Hôtel d'Argouges is conveniently located on one of its main squares, sheltered behind tall gates. A large courtyard and stone, semi-circular staircase lead up to the front entry of the hotel. French doors in the gracious salon-library lead out to the quiet back garden and terrace. Looking out over the beautiful garden or front courtyard, the bedrooms all have exposed beams, fabric covered walls and comfortable furniture as well as private shower or bath and phones. There are also two charming suites which have a small extra room for children. Additional bedrooms are found in an equally delightful adjacent home. Breakfast can be enjoyed in the privacy of your room, in the intimate, elegant breakfast salon, or on the back garden terrace overlooking Madame Auregan's brightly colored flowers. A veritable haven for travelers visiting Bayeux, the Hôtel d'Argouges offers good value in lovely surroundings plus gracious hosts Marie-Claire and Daniel Auregan who take great pride in their *metier. Directions:* From Paris follow directions to *Centre Ville* and you will find yourself on Rue St Patrice.

HÔTEL D'ARGOUGES
Hôtelier: Marie-Claire & Daniel Auregan
21, rue St Patrice
14400 Bayeux
Tel: 31.92.88.86, Fax: 31.92.69.16
25 Rooms
Double from 330F to 500F
Open all year
Credit cards: all major
No restaurant
Region: Normandy; Michelin Map: 231

La Tonnellerie, renovated from a wine-merchant's house, is located on a quiet street near the church in the country village of Tavers. Just 3 kilometers from the medieval city of Beaugency and only an hour-and-a-half drive from Paris by the autoroute, the Hôstellerie de la Tonnellerie is an ideal starting point for visiting the châteaux of the Loire Valley. The bedrooms and suites are invitingly decorated and each has its own immaculate bathroom. Two wings of the building border a central courtyard ablaze with flowers, next to the swimming pool. On the first floor of one wing La Tonnellerie's restaurant features regional specialties as well as *nouvelle cuisine*. A century ago, this is where coopers made barrels for wine merchants. The atmosphere of this lovely restored home is enhanced by antiques, floral arrangements, lovely watercolors and decorative wallpapers. The decor is warm and inviting and the welcome extended by the Aulagnon family is very gracious. *Directions:* Beaugency is 28 kilometers southwest of Orléans. The hotel is 3 kilometers southwest of Beaugency on the N152 in the direction of Blois.

HÔSTELLERIE DE LA TONNELLERIE
Hôtelier: Mme & M Aulagnon
12, rue des Eaux-Bleues
Tavers, 45190 Beaugency
Tel: 38.44.68.15, Fax: 38.44.10.01
12 Rooms, 8 Suites
Double from 705F to 1010F, Suite from 880F
Open Easter to mid-October
Credit cards: MC, VS
Restaurant, pool
Region: Loire Valley; Michelin Map: 238

La Réserve is described by the management as a "restaurant with rooms." It is certainly one of the most luxurious "restaurants with rooms" in France, and La Réserve is one of France's most accredited restaurants. You will be expertly catered to both in the dining room and in the hotel. You may dine in the very elegant restaurant with floor-to-ceiling windows overlooking the salt-water pool and ocean. This elegant room is bordered by an outside terrace which is used for lunch and dinner in the balmy summer months. There are also two small dining rooms in each wing that can be reserved for private functions—one opens onto the terrace and would make an ideal setting for any special occasion. The swimming pool (heated during the winter months) is filled with sea water and surrounded by a private dock where guests moor their boats when they come to lunch in summer. To accompany your meal, the wine cellar features an excellent selection of local wines and those of Bordeaux and Burgundy. Guests not only return year after year to La Réserve, but request the same rooms. There are fifty traditionally furnished bedrooms plus three apartments, each with a sitting room and private balcony. *Directions:* Located halfway between Nice and Monte Carlo (8 kilometers) right on the Mediterranean Sea. The N98 goes right through Beaulieu sur Mer and at one point becomes the Blvd Général-Leclerc.

HÔTEL LA RÉSERVE
Hôtelier: Jean François Marinalle
5, Blvd Général-Leclerc
06310 Beaulieu sur Mer
Tel: 93.01.00.01, Fax: 93.01.28.99
50 Rooms, 3 Suites
Double from 1180F, Suite from 4780F
Closed mid-November to mid-December
Credit cards: all major
Restaurant, pool
Region: Riviera; Michelin Map: 245

BEAUMONT (CHINON)   CHÂTEAU HÔTEL DE DANZAY   Map: 6B

The Château Hôtel de Danzay is located on the edge of a quiet little village surrounded by vineyards. It is largely of 15th-century construction though parts date back to the 12th century. While it is an imposing building, it is homey compared to the grand châteaux in the Loire Valley. The Sarfatis purchased the château in 1981 and completely renovated it, adding modern conveniences such as immaculate bathrooms and heating while retaining all the wonderful old features such as exposed stone walls and heavy beamed ceilings. Decorated with wonderful old furniture, tapestries, and armory there's a castle-like feel to the lofty sitting room where you enjoy drinks before dining in the candle-lit restaurant. Just off the lobby, what was once the family chapel is now a dramatic bedroom starkly modern, in shades of white, with the bathroom (except for the toilet) incorporated into the room. Well worn by generations of passage, circular stone steps lead up to the traditionally decorated bedrooms. All of these luxurious bedchambers have modern bathrooms and are furnished with large antique pieces, befitting the grand scale of this castle. Across the lawn, on the edge of the vineyard is a swimming pool. *Directions:* Take D749 towards Bourgeuil for 5 kilometers and look for signposts directing you left to the château.

CHÂTEAU HÔTEL DE DANZAY
Hôtelier: Mme & M J. Sarfati
37420 Chinon, Beaumont en Veron
Tel: 47.58.46.86, Fax: 47.58.84.35
8 Rooms, 2 Suites
Double from 650F to 1200F, Suite from 1200F
Closed mid-November to March
Credit cards: AX, VS
Restaurant closed October, pool
Region: Loire Valley; Michelin Map: 232

In the heart of the lovely, medieval town of Beaune, Le Cep offers a gracious welcome, charming and comfortable bedrooms decorated with elegance and taste, and very attentive service. The bedrooms all vary in size and decor and are all handsome—highly polished wooden antique furnishings are accented by the beautiful, softly colored fabrics used for the curtains, bedspreads and upholstery. In the bar and public areas, heavy-beamed ceilings, old gilt-framed portraits and fresh flower arrangements add character and elegance. The former wine cellar, a cozy room with a low, arched stone ceiling, is used as a breakfast room when the weather does not permit service outdoors in the pretty courtyard. If you are looking for less elegant fare than that offered in the hotel's restaurant (separate management), there are many very attractive restaurants just a few steps away in the heart of this delightful old town. While Beaune is a destination in itself, it is also a delightful base for touring the Burgundy wine region. Le Cep combines elegance and warmth in perfect proportions. *Directions:* Beaune is located at the heart of Burgundy, 45 kilometers south of Dijon. Circle the town on the road that follows the ramparts. Turn left into the center of town on Rue Maufoux (opposite Hôtel de la Poste). Le Cep is on the right side of the road.

HÔTEL LE CEP
Hôtelier: Mme & M Bernard
27, Rue Maufoux
21200 Beaune
Tel: 80.22.35.48, Fax: 80.22.76.80
49 Rooms, 3 Suites
Double from 600F to 1000F, Suite from 1200F
Open all year
Credit cards: all major
Restaurant
Region: Burgundy; Michelin Map: 243

Hôtel de la Poste is located on the busy ring-road that follows the ancient city walls of Beaune. With parts of it dating back to 1660, the hotel has in recent years undergone a complete renovation including the addition of double-paned windows to eliminate all traffic noise from rooms facing the boulevard. The lobby and bar have retained their old world ambiance, but the bedrooms are more contemporary in their decor. While I can appreciate that this is a very busy city hotel, I was disappointed to see that several of the rooms had stained carpets. The restaurant has maintained its standard of excellence and some of France's finest Burgundies are a perfect accompaniment to the hotel's outstanding menu selections. With Beaune as a base, you can easily venture out to explore and sample some of Burgundy's finest wines. A few minutes walk brings you to the heart of this delightful old walled town with its delightful pedestrian streets. *Directions:* Beaune is located at the heart of Burgundy, 45 kilometers south of Dijon. Circle the town on the ring-road to Blvd Clemenceau; the hotel is on the right side of the road.

HÔTEL DE LA POSTE
Hôtelier: Mme & M Stratigos Baboz
5, Blvd Clemenceau
21200 Beaune
Tel: 80.22.08.11, Fax: 80.24.19.71
22 Rooms, 8 Suites
Double from 750F to 1000F, Suite from 1200F
Open all year
Credit cards: all major
Restaurant
Region: Burgundy; Michelin Map: 243

L'Auberge de l'Abbaye is a very pretty, Norman, half-timbered inn in the picturesque village of Le Bec Hellouin. The medieval abbey, built along a stream and surrounded by half-timbered and thatched buildings, is a peaceful pastoral setting far removed from the hustle and bustle. When we entered the cozy, low-ceilinged restaurant of the 18th-century L'Auberge de l'Abbaye, we were greeted by the sight and aroma of a large, freshly baked apple tart. We were told by the welcoming owner, Madame Sergent, that her restaurant is renowned all over the world for apple tarts. Grand Marnier, a specialty of the region, is also featured here, with large bottles present on each table. The restaurant is full of old-world country-French charm. Lace curtains grace the windows, polished copper and faience ornament the walls, country-style tables are set with care and the low-beamed ceiling adds character. A narrow little staircase leads to the bedrooms which are small and rather drab in their decor with brown paintwork and dark flowered wallpaper. Each room is accompanied by a basic, but spotlessly clean bathroom. Inside and out, L'Auberge de l'Abbaye is the epitome of a simple, country French restaurant with rooms. *Directions.* Located 12 kilometers southwest of Rouen. Take the N138 from Rouen in the direction of Alençon to Maison Brulée. Just before Brionne turn right to Le Bec Hellouin.

L'AUBERGE DE L'ABBAYE
Hôtelier: Sergent Family
27800 Le Bec Hellouin
Tel: 32.44.86.02
10 Rooms, 1 Suite
Double from 350F to 380F, Suite from 480F
Closed mid-January to mid-February
Credit cards: MC, VS
Restaurant
Region: Normandy; Michelin Map: 231

Soon after the publication of the first edition of this guide, I was directed to the Hôtel Bonnet and have since returned for repeated visits. Picturesquely located on a bend of the Dordogne, in the shadow of the towering Château de Beynac, the Bonnet is indeed a "gem." The bedrooms are simple in decor, but the restaurant setting, either indoors with large windows looking onto a river panorama or on the vine-covered terrace, encourages you to linger for hours. The Dordogne meanders through the Périgord, a region whose products have attracted the recognition of true gourmets. Turkeys, ducks, geese, *foie gras*, mushrooms, truffles, vegetables and fruits (particularly strawberries and raspberries) are all found in abundance. Chef Monzie was trained in Périgord and his excellent cuisine reflects the regional specialties. With the vineyard regions of Bordeaux, Bergerac and Cahors nearby, the Restaurant Bonnet offers you a fine selection of wines to accompany your meal. Generations of the Bonnet family have managed this inn for almost a century and today Renée Bonnet is in residence to act as gracious hostess. Stay here for more than three nights and take advantage of the good value offered by their *pension* rates. This is a reasonably priced, simple, but delightful inn with an incomparable riverside setting. *Directions.* Take the D710 and D47 south from Périgueux to Sarlat. At Sarlat travel 10 kilometers on the D703 west to Beynac.

HÔTEL BONNET
Hôtelier: Mlle Renée Bonnet
24220 Beynac
Tel & Fax: 53.29.50.01
22 Rooms
Double from 310F to 335F
Open mid-April to mid-October
Credit cards: MC, VS
Restaurant
Region: Dordogne; Michelin Map: 235

Perched at the end of a rocky promontory in Brittany, the views from Domaine de Rochevilaine are stupendous, especially when the sun shines on the glistening sea or when the wind howls as the waves crash against the rocks below. The vast windows of the sitting room and the restaurant overlook a skywide expanse of open sea giving the distinct sensation of being shipboard. Oriental carpets grace old polished hardwood floors and a roaring fire burns in the grate on cool days. Bedrooms are found either in the little, old stone cottages or in a new (though traditionally styled) wing of rooms near the luxurious indoor swimming pool (there's also a salt water pool on the rocks). All of the bedrooms enjoy dramatic sea views, several have private terraces, handsome wood floors and mellow paneling. The most dramatic room is La Vigie, (the lookout), room 11, named for its 180 degree views. The health center offers a gymnasium, massages, and saunas. *Directions:* The Domaine de Rochevilaine is at Pointe de Pen Lan, 5 kilometers from Muzillac on the D5. Muzillac is located 25 kilometers southeast of Vannes on the road that travels between Vannes and Nantes.

DOMAINE DE ROCHEVILAINE
Hôtelier: Gilles Cotillard
Pointe de Pen Lan
Billiers, 56190 Muzillac
Tel: 97.41.61.61, Fax: 97.41.44.85
40 Rooms
Double from 680F to 1200F, Suite from 1600F
Closed mid-January to mid-February
Credit cards: all major
Restaurant, pools
Region: Brittany; Michelin Map: 230

Bléré is a delightful little town that is perfectly located for exploring the châteaux of the Loire Valley and quiet enough that it is not mobbed by tourists. Facing the town's pedestrian center, Le Cheval Blanc has a contemporary facade that disguises the fact that this is a very old building that was once an annex for the neighboring church. After the revolution, the building was converted to a café-bar and remained so for almost two centuries. It was purchased by Michel and Micheline Blériot several years ago and they have converted the café into a most attractive restaurant with pretty wallpaper, wooden chairs, and tables dressed with crisp linens. An inner courtyard latticed with vines and set with white outdoor tables is a delightful spot for breakfast. Michel is the chef while Micheline looks after the front of the house. Upstairs, the bedrooms are very simply decorated and all but one are small with either a tiny shower or bathroom. They are all spotlessly clean and provide very good value for the money. *Directions:* Bléré is on the N76, 27 kilometers east of Tours and 8 kilometers west of Chenonceaux. The rear of the hotel faces Place Charles Bidault and the hotel's car park.

LE CHEVAL BLANC
Hôtelier: Michel & Micheline Blériot
5, Pl. Charles Bidault, Pl. de l'Église
37150 Bléré
Tel: 47.30.30.14, Fax: 47.23.52.80
12 Rooms
Double from 270F to 380F
Closed January
Credit cards: all major
Restaurant
Region: Loire Valley; Michelin Map: 238

Brantôme, with its Benedictine abbey tucked into the cliffs, narrow streets lined with gray-stone houses and ancient footbridge spanning the River Dronne beside Le Moulin de l'Abbaye, is an enchanting setting. Owner Regis Bulot is president of Relais and Châteaux hotels and you can be certain that he ensures that his hotel is a flagship for this prestigious organization. From its picturesque, riverside setting the hotel looks across the river to Brantôme. Dinner is a real treat—we found it no more expensive than at far inferior places and its wine list had many well-priced wines. Dinner, whether served outdoor on the terrace or in the elegant dining room, profits from the idyllic riverside setting. The lovely bedrooms are found in three buildings: the mill, an adjacent home and a delightful riverside house just two minutes walk across the bridge and through the park. We particularly enjoyed our village bedroom atop a broad flight of spiral stairs. It enjoys delightful decor, views across the rooftops through tiny windows and a luxurious bathroom with an enormous circular tub. *Directions:* Brantôme is located 27 kilometers northwest of Périgueux on the N939. The mill is located on the edge of the village on the road to Bourdeilles.

LE MOULIN DE L'ABBAYE
Hôtelier: Regis Bulot
Directeur: Mme & M Bernard Dessum
1, Route de Bourdeilles
24310 Brantôme
Tel: 53.05.80.22, Fax: 53.05.75.27
17 Rooms, 3 Suites
Double from 700F to 950F, Suite from 1050F
Open May to 25 October
Credit cards: all major
Restaurant
Region: Dordogne; Michelin Map: 233

The Château de Brélidy is located in central Brittany, in an area surrounded by quiet woods and fishing streams. Monsieur and Madame Yoncourt-Pemezec are the gracious, English speaking hosts who solicitously attend to their guests' every need. They run a professional château hotel offering luxurious accommodation and a warm welcome to tourists and business travelers alike. Their fourteen bedrooms are located in a beautifully reconstructed 16th-century wing of the castle, and although decorated in period style furniture and tapestry-style fabrics, are modern and spotless. They all have private baths and direct dial phones. Guests are invited to relax in the castle's salon where tapestry chairs, a huge open fireplace, vases of fresh flowers and *objets d'art* create a refined setting. A stay here is as comfortable as it is atmospheric, for although the castle dates from the 16th century, the Yoncourt-Pemezec family has worked hard to restore it to its current polished state of perfection. For travelers with smaller pocketbooks, the Yoncourt-Pemezec's also offer modest bed and breakfast accommodation in four small attic rooms. These rooms each have private bath and toilet, are homey, comfortable and spotlessly clean. *Directions:* From St Brieuc take the N12 in the direction of Brest to the D767 and exit for Lannion Bégard. At Dégard take the D15 in the direction of Pontrieux, 11 kilometers to Brélidy.

CHÂTEAU DE BRÉLIDY
Hôtelier: Mme & M Yoncourt-Pemezec
Brélidy, 22140 Bégard
Tel: 96.95.69.38, Fax: 96.95.18.03
14 Rooms, 1 Suite
Double from 450F to 720F, Suite from 880F
Open April to November
Credit cards: AX, VS
Restaurant
Region: Brittany; Michelin Map: 230

The atmosphere of the Middle Ages prevails in the narrow, winding, cobblestoned streets leading to the Château Grimaldi, built by Raynier Grimaldi, the ruler of Monaco, in 1309. As the streets become narrower, you pass under buildings which form an archway, arriving at Le Cagnard, a hotel that has been in operation for over forty years. Monsieur and Madame Barel Laroche make guests feel welcome and at home. Dinner on the terrace, set under a full moon, or indoors with the atmosphere of a medieval castle with candlelight flickering against age-old walls, is a romantic experience and the presentation of the cuisine is exceptional. The elevator is charming, presenting biblical paintings changing with each floor. Guestrooms are located either in the main building with the restaurant or tucked off cobbled streets in neighboring buildings. Rooms have a medieval flavor to their decor and are comfortable, but not overly luxurious. A few prize rooms enjoy patios with wonderful views over the tiled rooftops out to the countryside. *Directions:* From Nice travel southwest on the N98 10 kilometers to Cros de Cagnes. Turn north on the D36 to Cagnes sur Mer and follow signposts to Haut de Cagnes. Turn right just after the private parking area onto a very narrow street.

LE CAGNARD
Hôtelier: Mme & M Barel Laroche
Rue Pontis Long
Haut de Cagnes, 06800 Cagnes sur Mer
Tel: 93.20.73.21 & 22, Fax: 93.22.06.39
18 Rooms, 10 Suites
Double from 600F to 1000F, Suite from 1100F
Open all year
Credit cards: all major
Restaurant
Region: Riviera; Michelin Map: 245

The Richeux Hôtel is situated on an old traveler's road that ran between Mont St Michel and St Malo, in the little hamlet of St Méloir des Ondes, just south of Cancale. Sitting high on a clifftop, and surrounded by gardens, the hotel overlooks the Bay of Mont St Michel with the outline of its famous island in the distance. Jane and Olivier Roellinger, who have an award winning restaurant, Maison de Bricourt in Cancale, purchased this splendid turreted Victorian in 1992, and after a complete renovation opened it as a luxurious hotel. The comfortable sitting room and small dining rooms offer stunning sea views. We were only able to see some of the hotel's most luxurious bedrooms and found them to be absolutely divine. Galanga has a massive curved window framing Mont St Michel one way and Cancale the other; Anis Etoile, once an enormous bathroom, has an art deco mosaic extending half way up its walls, and Benso is a particularly attractive room with tall French windows and a balcony. Guests are welcomed with a personal note, fruit and an aperitif, and a serving of tea and cakes. The hotel has a small seafood restaurant or, alternatively, guests can be driven to Maison de Bricourt for dinner. *Directions:* From Cancale take the D76 towards Dol and the first left signpost to Mont St Michel. The hotel is on your left when you reach the sea.

RICHEUX HÔTEL
Hôtelier: Jane & Olivier Roellinger
1, rue Duguesclin, St Méloir des Ondes
35260 Cancale
Tel: 99.89.64.76, Fax: 99.89.88.47
16 Rooms, 3 Suites
Double from 650F to 1250F, Suite from 1250F
Open all year
Credit cards: all major
Restaurant closed Tuesday & Wednesday
Region: Normandy; Michelin Map: 230

Explore the medieval fortress of Carcassonne and then settle for an evening behind its massive walls in the intimate Hôtel de la Cité. Recessed into the walls near the Basilica St Nazaire, the hotel is on the site of the ancient Episcopal palace and offers you the refined comfort of its rooms in a medieval atmosphere. The bar is a welcome spot to settle in for a drink, its walls paneled in ornately carved wood and topped by beautiful and colorful murals that portray the life of days gone by. Breakfast is served in a room where tables are regally set on a carpet of *fleur de lys* under a beamed ceiling and surrounded by walls painted with shields and crests. The hotel's bedrooms, many of which open up onto the ramparts and a large enclosed garden, vary in price according to size, decor and view. Carcassonne is a magnificent fortress, completely restored to look as it did when first constructed centuries ago. It is impressive when viewed at a distance, rising above the vineyards at the foot of the Cevennes and Pyrénées, but even more spectacular when it is explored on foot. *Directions:* Carcassonne is located 92 kilometers southeast of Toulouse. Although in principle the city is closed to all but pedestrian traffic, guests can enter the city by car (via Porte Narbonnaise), travel the Rue Mayrevieille, the Rue Porte d'Aude and the Rue St Louis and park at the hotel.

HÔTEL DE LA CITÉ
Hôtelier: Christophe Luraschi
Place de l'Église
11000 Carcassonne
Tel: 68.25.03.34, Fax: 68.71.50.15
23 Rooms, 3 Suites
Double from 820F to 1250F, Suite from 1600F
Open all year
Credit cards: all major
Restaurant
Region: Languedoc; Michelin Map: 235

The village of Castillon du Gard sits on a knoll surrounded by gray-green olive trees and stretches of vineyards. Housed within medieval walls, the hotel Le Vieux Castillon, runs the length of one small street in this village of sienna-tiled, sun-washed houses, so typical of Provence. The first floor is a maze of tile floors, light sandstone archways, hallways and intimate sitting rooms. The renowned restaurant, Le Fumoir, overlooks the pool through arched windows. Lunch is sometimes served at tables set in a tiled courtyard. The staging of the pool is magnificent, set against a backdrop of the town ruins with vistas that sweep out over the countryside and neighboring villages. The bedrooms, found in the main building and in a neighboring annex, are furnished with floral wallpapers, complementing curtains and bedspreads and a tasteful mix of antiques and reproduction furniture. The style is one of Mediterranean elegance and leisure. Le Vieux Castillon is a remarkable accomplishment—eight years were spent converting the village homes into this luxurious hotel. Care was taken to retain the character of the original buildings and amazingly, the stones were preserved, cleaned and reset within the walls. *Directions:* From Avignon travel in the direction of Nîmes on the N86. At Remoulins take the D981 in the direction of Uzès and then travel 2 kilometers on D228.

LE VIEUX CASTILLON
Hôtelier: Roger Traversac
30210 Castillon du Gard
Tel: 66.37.00.77, Fax: 66.37.28.17
35 Rooms, 2 Suites
Double from 620F to 1290F, Suite from 1390F
Closed January & February
Credit cards: all major
Restaurant, pool, tennis
Region: Provence; Michelin Map: 245, 246

On the western outskirts of Paris, the Abbaye des Vaux de Cernay offers elegant accommodation and dining within the walls and ruins of a dramatic 12th-century abbey. Sequestered at the end of a lovely forested drive that winds through the *Park Regionale de la Haute Vallée*, surrounded by expanses of lawn and fronted by a serene lake, the setting is magnificent. The Abbaye des Vaux de Cernay played an important role in French history and was restored as a family residence by the Rothschilds in the 19th century. Vaulted ceilings, arched entries, massive wood doors, lovely antiques, grand wide hallways, a handsome mix of stone, tile and parquet floors and old stone walls give this imposing hotel an elegant quality. The main dining room is very formal and exquisite with its intricately arched ceiling. Warmed by a large fireplace, the restaurant walls are hung with beautiful paintings and the tables are set with only the finest of linens, crystal and silver. Sixty bedrooms are found in the main building, with the remaining rooms found in the converted stables by the entrance gate. Within the grounds are tennis courts, a fishing lake, a swimming pool and a private hunting park. *Directions:* From Paris take the A6 then the A10 for approximately 14 kilometers, in the direction of Chartres. Take the Les Ulis exit, direction of Gometz along the D35 and then the D40 through Les Molières and on to Cernay la Ville. The Abbaye is west of town.

ABBAYE DES VAUX DE CERNAY
Hôtelier: André Charpentier
Cernay la Ville
78720 Dampierre-en-Yvelines
Tel: (1) 34.85.23.00, Fax: (1) 34.85.20.95
117 Rooms, 3 Suites
Double from 500F to 1050F, Suite from 1600F
Open all year
Credit cards: all major
Restaurant, tennis, hunting, fishing
Region: Île de France; Michelin Map: 237

Chambolle-Musigny is a delightful village nestled amongst the vineyards in the heart of the Burgundy wine region. On one of the village's narrow streets, secluded behind a high wall, lies the Château André Ziltener, which opened as an elegant hotel in 1993. Guests enjoy the grand drawing room where tall French windows look out to the garden. Breakfast is eaten together around the large oval table in the dining room. Since breakfast is the only meal served, guests dine for lunch and dinner in nearby restaurants. The bedrooms are decorated in an open and spacious manner, all have soft beige carpets, and splendid marble bathrooms are provided with every luxurious amenity. Many of those on the top floor have high beamed ceilings. Included in your hotel tariff is an informative guided tour (reserve a time for a tour in English) of the wine museum in the château's cellars and a sampling of the four grades of red wine produced in the area. *Directions:* Chambolle-Musigny is between Gevrey-Chambertin and Nuits-St-Georges on the D122, a country road that parallels the N74 which runs between Dijon and Beaune.

CHÂTEAU ANDRÉ ZILTENER
Hôtelier: Dagmar Ziltener
Rue de la Fontaine
21220 Chambolle Musigny
Tel: 80.62.41.62, Fax: 80.62.83.75
8 Rooms, 2 Suites
Double from 1000F to 1200F , Suite from 1800F
Closed December to February
Credit cards: all major
No restaurant
Region: Burgundy: Michelin Map: 243

Le Moulin du Roc is a small, picture-perfect 17th- and 18th-century stone mill hugging the bank of the River Drome on the edge of the village of Champagnac de Bélair. Flower-filled gardens surround the mill and a little wooden bridge arches across the river to the swimming pool set amidst gardens on the opposite bank. The intimate dining room utilizes the weathered old beams and wooden parts and mechanisms of the original mill in its cozy decor. The atmosphere is intimate and the service is very attentive. Madame Gardillou is responsible for the kitchen and the exquisite cuisine. Preserving the traditions of fine gastronomy and employing established Périgord recipes and specialties, she has earned accolades for her food. Menu prices are reasonable considering the excellence of the cuisine. Monsieur Gardillou is a most gracious and charming host. The bedrooms, although not large, are exquisite. One particularly enchanting suite bridges the river and offers a bedroom with a marvelous wood canopy double bed, and an adjoining small bedroom with a single bed. The suites windows overlook the lazy River Drome, the gardens and the birch-lined pastures. *Directions:* From Périgueux travel north on the D939 to Brantôme and on towards Angoulême. Just before you enter the village (after the cemetery) turn left and the hotel is on your right at the river.

LE MOULIN DU ROC
Hôtelier: Mme & M Gardillou
24530 Champagnac de Bélair
Tel: 53.54.80.36, Fax: 53.54.21.31
10 Rooms, 4 Suites
Double from 550F to 650F, Suite from 700F
Closed mid-November to mid-December
& mid-January to mid-February
Credit cards: all major
Restaurant, pool, tennis
Region: Dordogne; Michelin Map: 233

Every room at Royal Champagne has a private terrace and a stunning view of vineyards cascading down to the town of Épernay in the heart of the Champagne region. The decor is just as delightful as the view and the bathrooms modern and well equipped. If you want to splurge, request the suite with its sitting room on the upper level, and spiral staircase leading down to the bedroom with its dramatic two-story windows framing the countryside view. While the bedrooms are located in rows of single-story contemporary buildings, the sitting room and restaurant are found in a more traditional-style white-stucco building full of interesting military memorabilia. The hotel was at one time an inn on the post road from Reims to Lyon and many regiments both French and foreign broke their journey here (Napoleon being the most celebrated). Dinner and its impeccable service are a special treat in the vaulted dining room with a mural celebrating Dom Perignon's discovery of champagne. Located close to Épernay, Royal Champagne is an excellent choice for a base from which to explore the Champagne region. *Directions:* From Reims, take the N51 towards Épernay and 6 kilometers before Épernay; turn left on the *Route de Champagne.* The hotel is on your right at the first corner.

ROYAL CHAMPAGNE
Hôtelier: Alain Guichaoua
Champillon
51160 Ay
Tel: 26.52.87.11, Fax: 26.52.89.69
31 Rooms, 3 Suites
Double from 850F to 1000F, Suite from 1200F
Closed January
Credit cards: all major
Restaurant, driving range
Region: Champagne; Michelin Map: 241

Haute Provence is a region of France whose beauty is bounded by the snow-covered Alps, the fields of lavender and olive trees of Provence and the blue waters of the Riviera. Villages of soft stone and sienna tiled roofs cluster on hilltops and dot this picturesque landscape. Haute Provence serves as an ideal resting spot when traveling between the regions that bound it. La Bonne Étape is an old coaching inn, a gray-stone manor house with a tiled roof—blending beautifully and suited to the landscape. From its location, it enjoys panoramic views over the surrounding hills. Dating from the 17th century, the hotel has eleven bedrooms and seven apartments, all attractively decorated. The restaurant is recognized for the quality of its cuisine. Pierre Gleize and his son, Jany, employ local ingredients such as honey, lavender, herbs, lemon, pork, and rabbit to create masterpieces in the kitchen. Dine in front of a large stone fireplace and sample some of their specialties. Exceeding the praise for the cuisine are the superlatives guests use to describe the hospitality extended by your charming hosts, the Gleize family. *Directions:* Château Arnoux is situated 40 kilometers north of Aix en Provence, halfway between Albertville and Nice on the N85.

LA BONNE ÉTAPE
Hôtelier: Jany & Pierre Gleize
Chemin du Lac
04160 Château Arnoux
Tel: 92.64.00.09, Fax: 92.64.37.36
11 Rooms, 7 Suites
Double from 600F to 900F, Suite from 1300F
Open mid-February to January 3
Credit cards: all major
Restaurant, pool
Region: Haute Provence; Michelin Map: 245

On the main road, opposite the gates that open to the road winding to the Château de Chaumont, sits the Hôstellerie du Château. An attractive, timbered building, its location is its biggest drawback, for in summer it is hard to shut out the traffic noises unless you request a room that faces the river. However, it is a very moderately priced hotel for the tourist-thronged Loire Valley. You will be charmed by the beam-ceilinged dining room, the attractive salon and the Gourdins' hospitality. On warm summer days tables are set on the patio facing the street, providing an inviting spot to rest and enjoy a refreshing drink. Upstairs the prettily papered bedrooms are moderate in size and simply furnished. Each has an attractive modern bathroom—with either shower, small tub or large tub. Rooms are priced by size and location, so the largest rooms facing the river command the highest price. The Hôstellerie du Château is a well-located hotel for exploring the castles of the Loire. Accommodations are not luxurious, but comfortable and well priced. *Directions:* Chaumont sur Loire is located 36 kilometers northeast of Tours on the N751.

HÔSTELLERIE DU CHÂTEAU
Hôtelier: Mme & M Gourdin
2, Rue du Marechal de Lattre
Chaumont sur Loire, 41150 Onzain
Tel: 54.20.98.04, Fax: 54.20.97.98
15 Rooms
Double from 440F to 750F
Open March to November
Credit cards: MC, VS
Restaurant, pool
Region: Loire Valley; Michelin Map: 238

Château de Chaumontel is an enchanting hotel that once belonged to the family of the Prince de Conde. The castle gates and surrounding trees frame a breathtaking view of the castle. Staged with a moat and a glorious expanse of green, lush grass and mounds of colorful flowers, it is easy to understand why many French brides select the Château de Chaumontel as a setting for their wedding reception. As a guest of the hotel you can also enjoy the romance of the castle's numerous bedchambers. A labyrinth of narrow stairways winds up to rooms tucked under the beams or perhaps in one of the castle turrets. All individual in their decor, the twenty rooms of the hotel are furnished with handsome antiques and pretty decorative prints. A few of the bedrooms are a bit more private as they are located in a pavilion situated near the entrance. The château has facilities to cater large parties and weddings, but the guest dining room located in the castle proper is intimate and charming. Tables are set before a large fireplace, or on a warm day you can take advantage of the lovely white tables set in the garden. *Directions:* Follow A1 from Le Bourget or Charles de Gaulle-Roissy airports to D9 then turn on N16 towards Luzarches and Chantilly. Approximately 8 kilometers before Chantilly look for a large sign for the château.

CHÂTEAU DE CHAUMONTEL
Hôtelier: Mme & M Patrick Rigard
21, rue André Vassord
Chaumontel, 95270 Luzarches
Tel: (1) 34.71.00.30, Fax: (1) 34.71.26.97
20 Rooms
Double from 450F to 800F
Open all year
Credit cards: all major
Restaurant
Region: Île de France; Michelin Map: 237

Hôstellerie le Prieuré is a lovely château on the banks above the Loire. In season, Le Prieuré caters to tours and buses which do tend to invade the sense of "days gone by." However, if you travel off season and can obtain a room in the castle proper, you will be rewarded with a sense of regality. Stone steps wind up the castle turret to spacious rooms which are beautifully appointed with large windows set in thick stone walls opening up to fantastic vistas of the flowing Loire River. There are a few rooms built at the base of the château, called terrace rooms, that open onto private patios. They are also handsome in their decor, but not as luxurious in size. When heavily booked, Le Prieuré also offers more "motel-like" accommodations in bungalows near the pool. The hotel claims that they do advise guests when only the bungalow rooms are available, as they do not afford the castle experience that you would anticipate. The restaurant, an elegant room surrounded by windows, has earned a reputation for excellent cuisine. Situated in a large estate high above the Loire, this lovely hotel commands panoramic views of the river and is a convenient base for exploring the enchanting Château de Saumur and western stretches of the Loire Valley. *Directions:* From Saumur, travel northwest 8 kilometers on D751 in the direction of Gennes.

LE PRIEURÉ
Hôtelier: M P H Doumerc
Chênehutte les Tuffeaux, 49350 Gennes
Tel: 41.67.90.14, Fax: 41.67.92.24
35 Rooms
Double from 790F to 1640F
Closed mid-January to March
Credit cards: all major
Restaurant, pool, tennis
Region: Loire Valley; Michelin Map: 232

Traveling east from Tours on N76, look for signs before you reach Montrichard for the Château de Chissay in the small town of Chissay en Touraine. At the top of a small hill, the arched stone entry way between twin towers serves as the entrance to this *petite* château. Walk through the vaulted stone walls over old cobblestones to reach the inner courtyard with its fountain and open cloister side which lets in cool breezes and looks out over a vista of the Loire Valley. Tapestry covers the chairs in the intimate restaurant, and heavy antique furnishings dress the grand salons. At the time of our visit the bedrooms were all occupied, but a helpful management described them as all having private baths and beautifully traditional furnishings. From the lovely decor and refined taste evident throughout the public areas of the château, we are sure the bedrooms and apartments are very comfortable and pleasant. Located within a twenty-acre estate, this romantic castle is a former royal residence containing a dungeon that dates from the 11th century. Despite its white stone walls and floors, and heavy, forbidding old wooden doors, the Château de Chissay provides a warm and luxurious ambiance from which to explore the many other châteaux of the Loire Valley. *Directions:* From Tours travel 48 kilometers west in the direction of Chenonceaux and then Montrichard. Chissay is located 4 kilometers before the town of Montrichard.

CHÂTEAU DE CHISSAY
Hôtelier: M Longet
Chissay en Touraine
41400 Montrichard
Tel: 54.32.32.01, Fax: 54.32.43.80
24 Rooms, 7 Suites
Double from 690F to 1000F, Suite from 1240F
Closed mid-November to March
Credit Cards: all major
Restaurant, pool
Region: Loire Valley; Michelin Map: 238

Cipières is a beautiful hilltop village with a panoramic view of the Loup Valley. It was surprising to find in this lovely, but remote, setting the elegant Château de Cipières run like an exclusive bed and breakfast and priced like a luxury hotel, Monsieur and Madame Nerozzi are your hosts to welcome you and oversee your stay. Within the walls of this historic 13th-century and 18th-century castle the Capello Nerozzis have aristocratically appointed with fine period furnishings five spacious suites that enjoy fireplaces and magnificent views of the charming village of Cipières with the valley and foothills as a breathtaking backdrop. The suites are priced on a *demi-pension* basis, and for dinner a traditional "home-made" Italian and provincial meal is offered in a regal dining room. Lunch is available on an *à la carte* basis. A beautiful pool is set on the edge of the property, also enjoying the serene backdrop of the Loup Valley. While accommodations here are very high priced we have decided to include the Château de Cipières because it affords you an opportunity to overnight and linger in this dramatically beautiful region. *Directions:* Cipières is a lovely hilltop village tucked at the end of the Loup Valley, located 38 kilometers from either Nice or Cannes in the direction of Gorges du Loup.

CHÂTEAU DE CIPIÈRES
Hôtelier: M & Mme Capello Nerozzi
06620 Cipières
Tel: 93.59.98.00 Fax: 93.59.98.02
5 Suites
Suite from 1850F to 2350F includes dinner
Open April to November
Credit cards: all major
Restaurant for guests, pool
Region: Riviera; Michelin Map: 245

Set on the hillside on the edge of the quiet little village of Colroy la Roche is Hôstellerie La Cheneaudière, a luxurious Relais and Châteaux hotel built in recent years to resemble the surrounding Alsace houses—the hotel blends in beautifully with the adjacent village. The hotel is a world of formal, refined elegance where either Marcel or Mme François are on hand to make certain that everything is of the highest standard. Each luxurious bedroom is beautifully appointed and accompanied by a spacious bathroom—several enjoy a private patio. The largest suite is particularly impressive with large elegantly furnished rooms and a bathroom which sports a glinting golden colored tub and his and hers sinks. The hotel has two dining rooms whose formal atmosphere are warmed by large fires. The cuisine is prepared under the supervision of Chef Jean Paul Bossee and includes specialties such as *millefeuille de foie gras et truffes* and *tartare de saumon sauvage*. The hotel has a spacious lounge and a few elegant boutiques. Guests enjoy the large, heated indoor pool and the adjacent tennis courts. *Directions:* Colroy la Roche is located 62 kilometers southwest of Strasbourg. Travel the D392 first in the direction of Molsheim, then Schirmeck. Beyond Schirmeck at Saint Blaise la Roche take the D424 just a few kilometers to Colroy la Roche.

HÔSTELLERIE LA CHENEAUDIÈRE
Hôtelier: Mme & M Marcel François
Colroy la Roche, 67420 Saales
Tel: 88.97.61.64, Fax: 88.47.21.73
32 Rooms
Double from 1200F
Open March to December
Credit cards: all major
Restaurant, pool, tennis, sauna
Region: Alsace; Michelin Map: 242

Down a private drive enclosed by cornfields, Manoir d'Hautegente sits beneath shady trees in a garden bounded by stone walls, colorful flowers and a rushing stream. A flock of geese on a nearby lawn complete the postcard scene. The original core of this ivy-covered manor house was a forge for the local abbey and dates from the 13th century. The forge later became a mill and other sections were added with the distinctive arched windows and doors. The Hamelin family has lived here for over three hundred years and the next generation is in place, as Patrick and his young family have joined his mother in the hotel. In the evening Madam presides in the kitchen offering two seasonal set menus and a short *à la carte*. Family antiques decorate the salons, halls and bedrooms, including the tallest of grandfather clocks on the landing. With their high ceilings, fabric colored walls and coordinating drapes and bedspreads the bedrooms vary greatly in size, but all enjoy river views. Bounded by a cornfield, the swimming pool is a perfect retreat on warm summer days. The Manoir d'Hautegente is located in a quiet countryside within easy driving distance of tourist spots and is a tranquil base from which to explore Dordogne. *Directions:* From Brive go towards Périgueux on the N89 and turn at Le Lardin in the direction of Montignac for 1 kilometer to Condé where you turn east towards Coly on the D62. A sign before Coly directs you down a drive to the mill.

MANOIR D'HAUTEGENTE
Hôtelier: Edith & Patrick Hamelin
Coly, 24120 Terrasson
Tel: 53.51.68.03, Fax: 53.50.38.52
10 Rooms
Double from 500F to 850F
Closed mid-November to March
Credit cards: all major
Restaurant, pool
Region: Dordogne; Michelin Map: 233, 235

Concarneau is one of Brittany's busiest ports. Sitting in its large sheltered harbor is La Ville Close, a 14th-century fortified town, surrounded by colorful bobbing boats and joined to the mainland by a wooden bridge. Its narrow, cobbled streets and old houses are full of crêperies, gift shops, and restaurants. One of the most attractive of its restaurants is Le Galion which offers accommodation in the small house across the street. Each bedroom is immaculately but plainly decorated, a very tailored look softened by pretty pastel bedspreads. Each room has a tiny kitchen with a stove, microwave and all the fixings for coffee and tea tucked away in a small closet. At 7:30 am rolls and croissants are placed in a basket outside your door. You can do no better than dine with Henri and Marie-Louise Gaonac'h at Le Galion. Henri makes certain you are well fed while Marie-Louise sees that you are well taken care of in the romantic restaurant, with its stone walls and low, heavy beamed ceiling, where tapestry covered chairs are set around elegantly laid tables. The menu offers a tempting variety of set meals from "very good value for money" through *gourmand*, in addition to a short *à la carte*. *Directions:* Concarneau is on the coast almost midway between Quimper and Quimperlé. Follow signposts for the port. In summer you can take a car onto the island only after 7 pm (rest of year: no restrictions). Follow the main street to Le Galion.

LE GALION
Hôtelier: Marie-Louise & Henri Gaonac'h
15 Rue St Guénole, B. P. 115
29181 Concarneau
Tel: 98.97.30.16, Fax: 98.50.67.88
5 Rooms
Double from 420F
Closed mid-January & February
Credit cards: all major
Region: Brittany: Michelin Map: 230

Set on a cobblestoned street just a block from the entrance of Conques is the Hôstellerie de l'Abbaye, a small country hotel, whose chef is also the patron. While we found the welcome at the front desk to be cool, Prince Charles must have felt otherwise since he selected the inn for his weekend visit to Conques, and the Prince's photo is proudly displayed at the front desk. Conques was one of the main stopping places on the old pilgrimage route to Santiago de Compostela in Spain (known as the Way of St James), and as such, has been host to travelers for many years. While you are in Conques, if you are on a budget, the Hôstellerie de L'Abbaye makes a good choice for a hotel. New modern chairs and fabrics contrast with the ancient beams and old antiques that have long graced the public rooms. Guestrooms are clean and neat, and the bathrooms are modern. All rooms are spic and span and priced correctly for a moderately priced hotel. Hopefully, if you choose to stay here you will be greeted with a warm smile. *Directions:* Conques is a small village located 38 kilometers northwest of Rodez and 57 kilometers southwest of Aurillac. The Hôstellerie de l'Abbaye is located just off the main cobbled square.

HÔSTELLERIE DE L'ABBAYE
Hôtelier: M Etourneaud
Rue Charlemagne
12320 Conques
Tel: 65.72.80.30, Fax: 65.72.82.84
8 Rooms
Double from 340F to 460F
Closed: last two weeks January
Credit cards: all major
Restaurant
Region: Lot & Aveyron; Michelin Map: 235

The medieval village of Conques overlooks the Dourdou Gorge. Off the beaten track, the village is glorious in the gentle light of evening or in the mist of early morning. Conques' pride is an 11th-century abbey, directly across from a lovely hotel, the Ste Foy. The shuttered windows of our room opened to church steeples and we woke to the melodious sound of bells. The decor of the bedrooms is neat and attractive and the rooms have been recently refurbished and air conditioned. The dining rooms are a delight—tables topped with crisp linen, country French furniture, flagstone floors, ancient stone walls, low beamed ceilings. In summer you can dine in the sheltered courtyard or on the rooftop terrace that overlooks the abbey. You can order *à la carte* or select from a well-chosen three- or four-course fixed menu at a very reasonable price. The restaurant offers a number of regional dishes. The Roquefort cheese produced in the area is exceptional and the house *salade verte aux noix et roquefort et huile de noix* is a perfect first course to any meal. The wine list contains a wide selection of fine French wines. *Directions:* From Rodez take the D901 northwest for 37 kilometers in the direction of Decazeville and Figeac to Conques.

HÔTEL STE FOY
Hôtelier: Marie France Garcenot
12320 Conques
Tel: 65.69.84.03, Fax: 65.72.81.04
16 Rooms, 3 Suites
Double from 400F to 900F, Suite from 1000F
Open Easter to mid-November
Credit cards: all major
Restaurant, pool
Region: Lot & Aveyron; Michelin Map: 235

Vieux Cordes is an enchanting, medieval hilltop-village. Located at the center of this medieval city is the Hôtel du Grand Écuyer. Once the home and hunting lodge of Raymond VII, Comte de Toulouse, this is a grand hotel that seems to improve with age. Found along the upstairs hallway whose floors creak and slant, the bedrooms are very impressive in their decor. Decorated with period furnishings, a few of the rooms boast magnificent four poster beds and some even enjoy large fireplaces. The bedroom windows, set in thick stone walls, open on to glorious vistas of the surrounding countryside. The reputation of the hotel's restaurant reflects the expertise of Monsieur Yves Thuriès, under whose direction and guidance selections from the menu are further enhanced by artful and creative presentation. His specialty is desserts and they are divine in taste as well as presentation. If you want to try your own talent in the kitchen, purchase a copy of his book, *La Nouvelle Patisserie*. Vieux Cordes is a gem. It is a medieval village that proves to be a highlight of many a trip and the Hôtel du Grand Écuyer is the final polish that makes Cordes an ideal stopover for any itinerary. The Thuriès family is renovating the Hôstellerie du Vieux Cordes, a simpler hotel at the top of this charming village. *Directions:* Cordes is 25 kilometers northwest of Albi on the D600.

HÔTEL DU GRAND ÉCUYER
Hôtelier: Yves Thuriès
Rue Voltaire
81170 Cordes
Tel: 63.56.01.03, Fax: 63.56.16.99
12 Rooms, 1 Suite
Double from 620F to 850F, Suite from 1400F
Open April to mid-October
Credit cards: all major
Restaurant
Region: Tarn; Michelin Map: 235

Perched on a hill in the middle of a lovely valley in Provence is the charming medieval village of Crillon le Brave comprised of only a cluster of weathered stone houses and a picturesque church. The town is completely commercial except for one of Provence's jewels, the deluxe Hôstellerie de Crillon le Brave, which is terraced on the hillside just below the church. This small hotel exudes an aura of elegance, yet there is nothing stuffy or intimidating about staying here. The well-trained staff is friendly and the ambiance is delightful. The restoration has been beautifully accomplished maintaining all the wonderful wood and stone textures, which have been delightfully accented by the bold colors of Provençal print fabric. Fine country antiques are used throughout. The guest rooms, too, are decorated in the same style and most have magnificent views of the countryside. The hillside location lends itself well to romance—the dining room is located in a medieval looking vaulted ceilinged room which opens out onto a splendid terrace where meals are usually served. From the terrace, a path leads down to a lower garden where a swimming pool invites you to linger on comfortable lounge chairs and soak in the view. *Directions:* In Carpentras follow signs toward Mount Ventoux and Bédoin on the D974. Travel 10 kilometers northeast and just before the village of Bédoin, take the left turn marked Crillon le Brave.

HÔSTELLERIE DE CRILLON LE BRAVE
Hôtelier: Peter Chittick & Craig Miller
Place de l'Eglise
84410 Crillon le Brave
Tel: 90.65.61.61, Fax: 90.65.62.86
15 Rooms, 6 Suites
Double from 750 to 1250F, Suite from 1250F
Open April through December
Credit cards: all major
Restaurant, pool
Region: Provence; Michelin Map: 245, 246

The Dordogne River makes a panoramic journey through a rich valley studded with castles. The ancient village of Domme has for centuries stood guard high above the river and commands a magnificent panorama. The town itself is enchanting, with ramparts that date from the 13th century, and narrow streets that wind through its old quarter and past a lovely 14th century Hôtel de Ville. Visitors come to Domme for its spectacular views of the Dordogne River Valley and the best vantage point is from the shaded terrace of the Hôtel de l'Esplanade. Staying at this hotel enables you to savor the village long after the tour buses have departed. The Gillards extend a warm and friendly greeting at the Hôtel de l'Esplanade and Ren Gillard is both your host and chef. In either of the two dining rooms, charmingly country in their decor, he'll propose some excellent regional specialties. Bedrooms in the main building of the hotel are found down narrow, ornately decorated hallways and a few on the village edge open onto unobstructed million dollar views of the Dordogne. Other guestrooms are found not in the main building but down cobbled streets in neighboring buildings. Most accommodations are housed behind old stone walls of the village and, although attractively decorated and comfortable, are not luxurious. *Directions:* Domme is located 75 kilometers southeast of Perigueux. From Sarlat take the D45 for 12 kilometers to Domme.

HÔTEL DE L'ESPLANADE
Hôtelier: Ren Gillard
24250 Domme
Tel: 53.28.31.41, Fax: 53.28.49.92
24 Rooms, 1 Suite
Double from 350F to 600F, Suite from 800F
Open mid-February to mid-November
Credit cards: all major
Restaurant
Region: Dordogne; Michelin Map: 235

At first glance this hotel appears as a typical French roadside restaurant with natural wood shutters and flower boxes overflowing with a profusion of red, pink and white geraniums. The wonderful surprise is that behind a simple exterior lies a sophisticated hotel and gourmet restaurant run by Jean-Paul Perardel and his charming wife Denise. Bedrooms are located in quiet wings that stretch behind the hotel. The smaller, less expensive, rooms are decorated in what Denise Perardel terms a "rustic" style. Larger rooms are more county-house style in their decor. All are accompanied by an immaculate bath or shower room and are outfitted with telephone, TV, and mini-bar. Six plainer rooms are found in a modern house in the village. Patrick Michelon presides in the kitchen and his appealing cuisine ensures that the restaurant attracts a great many local patrons. The hotel is located in a farming region a half hour drive from the vineyards of Champagne. *Directions:* From Reims take the N44 south to Châlons sur Marne and then the N3 east in the direction of Metz for 8 kilometers.

AUX ARMES DE CHAMPAGNE
Hôtelier: Denise & Jean-Paul Perardel
31, avenue du Luxembourg
51460 L'Épine
Tel: 26.69.30.30, Fax: 26.66.92.31
35 Rooms, 2 Suites
Double from 370F to 780F, Suite from 1250F
Closed mid-January to mid-February
Credit cards: MC, VS
Restaurant closed Sunday evening & Monday
  November to March, tennis
Region: Champagne; Michelin Map: 241

The village of Eugénie les Bains is little more than a bend in the road and Les Prés d' Eugénie, Christine and Michel Guérard's ethereal complex that extends beyond the bounds of the thermal spa to include several old adjoining properties, refurbished into luxurious rooms and an exquisite restaurant. Guests are divided into four groups: those attracted to the fitness spa and hot springs; devotees of Michel Guérard's *gourmande* cuisine; devotees of Michel Guérard's *minceur* (slimming) cuisine; and those who want to try a bit of everything. The main building contains Les Prés d'Eugénie and the spa where wraps, massages, and every imaginable treatment with mineral water is designed to promote weight loss and relieve rheumatism, urinary and digestive problems. Alongside, there is La Maison Rose with more ordinary bedrooms and where only *minceur* cuisine is served. Across the garden, the most opulent country French bedrooms are found in a converted convent, Le Couvent des Herbes. Additional deluxe studios and a restaurant are found at La Ferme aux Grives. In the rustic farmhouse-style restaurant tables and chairs are arranged around an old country table groaning with fresh produce and meat is roasted on the spit in the enormous fireplace. *Directions:* From Bordeaux take the A66 south towards Bayonne to the N134 toward Mont de Marsan, then take N124 to Grenade sur l'Adour and the D11 to Eugénie les Bains.

LES PRÉS D' EUGÉNIE
Hôtelier: Christine & Michel Guérard
40320 Eugénie les Bains
Tel: 58.05.05.05, Fax: 58.51.13.59
33 Rooms, 10 Suites
Double from 450F to 550F, Suite from 1250F
Open late February through November
Credit cards: all major
Restaurant, pool
Region: Landes: Michelin Map: 234

The vine-covered Hôtel Cro-Magnon was built on the site where the skull of the prehistoric Cro-Magnon man was unearthed and, appropriately, a beautiful collection of prehistoric flints is on display in the hotel. Managed by the third generation of the Leyssales family, this is a tranquil country-style hotel with beautiful furnishings from the Perigord region. The hotel has a large swimming pool, perfect for warm summer days, and a park of four acres. There are 22 rooms, some of which are in the annex added in 1962. Rooms are priced according to their location and size. Back bedrooms in the annex look out through shuttered windows onto the expanse of colorful garden and pool. The restaurant is truly delightful in its country-French decor and the menu features Périgordian specialties that are a prime attraction of the region. The hotel's front terrace is set under the shade of draping vines and is an ideal place to linger over lunch or enjoy an aperitif. Les Eyzies is a popular tourist destination and the town is rich in accommodation. The Cro-Magnon hotel proves to be a choice and favorite of many, which is a direct reflection on the standards of service and welcome set by the Leyssales family. We continue to receive only words of praise from our readers who have experienced the hospitality of the Leyssales family in this lovely hotel. *Directions:* Les Eyzies is located 45 kilometers southeast of Périgueux.

HÔTEL CRO-MAGNON
Hôtelier: Christiane & Jacques Leyssales
24620 Les Eyzies
Tel: 53.06.97.06, Fax: 53.06.95.45
18 Rooms, 4 Suites
Double from 350F to 550F, Suite from 650F
Open end April to mid-October
Credit cards: all major
Restaurant, pool
Region: Dordogne; Michelin Map: 233

For more than a thousand years this majestic château has soaked up the sun and looked across the beautiful blue water of the Mediterranean. Rising 400 meters above sea level, the medieval village of Èze looks down upon Cap Ferrat and Nice. You can happily spend an entire afternoon on the secluded hotel terrace overlooking the pool and the stunning coastline vistas. In the sparkle of evening lights, the coastal cities seem to dance along the waterfront. The bedchambers open onto views of the Riviera or surrounding hillsides. Housed within the walls of this medieval village, the rooms are not grand or large, but tastefully appointed with modern conveniences. Enjoy a drink in the bar just off the pool while studying the day's menu selections. For lunch or dinner, a meal at the Château de la Chèvre d'Or is a wonderful experience, a combination of marvelous cuisine and incredible views. The restaurant is popular with the local community and the many celebrities who have homes on the Riviera, so reservations are a must. Attentive service, superb cuisine, beautiful views and a peaceful, serene medieval atmosphere make the Château de la Chèvre d'Or a hotel to which you will eagerly return. *Directions:* Èze Village is located on the *Moyenne Corniche*, the N7, between Nice and Monaco (13 kilometers east of Nice). Exit the Autoroute, A8, at La Turbie.

CHÂTEAU DE LA CHÈVRE D'OR
Hôtelier: Pierre de Daeniken
Directeur: Randrianasolo Simon
Rue du Barri, 06360 Èze Village
Tel: 93.41.12.12, Fax: 93.41.06.72
15 Rooms, 5 Suites
Double from 1300F to 2500F, Suite from 2650F
Open March to New Year
Credit cards: all major
Restaurant, pool
Region: Riviera; Michelin Map: 245

Monsieur André Rochat, in the fabled tradition of Swiss excellence, has renovated the former château of Prince William of Sweden and converted the magnificent residence into a hotel of superb luxury. The Château Eza is located in the medieval village of Èze, perched 400 meters above the coastline of the Riviera. The hotel's bedrooms are found in a cluster of buildings that front onto Èze's narrow, winding, cobblestoned streets. Most of the rooms have a private entry and blend in beautifully as part of the village scene. Accommodation can only be described as extremely luxurious apartments or suites. The decor is stunning, with priceless antiques and Oriental rugs. Each room enjoys spectacular views and wood-burning fireplaces and some have private terraces, with views extending out over the rooftops of the village. The Château Eza has a renowned restaurant with views and service to equal the excellent cuisine. A multi-level tea room with its hanging garden terraces is a delightful and informal spot for afternoon tea or a light meal. The Château Eza is a wonderful final splurge before departing France—the airport at Nice is just fifteen minutes from Èze Village. As Èze is closed to cars, look for the reception at the base of the village—it is easy to spot as two donkeys, *les bagagistes*, are stabled out front. *Directions:* Èze Village is located on the *Moyenne Corniche*, the N7, between Nice and Monaco. Exit the Autoroute, A8, at La Turbie.

CHÂTEAU EZA
Hôtelier: André Rochat
06360 Èze Village
Tel: 93.41.12.24, Fax: 93.41.16.64
6 Rooms, 2 Suites
Double from 1500F, Suite from 2500F
Open April through October
Credit cards: all major
Restaurant
Region: Riviera; Michelin Map: 245

William the Conqueror, the famous Frenchman who conquered England, was born in the town of Falaise's mighty fortress. Just a five minute drive from the castle's ramparts you come to Château du Tertre, a stylish little 18th century château, set in parklike grounds. It has only recently opened as a hotel and has in a surprisingly short time received accolades for the culinary creations of its young chef, Pierre Gay. His vivacious, young, wife Nathalie manages the château. Owner Roger Vickery, a transplanted Englishman, chose to go with an uncluttered decor mixing contemporary and traditional in a very pleasing way which gives the hotel a very sophisticated look. Guests enjoy drinks in a clubby little parlor before going into dinner in the former grand salon which is now an elegant restaurant. Each bedroom is named after a famous French writer who wrote about Normandy. We particularly enjoyed Madame Bovary, which can be a suite of rooms when joined with the adjacent room, Gustave Flaubert. We found Alphonse Allais to be a little too busy for our taste, but would gladly have settled into any of the other rooms. All but one of the bathrooms has a vast Victorian claw-foot tub. Television is available on request. The staff is young and very enthusiastic. *Directions:* Leave Falaise on D5111 toward Pont d'Oully. After 1 kilometer, at the roundabout, take D44 toward Foueneau le Val and the château is on your right after 1 kilometer.

CHÂTEAU DU TERTRE
Hôtelier: Roger Vickery, Nathalie & Pierre Gay
St Martin de Mieux
14700 Falaise
Tel: 31.90.01.04, Fax: 31.90.33.16
9 Rooms
Double from 750F to 950F, Suite from 1100F
Closed February
Credit cards: all major
Restaurant closed Sunday evening & Monday
Region: Normandy: Michelin Map: 231

The Château de Fère is a delightful château hotel an hour's drive from Charles de Gaulle-Roissy airport. Set in parklike grounds, there are actually two castles. One built in 1206 by Robert de Dreux is now in ruins and serves as a background to the second, the 16th-century Château de Fère. The owner, Richard Blia, is an architect, and he has remodeled and decorated his hotel in a style that he finds pleasing, with fabric covered walls and matching draperies and bedspreads. Some of his choices are delightful pastels while others are very flowery or very dark in color. We particularly enjoyed our bedroom (25) with its heavy beams and pale yellow walls. Other favorites include the dramatic suite (33) with its huge circular tub and two bedrooms, and rooms 20, 36, 29 and 41. Most bedrooms have twin beds, which can be made into one large bed. The restaurants look out to the wooded grounds through tall windows, and display elegant linens, silver and crystal. Ask for a seat in the pine-paneled restaurant if the large folkloric animal murals in the main restaurant are not to your taste. A magnificent menu and an excellent wine list are offered with the estate's champagne being a specialty. *Directions.* From Paris take A4 and exit at Château Thierry following directions to Soissons. Then take D967 north to Fère en Tardenois. The Château de Fère is located 3 kilometers outside Fère en Tardenois.

CHÂTEAU DE FÈRE
Hôtelier: Richard Blia
Directrice: Jo-Andréa Finck
02130 Fère en Tardenois
Tel: 23.82.21.13, Fax: 23.82.37.81
19 Rooms, 6 Suites
Double from 860F to 1130F, Suite from 1300F
Closed January and February
Credit cards: all major
Restaurant, pool, tennis, golf
Region: Champagne; Michelin Map: 237

La Régalido, converted from an ancient oil mill, is a lovely Provençal hotel, with its cream stone facade, sienna tile roof, and shuttered windows peeking out through an ivy-covered exterior. Running the length of this hotel is a beautiful garden bordered by brilliantly colored roses. In the entry, lovely paintings and copper pieces adorn the walls, and plump sofas and chairs cluster before a large open fireplace. An arched doorway frames the dining room, which opens onto a verandah and the rose garden. The restaurant, with its tapestry-covered chairs placed around elegantly set tables, is renowned for its regional cuisine and its wine cellar. Monsieur Michel spends much of his day tending to the kitchen and is often seen bustling about the hotel, dressed in his chef's attire, but is never too busy to pause for a greeting. His wife's domain is the garden—the French say that she has a "green hand" instead of just a "green thumb," and it shows. The bedrooms of La Régalido are very pretty in their decor and luxurious in size and comfort. About half of the rooms have terraces that look out over the tile rooftops of Fontvieille. *Directions:* From Avignon take N570 south in the direction of Arles. Ten kilometers before Arles turn southeast on the D33 to Fontvieille.

LA RÉGALIDO
Hôtelier: Mme & M Jean Pierre Michel
Rue Frédéric Mistral
13990 Fontvieille
Tel: 90.54.60.22, Fax: 90.54.64.29
14 Rooms
Double from 600F to 1350F
Closed January
Credit cards: all major
Restaurant closed Monday & Tuesday lunch
Region: Provence; Michelin Map: 245, 246

Set across the street from a stretch of lawn that borders the meandering River Loire, this is an attractive city hotel that is known for its restaurant. We chose to overnight in Gien to be first in line to visit the *Gien Faience* museum and factory which opens at 9:00 am. The hotel looked as if it might be the best in town, and although we were just looking for a comfortable overnight, we were surprised and rewarded with exceptionally courteous service, and a very attractive room. All employees of the hotel seem to have taken a course in hospitality—from the girls cleaning the rooms who always wear a warm smile, to the young man who appeared from the kitchen with a cold bottle of Evian, prompted only by the fact that he had seen us discard an empty bottle. This restaurant with rooms is reasonably priced, and the deluxe apartments are spacious. Our room, which overlooked the back parking area, was quiet. The rooms at the front enjoy river views and have double-glazed windows to block out traffic noise. *Directions:* Gien is located on the Loire River, 64 kilometers southeast of Orléans. Arriving from the northwest follow the D952 as it parallels the river through town. Just past the center of town, look for the Hôtel du Rivage, on the left hand side opposite the river.

HÔTEL DU RIVAGE
Hôtelier: Mme & M Christian Gaillard
1, quai de Nice
45500 Gien
Tel: 38.37.79.00, Fax: 38.38.10.21
16 Rooms, 3 Suites
Double from 370F to 510F, Suite from 695F
Open all year
Credit cards: all major
Restaurant closed mid-February to mid-March
Region: Loire Valley; Michelin Map: 238

Just outside the medieval village of Gordes, in the direction of Sénanque, is a complex of cream-colored stone houses converted to a delightful hotel, the Domaine de l'Enclos. The hotel sits on the hillside amongst gardens and stretches of green lawn. The main building was once a private home, regionally referred to as a *mas*, and houses a beautiful restaurant and six bedrooms. The restaurant occupies most of the first floor. Tables are spaciously set before floor-to-ceiling windows that look out over the valley, in front of a magnificent stone fireplace, or in a secluded corner. A quiet sitting room and bar are also available for guests' use. The Bergerie and Fermettes are neighboring, newly constructed buildings that offer luxurious suites and apartments. With cream-colored stone walls and tile roofs, the exteriors are attractively modeled after the original home and in keeping with the flavor of the region. All but two rooms in this section of the complex have a private terrace, patio or garden. The accommodations at the Domaine de l'Enclos are superlative, decorated with Provençal prints and treasured antiques. The bathrooms are spacious and equipped with every modern convenience. The Domaine's buildings are set to maximize views of the countryside and the setting is rural and tranquil. *Directions:* Traveling the Autoroute, A7, take the Avignon *Sud* exit and go to Apt on N573 and then Coustellet on D22. then north on D2 and D15 to Gordes.

DOMAINE DE L'ENCLOS
Hôtelier: Serge Lafitte
Route de Sénanque, 84220 Gordes
Tel: 90.72.08.22, Fax: 90.72.03.03
14 Rooms, 3 Suites
Double from 400F to 1300F, Suite from 1200F
Open all year
Credit cards: all major
Restaurant, pool, tennis
Region: Provence; Michelin Map: 245, 246

When the Konings family (from Holland) asked a realtor to find a place for them to retire in Provence, they expected the search to take years. To their delight, the perfect property, a very old stone farmhouse with great potential charm, was found almost immediately. The Konings bought the farmhouse and restored it into an absolute dream. The six guest rooms are in a cluster of weathered stone buildings forming a small courtyard. The name of each room gives a clue as to its original use such as The Old Kitchen, The Hayloft, and The Wine Press. Arja Konings has exquisite taste and each room is decorated with country antiques and Provençal fabrics. The Konings' son, Gerald, (who was born in the United States) is a talented chef. He oversees the small restaurant which is delightfully appealing, with massive beamed ceiling, tiled floor, exposed stone walls and country-style antique furnishings. The dining room opens onto a terrace which overlooks the swimming pool. *Directions:* Gordes is located about 38 kilometers northeast of Avignon. From Gordes go towards Apt on D2 for about 3 kilometers. Turn right (south) on D156 and in two minutes you will see La Ferme de la Huppe on your right.

LA FERME DE LA HUPPE
Hôtelier: Family Konings
Route D156
84220 Gordes
Tel: 90.72.12.25, Fax: 90.72.01.83
6 Rooms
Double from 500F
Open April to November
Credit cards: MC, VS
Restaurant
Region: Provence; Michelin Map: 245, 246

Tucked into a delightful village in the southwestern corner of France is an adorable romantic hotel, Pain Adour et Fantasie (which translates roughly to "bread, the River Adour and fantasy"). The 17th-century, half-timbered building faces the old-fashioned village square and backs on to the lazily flowing River Adour. The sunny restaurant overlooks a broad, river terrace where you can dine on warm summer evenings. Food is the premier reason for coming here. Owner and chef Didier Oudill has gained a reputation for outstanding fare (the restaurant has received a two-star rating from *Michelin*). The large guestrooms, several of which have river views, are decorated in a sophisticated, uncluttered manner, in soft, sunny pastels and furnished with country-French antiques. The bathrooms are modern and immaculate. The staff is young and very helpful. All in all, Pain Adour et Fantaisie has the ingredients to make your fantasies come true. *Directions:* From Bordeaux take A66 south towards Bayonne to N134 toward Mont de Marsan, then N124 to Grenade sur l'Adour.

PAIN ADOUR ET FANTAISIE
Hôtelier: Jeanine & Didier Oudill
7 Place des Tilleuls
40270 Grenade sur l'Adour
Tel: 58.45.18.80, Fax: 58.45.16.57
11 Rooms
Double from 480F to 900F
Open all year
Credit cards: all major
Restaurant closed Sunday evening & Monday
Region: Landes: Michelin Map: 234

The Château de Locguénolé, isolated by acres of woodland, presents an imposing picture as it sits high above the Lavet River with lawns sloping down to the water's edge. This magnificent château has been the family home of the De la Sablière family since 1600 and today Madame de la Sablière and her son Bruno run it as an elegant Relais & Châteaux hotel. Family antiques abound in the four elegant salons. Down the grand curving staircase is the restaurant where Denis Cros presents a wonderful menu complemented by an excellent wine list. The principal bedrooms are grand, lofty, and high-ceilinged overlooking a panorama of lawn forest and river. It is hard to beat the luxury offered by room 2, a decadent suite, and rooms 4 and 1, large rooms with massive bay windows. The low-beamed ceilinged attic rooms are delightful, but Bruno assured me that Americans prefer the cozy, comfortable rooms in the adjacent manor. With its close proximity to the coast, Château de Locguénolé is a lovely spot for exploring Brittany's coastline as well as visiting its historic hinterland. *Directions:* Hennebont is located 10 kilometers east of Lorient on N165, and approaching Lorient, take the exit Port Louis on D781 for 4 kilometers to the château.

CHÂTEAU DE LOCGUÉNOLÉ
Hôtelier: Mme & M Bruno de la Sablière
Route de Port Louis
56700 Hennebont
Tel: 97.76.29.04, Fax: 97.76.39.47
34 Rooms, 4 Suites
Double from 690F to 1460, Suite from 1295F
Closed January
Credit cards: all major
Restaurant, pool, tennis, sauna
Region: Brittany; Michelin Map: 230

If you are looking for a simple budget hotel, in an excellent location in the picturesque port town of Honfleur, we recommend Hôtel du Dauphin. Set on Place Berthelot, just off the town main square, St Catherines, the hotel is a hundred meters from the harbor. By day throngs of tourists and cars clog the town's narrow streets, but the nights are quiet. The lobby, sitting room and breakfast room are one large functional room. A maze of stairways and double doors ramble through the building and lead to the bedrooms. Most of the bedrooms are clean, basic and priced accordingly. However, five bedrooms are more "up market." Flower boxes adorn the timbered facade. The Hôtel du Dauphin has no restaurant, but there are numerous tempting little seafood restaurants lining the town's narrow winding streets. The Hôtel du Dauphin offers basic, clean and inexpensive accommodation at the heart of picturesque Honfleur. *Directions:* Arriving from Paris (180 kilometers) take the Autoroute, A13, direction Caen via Rouen. Exit the Autoroute at Beuzeville and travel north on D22 and then west on D180 to Honfleur. The hotel is at 10, Place Pierre Berthelot south of the harbor. Parking is difficult to find.

HÔTEL DU DAUPHIN
Hôtelier: Michel François
10, Place Pierre Berthelot
14600 Honfleur
Tel: 31.89.15.53, Fax: 31.89.92.06
35 Rooms, 2 Suites
Double from 330F to 500F, Suite from 700F
Closed January
Credit cards: all major
No restaurant
Region: Normandy; Michelin Map: 231

Narrow cobbled streets, lined with ancient houses, wind up from the picturesque sheltered harbor in Honfleur. Just a short stroll from the bustle of St Catherine's Square, you find yourself on the quiet cobbled street that leads to Hôtel L'Écrin. Set behind tall gates and fronted by a large courtyard, Hôtel l'Écrin was once a grand home and it retains that feel today. The decor, to say the least, is flamboyant—red velvet and gilt, lavishly applied, the fanciest French furniture, a multitude of paintings of all sizes and descriptions, and a wide assortment of decorations including stuffed birds, a larger-than-life-size painted statue of a Nubian slave, and two enormous wooden Thai elephants. The same lavish taste extends to the bedrooms in the main house where several large high-ceilinged rooms are ornately decorated. The bathrooms are modern and well equipped. On either side of the courtyard are additional, less ornate bedrooms. The staff is friendly, helpful and always happy to recommend restaurants to fit your budget. Honfleur is truly one of France's most picturesque port towns and the Hôtel l'Écrin offers quiet, convenient, moderately priced, colorful accommodation. *Directions:* Arriving from Paris (180 kilometers) take the Autoroute, A13, direction Caen via Rouen. Exit A13 at Beuzeville, travel north on D22, then west on D180 to Honfleur.

HÔTEL L'ÉCRIN
Hôtelier: Mme & M Jean-Louc Blais
19, Rue Eugéne Boudin
14600 Honfleur
Tel: 31.89.32.39, Fax: 31.89.24.41
20 Rooms
Double from 350F to 900F
Open all year
Credit cards: all major
No restaurant
Region: Normandy; Michelin Map: 231

Set on the coastal hills just outside the picturesque port town of Honfleur, La Ferme St Siméon is a lovely 17th-century Normandy home with flower boxes adorning every window. In the garden where painters such as Monet, Boudin and Jongkind set up their easels, seventeen rooms have been added. Of these new rooms, three are suites and like the other rooms, all are individually styled and handsomely decorated with fine antiques. The intimate decor of the restaurant is beautifully accented by a beamed ceiling and colorful flower arrangements decorate each table. The chef, Denis Le Cadre, has earned recognition in some of France's most prestigious restaurants. He uses only high quality fresh produce, for which the region is famous, to create exquisite dishes. Offered on an *à la carte* basis, the cuisine is delicious and expensive. Reservations for the hotel and the restaurant are a must and should be made well in advance. La Ferme offers a convenient base from which to explore enchanting Honfleur, and the D-Day beaches and Monet's home at Giverny are both just an hour's drive away. *Directions:* From Paris (180 kilometers) take the Autoroute, A13, direction Caen via Rouen. Exit A13 at Beuzeville, travel north on D22, then west on D180 to Honfleur. La Ferme is located just beyond the town on the coastal road (D513) in the direction of Deauville

LA FERME ST SIMÉON
Hôtelier: Mme & M Roland Boelen
Rue Adolphe-Marais
14600 Honfleur
Tel: 31.89.23.61, Fax: 31.89.48.48
31 Rooms
Double from 1350F to 2210F
Open all year
Credit cards: MC, VS
Restaurant, pool, tennis, sauna
Region: Normandy; Michelin Map: 231

Winding through the foothills of the Vosges Mountains, the wine route of Alsace is extremely picturesque. It meanders through delightful towns and is exposed to enchanting vistas of a countryside carpeted with vineyards and dotted by neighboring towns clustered around their church spires. The village of Itterswiller, nestled on the hillside amongst the vineyards, is a wonderful base from which to explore the region and the Hôtel Arnold is a charming country hotel. The accommodation and restaurant are in three separate buildings. The color wash of the individual buildings varies from white to soft yellow to burnt red. Each building is handsomely timbered and the window boxes hang heavy with a profusion of red geraniums. Most bedrooms are located in the main building of the Hôtel Arnold, set just off the road on the edge of the village. These simply decorated bedrooms are at the back of the hotel and look out over vineyards. Premier bedrooms (our favorites) are found in the delightful little home, (La Reserve), next to Winestub Arnold, the hotel's restaurant. Winestub Arnold, set under lovely old beams with pretty cloths and decorative flower arrangements adorning the tables, is an appealing place to dine on regional specialties and to sample the estate's wines. Arnold's also has a delightful gift shop. *Directions:* From Strasbourg, take N392 and continue on N425 39 kilometers south to Epfig and travel west to Itterswiller on D335.

HÔTEL ARNOLD
Hôtelier: Marléne & Gérard Arnold
98 Route du Vin
67140 Itterswiller
Tel: 88.85.50.58, Fax: 88.85.55.54
27 Rooms
Double from 380F to 695F
Open all year
Credit cards: MC, VS
Restaurant closed Sunday evening & Monday
Region: Alsace; Michelin Map: 242

The Château du Plessis is a lovely, aristocratic country home, truly one of France's most exceptional private châteaux-hôtels, and a personal favorite. Madame Benoist's family has lived here since well before the revolution, but the antiques throughout the home are later acquisitions of her great, great, great grandfather. The original furnishings were burned on the front lawn by revolutionaries in 1793. Furnishings throughout the home are elegant, yet the Benoists have established an atmosphere of homey comfort. Artistic fresh flower arrangements abound and you can see Madame's cutting garden from the French doors in the salon that open onto the lush grounds. The well-worn turret steps lead to the beautifully furnished accommodations. In the evening a large oval table in the dining room provides an opportunity to enjoy the company of other guests and the country-fresh cuisine of Madame Benoist. She prepares a four-course meal and Monsieur Benoist selects regional wines to complement each course. Advance reservations must be made. The Benoists are a handsome couple who take great pride in their home and the welcome they extend to their guests. *Directions:* To reach La Jaille-Yvon travel north of Angers on N162. At the town of Le Lion d'Angers clock the odometer 11 kilometers further north to an intersection, Carrefour Fleur de Lys. Turn east and travel 2½ kilometers to La Jaille-Yvon. Château du Plessis is on the southern edge of the village.

CHÂTEAU DU PLESSIS
Hôtelier: Mme & M Paul Benoist
49220 La Jaille-Yvon
Tel: 41.95.12.75, Fax: 41.95.14.41
8 Rooms
Double from 600F to 800F
Open March to November
Credit cards: all major
Restaurant for guests
Region: Loire Valley; Michelin Map: 232

Hôtel l'Arbre Vert with its shuttered windows, fragrant wisteria and windowboxes brimful of flowers is picturebook-perfect. The interior is as attractive as the exterior, with a rustic breakfast room, a sophisticated restaurant, and upstairs pretty bedrooms with sprigged wallpaper and country pine furniture. In summer, request one of the six smaller, contemporary rooms with terraces, each just large enough for a table and two chairs. The atmosphere is very friendly and the Kieny and Wittmer families extend a personal welcome. Monsieur Kieny who supervises the kitchen offers a number of interesting Alsatian specialties that are complemented by the regional wines. The hotel also has a cozy wine cellar where you can sample some famous as well as local Alsatian wines. Should the Hôtel l'Arbre Vert be full, the Hôtel la Belle Promenade (Tel: 89.47.11.51), directly across the square, is also attractive—somewhat more modern in decor, but benefiting from the same gracious and hospitable management. Kaysersberg's streets are lined with colorful old houses, many of which date back to the 16th century. *Directions:* Kaysersberg is located 11 kilometers northwest of Colmar by traveling on N83 and N415. L'Arbre Vert is located in Haute Kaysersberg. Once in town, follow the hotel's signposts through the town's narrow streets up to Haute Kaysersberg and to the hotel.

HÔTEL L'ARBRE VERT
Hôtelier: Kieny & Wittmer Families
1, Rue Haute du Rempart
68240 Kaysersberg
Tel: 89.47.11.51, Fax: 89.78.13.40
23 Rooms
Double from 379F to 429F
Closed January
Credit cards: MC, VS
Restaurant closed Monday
Region: Alsace; Michelin Map: 242

Just inside the walls of the charming town of Kaysersberg is the Résidence Chambard. The inn was built in 1981 but it blends in comfortably with the surrounding old buildings. The old-world facade shelters a more contemporary style hotel. The sixties-style hallways with orange velvet curtains lead to the bedrooms with their modern decor, but there are several more traditionally furnished rooms. Part of the entrance hall is a small lounge, and downstairs in the basement is a comfortable bar. The Restaurant Chambard, Pierre Irrmann's pride and joy, is in a separate building, just in front of the hotel. The decor is handsome—high-back, tapestry-covered chairs set around intimate tables before a large, open stone fireplace. Specialties of the house include *foie gras frais en boudin, turbot au gingembre frit* and *mousse chambard*. The wine list highlights some delicious Rieslings and Pinot gris. *Directions:* Kaysersberg is located 11 kilometers northwest of Colmar by traveling on N83 and N415. The Hôtel Rêsidence is located just inside the town gates.

HÔTEL RÉSIDENCE CHAMBARD
Hôtelier: Pierre Irrmann
13, Rue du Général de Gaulle
68240 Kaysersberg
Tel: 89.47.10.17, Fax: 89.47.35.03
18 Rooms, 2 Suites
Double from 700F to 750F, Suite from 850F
Closed March & Christmas
Credit cards: all major
Restaurant closed Monday
Region: Alsace; Michelin Map: 242

Perched above the flowing River Dordogne and backed by formal French gardens and acres of parkland, the Château de la Treyne has been renovated and returned to its earlier state of grandeur. A fairy-tale fortress, the château will enchant you with its presence, its grace, its regal accommodation and excellent restaurant. Michèle Gombert-Devals has opened her home as a luxury Relais & Châteaux hotel. Inside, heavy wood doors, wood paneling and beams contrast handsomely with white stone walls and the rich, muted colors of age-worn tapestries. Public rooms are furnished dramatically with antiques and warmed by log burning fires. In summer, tables are set on a terrace with magnificent views that plunge down to the Dordogne. On brisk nights a fire is lit in the elegant Louis XIII dining room, the tables are elegantly set with silver, china and crystal, and a pianist softly plays the grand piano. Up the broad stone staircase the château's bedrooms are all luxuriously appointed and furnished. Individual in their decor, size and location, the windows of the bedrooms open either onto dramatic river views or onto the lovely grounds. *Directions:* From Souillac on the N20 take D43 3 kilometers west towards Lacave and Rocamadour. Cross the Dordogne River and the gates to the château are on your right.

CHÂTEAU DE LA TREYNE
Hôtelier: Mme Michèle Gombert-Devals
Lacave, 46200 Souillac
Tel: 65.32.66.66, Fax: 65.37.06.57
14 Rooms, 2 Suites
Double from 900F to 1800F, Suite from 1600F
Closed mid-November to Easter
Credit cards: all major
Restaurant, pool, tennis
Region: Dordogne; Michelin Map: 239

The lovely Château d'Urbilhac, set high above the town, is a beautiful château with extensive grounds and a stunning swimming pool surrounded by statues. Very reasonable in price, the château attracts European families on holiday who appear at home here and comfortable in their regal surroundings. Madame Xompero, the owner, extends a gracious welcome and genuinely cares that her guests enjoy their holiday. There is no elevator and the bedrooms are scattered on three floors. We stayed in a small room on the third floor which was once the servants' quarters. There are a number of more spacious, grand rooms. Rooms 14 and 15 both have beautiful antique double beds; room 12, a corner room, has antique twin beds; and room 24 has twin brass beds. The dining room is small and friendly and the menu boasts a number of regional specialties—beautifully prepared and thoughtfully served. Removed from any tourist destination, the Château d'Urbilhac offers calm and quiet, a perfect hideaway for those who want to relax. *Directions:* Lamastre is located 40 kilometers northwest of Valence traveling on D533. The château is tucked away in the wooded hills above Lamastre: travel on D2, Route de Vernoux, for 2 kilometers.

CHÂTEAU D'URBILHAC
Hôtelier: Mme Xompero
Route de Vernoux
07270 Lamastre
Tel: 75.06.42.11, Fax: 75.06.52.75
13 Rooms
Double from 1000F to 1150F includes dinner
Open May to mid-October
Credit cards: all major
Restaurant, pool, tennis
Region: Rhône Valley; Michelin Map: 244, 246

Levernois is a country village located just five minutes by car on D970 from Beaune. Here the ivy-clad Hôtel le Parc offers a delightful alternative to Beaune for those travelers who prefer the serenity of the countryside. Christiane Oudot owns and manages this delightful hotel which comprises two lovely ivy-covered homes facing each other across a courtyard. A measure of her success as a hôtelier is the great many returning visitors. Guests congregate in the evening in the convivial little bar, just off the entry salon. In the summer, tables are set for breakfast in the courtyard; in winter guests are served in the attractive breakfast room. Breakfast is the only meal served. Wide, prettily papered hallways lead to bedrooms in the main building. The rooms are very attractive and simply decorated; all but two have their own spotlessly clean bath or shower. Across the courtyard are the larger bedrooms furnished with attractive pieces of antique furniture. Reserve early to enjoy the warm hospitality of Madame Oudot in this tranquil setting. *Directions:* Travel 3 kilometers southeast of Beaune on Route de Verdun-sur-le-Doubs D970 and D111.

HÔTEL LE PARC
Hôtelier: Mme Christiane Oudot
Levernois, 21200 Beaune
Tel: 80.24.63.00 & 80.22.22.51
25 Rooms
Double from 190F to 420F
Open all year
Credit cards: MC, VS
No restaurant
Region: Burgundy; Michelin Map: 243

Domaine de Beauvois is a 15th- and 17th-century château surrounded by a lovely wooded estate. Its bedrooms, furnished with antiques, offer you a holiday equal to that enjoyed by the many lords and ladies who came to the Loire Valley for relaxation long ago. It was also once a residence for knights. In the original tower some rooms have exposed old stone walls. The ceiling of one bedroom looks up to the original old oak beams that form a stunning pattern, and a chamber once occupied by Louis XII has its own fireplace and vaulted ceiling. From the bedrooms you have a lovely view of the pool, the courtyard, and the dense forest. On most nights one large, beautiful room, whose floor-to-ceiling windows overlook the courtyard terrace, is elegantly set for dinner. There is also a smaller, more intimate dining room. The service is professional and it is worth asking the *sommelier* for a tour of the remarkable wine cellar. For sports enthusiasts there are also tennis courts, trails in the surrounding forest and fishing nearby. *Directions:* Take N152 north out of Tours (right bank) in the direction of Saumur. After 12 kilometers, turn right at the Port de Luynes on the D49. Continue on D49 in the direction of Cléré les Pins for 2 kilometers to the Domaine.

DOMAINE DE BEAUVOIS
Hôtelier: Jean Claude Taupin
P. O. Box 27
37230 Luynes
Tel: 47.55.50.11, Fax: 47.55.59.62
33 Rooms, 4 Suites
Double from 920F to 1390F, Suite from 1460F
Open mid-March to mid-January
Credit cards: all major
Restaurant, pool, tennis
Region: Loire Valley; Michelin Map: 232

In a renaissance setting, encased within the walls of Old Lyon, this hotel is unique in Europe and has been described as a masterpiece. Housed in four buildings that once belonged to the Dukes of Burgundy, the decor of the Cour des Loges is a stunning contrast of modern and old. Old stone walls and massive beams stage a backdrop for bright fabrics, chrome, glass and dried flowers. Tapas is the hotel's one informal restaurant that offers light fare. Double windows buffer city noises, automatic shutters block out the light, televisions offer CNN, mini-bars are stocked with complimentary beverages and snacks, and bathrooms are ultra modern. Accommodations are expensive and surprisingly small. In some cases bathrooms are located on a terraced level in the room—not for the modest. While the hotel is popular with businessmen, it is also perfect for tourists because it is in the heart of this lovely old city. *Directions:* From A6 going south exit *Vieux Lyon* (after Tunnel Fourvière). Follow the Quai Fulchiron to where it becomes the Quai Romain Rolland. At the bridge turn left on Rue Octavio-Mey, first left on Rue de l'Angile. At the end of the street on the right is a Welcome-Accueil Garage (in front of the pedestrian zone); an employee will open the barrier so you can drive to the hotel.

COUR DES LOGES
Hôtelier: Jean-François Piques
2,4,6,8 Rue du Boeuf
69005 Vieux Lyon
Tel: 78.42.75.75, Fax: 72.40.93.61
53 Rooms, 10 Suites
Double from 980F to 1700F, Suite from 2000F
Open all year
Credit cards: all major
Restaurant, pool, sauna
Region: Rhône Valley; Michelin Map: 244, 246

Château de la Caze is a fairytale 15th-century castle, majestically situated above the Tarn. With its heavy doors, turrets and stone facade, it is a dramatic castle, yet intimate in size. It was not built as a fortress, but rather as a honeymoon home for Sonbeyrane Alamand, a niece of the Prior François Alamand. She chose the idyllic and romantic location and commissioned the château in 1489. Today this spectacular château is a professionally run hotel. The grand rooms with their vaulted ceilings, rough stone walls, tile and wood-planked floors are warmed by tapestries, Oriental rugs, dramatic antiques, paintings, copper, soft lighting and log-burning fires. Each bedroom in the castle is like a king's bedchamber. Room 6, the honeymoon apartment of Sonbeyrane, is the most spectacular room. It has a large canopied bed and an entire wall of windows overlooking the Tarn and its canyon. On the ceiling there are paintings of the eight, very beautiful sisters who later inherited the château, and according to legend, had secret rendezvous each night in the garden of the castle with their lovers. Just opposite the château, La Ferme offers six additional, attractive apartments. The restaurant enjoys spectacular views of the canyon. *Directions:* La Malène is located 42 kilometers northeast of Millau traveling on N9 and D907. From La Malène travel northeast 5½ kilometers on D907.

CHÂTEAU DE LA CAZE
Hôtelier: Mme & Mlle Roux
La Malène
48210 Ste Enimie
Tel: 66.48.51.01, Fax: 66.48.55.75
12 Rooms, 7 Suites
Double from 750F to 990, Suite from 1100
Open May to November
Credit cards: all major
Restaurant closed Tuesday.
Region: Tarn; Michelin Map: 240

For fifteen hundred years the Manoir de Montesquiou was the residence of the Barons de Montesquiou. With the canyon walls at its back, the Manoir de Montesquiou faces onto a street of the small town of La Malène at the center of the Tarn Canyon. This is a moderately priced château hotel, not luxurious but very traditional in furnishings. The welcome and service is warm and friendly. The Manoir de Montesquiou serves as a delightful and comfortable base from which to explore the spectacular beauty of the Tarn Canyon (*Gorges du Tarn*). Here you can enjoy a wonderful meal and then climb the tower to your room. All the bedrooms have private bath and those that overlook the garden at the back are assured a quiet night's rest. Each bedroom is unique in its decor, some with dramatic four-poster beds—the carvings on the headboard in room 6 are magnificent. Although the setting of the Manoir de Montesquiou is not as spectacular as the Château de la Caze, it is a less expensive alternative, excellent value and well located in the heart of the Tarn Canyon. From the hotel you can venture out by day to boat, fish, hunt, explore and walk. *Directions:* La Malène is located 42 kilometers northeast of Millau by traveling on N9 and then D907. The Manoir is located 5½ kilometers northeast of La Malène on N907.

MANOIR DE MONTESQUIOU
Hôtelier: Bernard Guillenet
La Malène
48210 Ste Énimie
Tel: 66.48.51.12, Fax: 66.48.50.47
10 Rooms, 2 Suites
Double from 420F to 570F, Suite from 785F
Open April to October
Credit cards: all major
Restaurant
Region: Tarn; Michelin Map: 240

Tucked away in the beauty and quiet of the Black Mountains is a fantastic hotel—the Château de Montlédier. Once you've arrived at the Château de Montlédier and developed a taste for the splendor and elegance it offers, you will not want to leave, and when you do, you will resolve to return. With just nine guest rooms, the Château de Montlédier is intimate in size and atmosphere. The accommodations are magnificent in their furnishings, luxuriously appointed, with commodious, modern bathrooms. Raymond, with its two stunning canopied beds, is one of the loveliest bedrooms. The restaurant of the hotel is in the cellar—cozy and intimate, it is a romantic setting in which to sample the excellent cuisine. The château also has a lovely swimming pool with views of the surrounding woodlands. The Château de Montlédier is a delightful hotel where everything—service, decor, cuisine—is done to perfection and with superb taste. *Directions:* Mazamet is located 47 kilometers north of Carcassonne. The Château de Montlédier is 5 kilometers from Mazamet. From Mazamet take N112 in the direction of Béziers.

CHÂTEAU DE MONTLÉDIER
Hôtelier: Chantal Thiercelin
Route d'Anglès, Mazamet
81660 Pont de Larn
Tel: 63.61.20.54, Fax: 63.98.22.51.
9 Rooms
Double from 400F to 600F
Closed January
Credit cards: all major
Restaurant closed Sunday evening & Monday, pool
Region: Tarn; Michelin Map: 235

There is an enchantment about this beautiful castle high above Mercuès and the Lot Valley. Once you have seen it you will not be able to take your eyes away or to drive through the valley without stopping. It appears to beckon you. Here you can live like "royalty" with all the modern conveniences. The château has been restored and decorated in keeping with formal tradition. The thirty-two guest rooms in the château are magnificent—the furnishings are handsome and the windows open to some splendid valley views. Unique and priced accordingly, Room 419 (in a turret) has windows on all sides and a glassed-in ceiling that opens up to the beams. In recent years an additional twenty-two rooms have been added in the newly constructed annex, the Hôtel des Cèdres. Here bedrooms are modern in decor and less expensive. Enjoy a memorable dinner in the elegantly beautiful restaurant. The Vigouroux family own vineyards which produce sumptuous wines bottled under the *Château de Haut Serre* label. They have just built some large cellars under the gardens connecting the château to store their produced and acquired wines. *Directions:* Located 8 kilometers from Cahors take D911 from Cahors to Mercuès and then turn right at the second light.

CHÂTEAU DE MERCUÈS
Hôtelier: Georges Vigouroux
Directeur: Bernard Denegre
Mercuès, 46090 Cahors
Tel: 65.20.00.01, Fax: 65.20.05.72
47 Rooms, 7 Suites
Double from 700F to 1600F, Suite from 1500F
Open April to mid-November
Credit cards: all major
Restaurant, pool, tennis
Region: Lot; Michelin Map: 235

Overpowered by the walls of the towering Jonte Canyon, the picturesque houses of Meyrueis huddle along the banks of the River Jonte. From this quaint village you take a farm road to the enchanting Château d'Ayres. A long wooded road winds through the grounds and hidden behind a high stone wall, the château has managed to preserve and protect its special beauty and peace. Built in the 12th century as a Benedictine monastery, it had been burned and ravaged over the years, and was at one time owned by an ancestor of the Rockefellers. In the late 1970s the property was sold to an enthusiastic couple, Jean-François and Chantal de Montjou, under whose care and devotion the hotel is managed today. A dramatic wide stone stairway sweeps up to the handsome bedchambers. Rooms vary in their size and bathroom appointments, which is reflected in their price, but all enjoy the quiet of park and setting. The decor throughout the château is lavished with personal belongings and is well-worn, comfortable and homey. Tables are intimately set in a few small cozy niches in rooms as opposed to one large formal room and serve as the restaurant. Works of culinary art are created in the kitchen daily. The Château d'Ayres is a lovely and attractive hotel. *Directions:* From Millau take N9 (signpost Clermont) for 7 kilometers to Aguessac where you turn right (signpost Gorges du Tarn).

CHÂTEAU D'AYRES
Hôtelier: Chantal & Jean-François de Montjou
48150 Meyrueis
Tel: 66.45.60.10, Fax: 66.45.62.26
23 Rooms, 3 Suites
Double from 420F to 780F, Suite from 780F
Open April to mid-November
Credit cards: all major
Restaurant, pool, tennis
Region: Tarn; Michelin Map: 240

Relais la Métairie is a charming country hotel nestled in one of the most irresistible regions of France, the Dordogne. La Métairie is an attractive soft yellow stone manor set on a grassy plateau. Views from its tranquil hillside location are of the surrounding farmland and down over the *Cingle de Trémolat,* a scenic loop of the River Dordogne. The nine bedrooms and one apartment are tastefully appointed and profit from the serenity of the rural setting. Rooms open onto a private patio or balcony terrace. The bar is airy, decorated with white wicker furniture. The restaurant is intimate and very attractive with tapestry-covered chairs and a handsome fireplace awaits you in the lounge. In summer, grills and light meals are served on the terrace by the swimming pool. Relais la Métairie is found on a country road that winds along the hillside up from and between Mauzac and Trémolat. Without a very detailed map, it is difficult to find. We found the reception to be somewhat cool, but will hope for a warmer welcome on our next visit as this is a lovely country inn with an idyllic, peaceful setting. *Directions:* From Trémolat travel west on C303 and then C301 to La Métairie. Both Trémolat and Millac are approximately 50 kilometers south of Périgueux.

RELAIS LA MÉTAIRIE
Hôtelier: Françoise-Vigneron & Gerard Culis
Millac,
24150 Mauzac
Tel: 53.22.50.47, Fax: 53.22.52.93
9 Rooms, 1 Suite
Double from 448F to 862F, Suite from 1138F
Open April to mid-October
Credit cards: MC, VS
Restaurant closed Tuesday lunch, pool
Region: Dordogne; Michelin Map: 235

Just a few minutes from the picturesque, rugged, Brittany coast, secluded by vast acres of woodland and park, Manoir de Kertalg was built as a grand stable block and used for many years as a cider press before being converted into a delightful hotel in 1986. We were shown around by Brann, Madame Lïer Le Goarnig's son, who forsakes his career as an artist during the season to help in the hotel. An exhibition of his fantasy style paintings decorates the large sitting room with its formal arrangements of red velvet chairs and small tables. All the bedrooms are very sophisticated in their decor. The less expensive rooms are those found on the three floors of the tower. Mickey (named after its ear shaped bedhead), the tiny room in the roof of the tower, is the least expensive room because of its size and having to climb three storeys of spiral staircase. A duplex of two bedrooms and one bathroom is available for families. Breakfast is the only meal served. There are many places nearby to eat dinner, between 5 and 15 minutes from the hotel by car. Madame Lïer Le Goarnig and her family live across the garden in the elegant château. *Directions:* Moëlan sur Mer is located 10 kilometers south of Quimperlé, traveling on D16 south and D116 west. From the village take D24 towards Riec-sur Belon and Pont Aven. The hotel is on your right after 2 kilometers.

MANOIR DE KERTALG
Hôtelier: Mireille Lïer Le Goarnig
29350 Moëlan sur Mer
Tel: 98.39.77.77, Fax: 98.39.72.07
9 Rooms, 1 Suite
Double from 490F to 980F, Suite from 1100F
Closed November to Easter
Credit cards: MC, VS
No restaurant
Region: Brittany: Michelin Map: 230

This charming 16th-century complex of mills and little cottages beside a peaceful lake and rushing millstream is absolutely picture-perfect. The largest mill now houses a reception area, sitting rooms (one of which incorporates the grinding machinery) and a beamed dining room which overlooks the rushing waters of the millstream. Both the enchanting atmosphere and excellent cuisine ensure a perfect evening. The owner, Monsieur Quistrebert, is ever present. He bustles about ensuring that the service is professional and attentive. Bedrooms are found in quaint little stone cottages around the lake or just a short distance downstream surrounding an additional mill. In the last edition of this guide, we expressed our dissatisfaction with the decor of the bedrooms and hoped to report in this edition that all is now in order. While things have certainly improved (many of the rooms were delightfully decorated) we found several, including our own, to be in need of redecoration and new carpet. However we continue to recommend this hotel because Les Moulins du Duc is picturesque, the service is excellent and the staff friendly and helpful. Once again we look forward to the day when we wholeheartedly recommend this most idyllic of hotels. *Directions:* Moëlan sur Mer is located 10 kilometers south of Quimperlé. The mill is 2 kilometers northwest of the village.

LES MOULINS DU DUC
Hôtelier: Quistrebert Family
29350 Moëlan sur Mer
Tel: 98.39.60.73, Fax: 98.39.75.56
27 Rooms
Double from 850F, Suite from 1050F
Closed mid-January to March
Credit cards: all major
Restaurant, pool
Region: Brittany; Michelin Map: 230

Haute Provence is a beautiful region of rugged terrain and villages of warm sandstone buildings and tiled roofs, nestled between the Riviera, the Alps and Provence. Monsieur and Madame Vernet built Le Calalou in the shadow of Moissac to match the village architecturally and blend beautifully into the landscape. Madame Vernet is a perfectionist and the guests benefit as she demands that rooms be spotlessly clean, the public areas fresh, the garden immaculately groomed and the terrace swept. Monsieur Vernet is very approachable and the staff is accommodating. The bedrooms are freshly decorated, simple and basic in their decor, and have very comfortable beds and modern bathrooms. The rooms look out over the swimming pool to spectacular valley views or open on to a private terrace. You can dine either in the glass-enclosed restaurant, a smaller more intimate dining room, or on the garden terrace. During season, May through mid-September, the Vernets request that guests stay at Le Calalou on a *demi-pension* basis. Off season, take advantage of the hotel's proximity to the village of Tourtour, *village dans le ciel*, and discover its many charming restaurants along medieval streets. *Directions:* Moissac Bellevue is about 86 kilometers from Aix. From Aix take the A8 to St Maxime and follow the D560 northeast through Barjols to Salernes where you take the D31 north to Aups and D9 to Moissac Bellevue.

HÔTEL LE CALALOU
Hôtelier: Mme & M Armande Vernet
83630 Moissac Bellevue
Tel: 94.70.17.91, Fax: 94.70.50.11
38 Rooms, 1 Suite
Double from 440F to 610F, Suite from 880F
Open March to November
Credit cards: all major
Restaurant, pool, tennis
Region: Haute Provence; Michelin Map: 245

Domaine de la Tortinière, built in 1861, has a most impressive exterior, an inviting interior and charming hosts in Madam Olivereau-Capron and her son Xavier. Xavier explained that his mother did not want a hotel that was a historical museum, but rather a blend of contemporary and traditional decor with modern and antique furniture. In the drawing room old paneling painted in soft yellows combines with modern sofas and tables and traditional chairs to create a very comfortable room. Bedrooms continue in the same vein with a pleasing blend of traditional and contemporary, and are found in the main château, the adjacent pavilion, and a little cottage by the entrance to the property. In autumn the surrounding woodlands are a carpet of cyclamens, while in summer the heated swimming pool and tennis courts are great attractions for guests. Several times a year the château offers cooking courses that serve as an introduction to regional cuisine. Recipes are selected from those served at the finest tables among the privately owned châteaux and manors of the Touraine. Instruction includes preparation of complete menus and you have the opportunity to dine with the owners in their châteaux. *Directions:* The château is located just off N10, on D287 leading to Ballan-Miré, 2 kilometers north of Montbazon and 10 kilometers south of Tours (follow signposts for Poitiers).

DOMAINE DE LA TORTINIÈRE
Hôtelier: Mme & Xavier Olivereau-Capron
Les Gués de Veign
37250 Montbazon
Tel: 47.26.00.19, Fax: 47.65.95.70
14 Rooms, 7 Suites
Double from 455F to 870F, Suite from 11550F
Open March to mid-December
Crèdit cards: MC, VS
Restaurant, pool, tennis
Region: Loire Valley; Michelin Map: 232, 238

A romantic château from the age of Napoleon the III, the Château de Puy Robert is an intimate castle set in its own beautiful park, just 2 kilometers from the famous prehistoric Lascaux caves. This pretty cream colored stone castle with its turrets and gray roof offers fifteen guestrooms. The remainder of the rooms are found in a nearby newly constructed annex. The bedrooms in the main château are more intimate, particularly those which have a turret incorporated into their living space. Those in the annex are spacious and enjoy either a terrace or patio that overlooks the grounds and the lovely pool. The Parveaux Family also owns the fabulous Château de Castel Novel, and their years as professional hôteliers show in the way they run this hotel. Guestrooms are all well appointed, many are decorated in pastel florals and all enjoy the quiet of the setting. The large dining room prides itself on local cuisine—some of the finest France has to offer. The grounds are immaculate, geraniums overflow from terra-cotta pots, pink impatiens fill the borders, the lawn is mowed to perfection, and well-kept tables and chairs invite you to repose in the leafy shade. *Directions:* From the town of Montignac follow D 65 which leads directly to the gates of the château.

CHÂTEAU DE PUY ROBERT
Hôtelier: Albert Parveaux
Directeur: Vincent Nourrisson
Route de Valojoulx
24290 Montignac
Tel: 53.51.92.13, Fax: 53.51.80.11
36 Rooms, 2 Suites
Double from 580F to 1120F, Suite from 950F
Open all year
Credit cards: all major
Restaurant, pool
Region: Dordogne; Michelin Map: 239

The Château de la Salle is romantically tucked away in the scenic Normandy countryside. Once part of a private estate, this 16th-century mansion was remodeled in the 17th and 18th centuries and has 10 spacious bedchambers with either a small bath or shower-room. Several are handsomely decorated with period pieces, while our room (8) was more contemporary in decor. Two rooms are furnished with antique four-poster beds; one has been enlarged to fit a double bed, while the other remains its original size—perhaps a bit small for some couples. The small restaurant has a few heavy wooden tables and tapestry-covered chairs positioned before a large open fireplace underneath a low barrel-vaulted ceiling. With its tiny windows set in massively thick walls, this was long ago the manor's kitchen, and was actually very modern for its time. If you are lucky perhaps you will secure the table next to the hearth where a small wooden door at table height opens to a small round pastry oven. Our arrival coincided with a wet, gray day, but we were greeted by Madame Lemesle with a warm welcome reinforced by her tail-wagging dog. *Directions:* The hotel is 13 kilometers southeast of Coutances. From Coutances go towards Villedieu (D7) and then head for Cerisy la Salle (D27). A small road (D73) turns off before Cerisy and continues straight through the village where signposts direct you down country lanes to the château.

CHÂTEAU DE LA SALLE
Hôtelier: Cecile Lemesle
50210 Montpinchon
Tel: 33.46.95.19, Fax: 33.46.44.25
10 Rooms
Double from 700F to 750F
Closed January & February
& weekdays November to New Year
Credit cards: all major
Restaurant
Region: Normandy; Michelin Map: 231

Mont St Michel is an overcrowded tourist destination, but if you have your heart set on an overnight stay, we recommend Hôtel Mère Poulard simply because it offers the nicest accommodations on the island. However, the accommodations are expensive for what you get, the restaurant and menu is astronomically priced, and the staff is understandably weary of the great number of non-French speaking guests. Found just inside the town walls, Mère Poulard is famous for its omelets. The preparation of omelets can be seen from the street and is an attraction in its own right. The eggs are whisked at a tempo and beat set by the chef and then cooked in brightly polished copper pans over a large open fire. Bedrooms above the restaurant are uniform in size and all have the same tariff—those at the back are darker because they look out on the hillside. Bedrooms in the adjacent building are more spacious and also more expensive. All the bedrooms have an attractive country decor with matching wallpaper drapes and bedspreads using a different color for each room. The hotel owns a similar hotel nearby and both are members of *Best Western* hotels and can be easily booked through their reservation service. *Directions:* Mont St Michel is located 66 kilometers north of Rennes traveling on N175.

HÔTEL MÈRE POULARD
Hôtelier: M Vannier
BP 18 Grand Rue
50116 Mont St Michel
Tel: 33.60.14.01, Fax: 33.48.52.31
27 Rooms
Double from 600F to 800F
Open all year
Credit Cards: all major
Region: Normandy; Michelin Map: 231

Standing at the entrance to the village Les Muscadins is an eye-catching sight with its green shuttered windows and terrace hung with a profusion of deep red geraniums. With just eight guestrooms, Les Muscadins is intimate and enjoys a lovely restaurant that has earned a Michelin star. Edward Bianchini, an American, came to France never expecting to open a hotel, fell in love with the property and negotiated its purchase within an hour of having first seen it—love at first sight. A hallway winds from the reception area to the guestrooms that either overlook the rooftops of the village, out to the ocean, or back onto the walls of the old village. Rooms are comfortable, not large, but fresh in their decor—fabrics are attractive and well chosen. The restaurant, decorated in blues and whites, is extremely attractive and Edward Bianchini's menu is very reasonable in price and offers an excellent selection. In warm months, guests dine on the terrace and enjoy vistas that almost seem a painting of the surrounding landscape. The true *Muscadins* —loyalists for the king who were in constant search of the good life—would have enjoyed this country hotel. Charming and accommodating, Les Muscadins is also well located—one can walk from the hotel's doorstep to the heart of the village. *Directions:* Take the Cannes\Mougins exit off A8 and continue in the direction of Mougins. Take the *Voie rapide* to the Mougins Ave\Notre Dame Vie exit, turn left and continue to the old village.

LES MUSCADINS
Hôtelier: Edward W. Bianchini
18, boulevard Georges Courteline
06250 Mougins
Tel: 93.90.00.43, Fax: 92.92.88.23
8 Rooms
Double from 750F to 1200F
Open March through January
Credit cards: all major
Restaurant
Region: Provence; Michelin Map: 245

Noizay is a quiet town on the north side of the Loire River to the west of Amboise. The Château de Noizay, a lovely hotel tucked into the hillside, played a role in a turbulent period of French history. It was here in 1560 that Castelnau was held prisoner by the Duc de Nemours after a bloody assault in the town. Castelnau was then taken to Amboise where heads were guillotined and then speared and displayed on the balcony of that château. It was the massacre that marked the defeat of the Calvinists. The Château de Noizay entered a new era as a luxury hotel. Fourteen rooms, at the top of the grand central stairway, have been decorated with attractive fabrics, period furniture and each is accompanied by a modern bathroom. From the smallest third floor rooms tucked under the eaves looking out through small circular windows, to the more dramatic and spacious second floor bedchambers, accommodations are commodious and quiet. Off the entry, an elegant dining room decorated in a warm yellow and soft blue promises gastronomic cuisine and the wine selection comes from an impressive cellar. The grounds of the château include a lovely forested park, formal garden, pool and tennis courts. *Directions:* Cross the Loire River to the north from Amboise, then travel west on N152 approximately 10 kilometers. Turn north on D78 to Noizay.

CHÂTEAU DE NOIZAY
Hôtelier: François Mollard
37210 Noizay
Tel: 47.52.11.01, Fax: 47.52.04.64
14 Rooms
Double from 680F to 1150F
Open mid-March to mid-November
Credit cards: all major
Restaurant, pool, tennis
Region: Loire Valley; Michelin Map: 232, 238

After spending the day visiting the elegant châteaux of the Loire Valley, there is nothing more inviting than retiring to your château in an evening, and we have yet to find a château hotel that we enjoy more than Domaine des Hauts de Loire. Built as a grand hunting lodge in the 19th century for the Count de Rostaing, the ivy-covered château is framed by tall trees and reflected in a tranquil lake where swimming swans glide lazily by. To complete the attractive picture are acres of woodland with inviting forest paths, tennis courts and a swimming pool. The beautiful salon sets a mood of quiet elegance and it is here that guests gather for drinks and peruse the tempting dinner menu. The restaurant is gorgeous, with soft pastel linens, silver candlesticks, china and silver dressing every table. During our stay we were very impressed by the professional, friendly staff and attentions of M and Mme Bonnigal. Whether you secure a room in the château or the adjacent timbered wing, each luxurious room accompanied by a spacious modern bathroom is delightful. *Directions:* Onzain is located northeast of Tours traveling 44 kilometers on N152. From Onzain follow signs for Mesland and Herbault for 3 kilometers to the hotel.

DOMAINE DES HAUTS DE LOIRE
Hôtelier: Marie-Noëlle & Pierre-Alain Bonnigal
41150 Onzain
Tel: 54.20.72.57, Fax: 54.20.77.32
25 Rooms, 9 Suites
Double from 650F to 1300F, Suite from 1600F
Open March through November
Credit cards: all major
Restaurant, pool, tennis
Region: Loire Valley; Michelin Map: 238

Vieux Pérouges is a charming, medieval village with the atmosphere of a time long gone by. In one of the quaint old timbered buildings that lean out over the narrow, cobblestoned streets, you will find a captivating restaurant, the Ostellerie du Vieux Pérouges. Traditional and regional cuisine of the Bressane and Lyonnaise districts, which are the pride of the chef, are served in the 13th-century dining room of this charming hotel. Enhancing the atmosphere are waiters dressed in regional costumes. Open for breakfast, lunch and dinner, the restaurant also profits from a wine cellar with a wonderful selection of fine Burgundies. The bedrooms are located in two separate buildings. The fifteen rooms in the St Georges manor are fabulously decorated with antiques and a few even have their own garden. The annex houses more simply decorated rooms—not as attractive as those in the main building, but quite pleasant and perhaps more appealing since they are less expensive. *Directions:* Pérouges is located 35 kilometers northeast of Lyon. Take the Autoroute A42 from Lyon and leave at Pérouges (exit 7). Pérouges is located 6½ kilometers to the northeast by taking D65 to D4.

OSTELLERIE DU VIEUX PÉROUGES
Hôtelier: Georges Thibaut
Place du Tilleul
Vieux Pérouges
01800 Pérouges
Tel: 74.61.00.88, Fax: 74.34.77.90
25 Rooms, 3 Suites
Double from 600F to 1100F, Suite from 1100F
Open all year
Credit cards: MC, VS
Restaurant closed Wednesday
Region: Rhône Valley; Michelin Map: 244

Several years ago Even O'Neill gave up a high-powered role in the business world to purchase his aunt's 15th-century manor house hotel. His deep love for his new home shows in every aspect of his solicitous management of the Manoir de Vaumadeuc. All the rooms have been renovated and redecorated under Even's direction, ushering in a new era of freshness and elegant style to the ancient medieval surroundings. In spite of the thick stone walls and huge walk-in fireplaces, the feeling throughout is light, airy and very comfortable. We particularly liked our large paneled bedroom, but found the bathroom rather small and awkward for a deluxe bedroom. The library with its tall bookcases is another delightful deluxe room. Under the eaves are several lovely bedrooms with modern bathrooms. Pleasing floral fabrics, paintings and antiques lend a luxurious, yet personalized atmosphere. There are also two cottage style bedrooms located in the carriage house that are smaller and cozier than those in the manor. During the summer season delicious dinners are graciously served in the intimate restaurant by Even and his wife, Carol. *Directions:* From Plancoët, take D768 towards Lamballe for 2 kilometers. Go left on D28 for about 7 kilometers to the village of Pléven. Go through the village and you will see the Manoir de Vaumadeuc on the right.

MANOIR DE VAUMADEUC
Hôtelier: Carol & Even O'Neill
Pléven 22130 Plancoët
Tel: 96.84.46.17, Fax: 96.84.40.16
14 Rooms
Double from 750F to 1050F
Open mid-March to January
Credit cards: MC, VS
Restaurant closed in low season
Region: Brittany, Michelin Map: 230

This handsome stone manor is the result of one man's lifelong dream and years of hard work. Monsieur Bernard had a vision of owning a château, purchased Château de la Motte, a part 14th- and part 18th-century château, and lovingly restored it as a hotel. Éric Bernard, his son, manages the hotel and welcomes and escorts guests to one of the château's eight bedchambers. Each room is different in its decor, but all reflect the artistry of Monsieur Bernard, offering luxury, spaciousness and modernly appointed bathrooms. The large bedroom windows frame enchanting scenes of either the lake or forest and it's a real treat to wake to the sight and sounds of swans taking flight. In the evening, the Bernard's are often present, as guests gather for before dinner drinks in the airy salon where tables are set before French doors opening on to the lake. The restaurant is lovely and there is a very homey atmosphere to this intimate hotel. *Directions:* From St Malo take R137 towards Rennes for 30 kilometers. One kilometer before the village of Pleugueneuc, turn right at the signpost for Plesder. The entrance to the château is just before Plesder.

CHÂTEAU DE LA MOTTE BEAUMANOIR
Hôtelier: Mme & M Charles Bernard
35720 Pleugueneuc
Tel: 99.69.46.01, Fax: 99.69.42.49
6 Rooms, 2 Suites
Double from 820F, Suite from 920F
Open all year
Credit cards: all major
Restaurant closed December to April, pool
Region: Brittany; Michelin Map: 230

Pull off the busy main road into L'Auberge du Vieux Puit's parking, and the bustle of the 20th century slips away as you enter a courtyard surrounded by ancient timbered buildings. This is a typical Normandy home dating from the 17th century. The complex was used as a tannery in the 19th century, was converted to an inn in 1921, and has been in the Foltz family for two generations. Hélène Foltz is your gracious hostess and Jacques Foltz oversees the kitchen. A leaning timbered 17th-century cottage contains five characterful bedrooms, only one has complete ensuite facilities. The adjacent house has an old exterior and a modern more spacious interior, where all of the bedrooms have ensuite facilities. Facing the street, the restaurant is a maze of low timbered rooms with tables set under heavy beams before a large open fireplace and surrounded by copperware, paintings and country style antiques. This is a "restaurant with rooms" and guests are expected to dine at the restaurant. A stroll away are the narrow timbered streets of Pont Audemer. Jacques speaks excellent English and is happy to suggest enough daytrips through Normandy to keep you busy for a week. *Directions:* From Paris/Rouen (A13) exit at Pont Audemer *Nord*, follow signposts for Caen. At the bridge, continue straight for 300 meters and the hotel is on your left.

L'AUBERGE DU VIEUX PUITS
Hôtelier: Hélène & Jacques Foltz
6, Rue Notre-Dame du Pré
27500 Pont Audemer
Tel: 32.41.01.48
12 Rooms
Double from 290F to 440F
Closed Christmas & January
 & every Monday & Tuesday except high season
Credit cards: MC, VS
Restaurant closed Monday & Tuesday except summer
Region: Normandy; Michelin Map: 231

Typically we do not include hotels in our book unless we have seen the bedrooms. We were so taken by Hôtel du Vieux Moulin's spectacular location on a hillside overlooking the meandering River Gard with the most breathtaking view of the ancient Pont du Gard aqueduct that we decided, after having seen photographs of bedrooms, to make an exception. The photos showed some most attractive rooms, each individual in their decor with country prints and reproduction furniture. Several of the bedrooms have a spectacular view of the Pont du Gard. The public rooms are furnished in a comfortable Provençal style. The restaurant, on the Sunday of our visit, was filled with patrons, all enjoying a lazy, warm afternoon. Copper pots hang on the walls, and tables with ladder back chairs are set under handsome old beams. Outdoors, the shaded terrace, enjoys an unparalleled vantage point from which to view the Pont du Gard. *Directions:* From Remoulins (23 kilometers north of Nimes, 25, kilometers west of Avignon), follow signs that direct to the left bank of the Gard River. The turnoff to the Hôtel du Vieux Moulin is just before the paid parking area for the Pont du Gard.

HÔTEL DU VIEUX MOULIN
Hôtelier: William Dec
Directeur: Raymond Aparis
Face Pont Du Gard (rive gauche)
30210 Remoulins
Tel: 66.37.14.35, Fax: 66.37.26.48
16 Rooms
Double from 330F to 460F
Open March to October
Credit cards: all major
Restaurant
Region: Provence; Michelin Map: 245, 246

The village of Riquewihr is encircled by a tall wall and surrounded by vineyards. Within the walls the narrow pedestrian streets are lined with ancient brick and timber houses. Houses were built to produce wine on the ground floor while the family residences were upstairs. Riquewihr is an idyllic little town and the Hôtel L'Oriel is ideally situated for using as your base to explore the Alsace wine region. On a narrow side street, Hôtel L'Oriel occupies a 450-year-old building. Guests have a large breakfast room and a small sitting area. Steep stairs and narrow corridors lead to the guestrooms that either overlook the narrow street or a tiny central courtyard (it's not a place for large suitcases). Bedrooms are all very nicely decorated and outfitted with TV and phone. We particularly liked the rooms on the first floor (second floor for Americans) with their windows overlooking the narrow street. Serge Wendel speaks German and French and is very welcoming. He is happy to recommend restaurants in the village for dinner. *Directions:* Riquewihr is just south of Ribeauvillé. When you arrive at the entrance to the town turn right, park in the first available parking space beneath the wall and walk back to the first entrance through the wall. The hotel is on your right after 50 meters. Monsieur Wendel will provide you with a map so that you can drive your car to the hotel to unload luggage before parking it in a carpark.

HÔTEL L'ORIEL
Hôtelier: Serge Wendel
3 Rue des Ecuries Seigneuriales
68340 Riquewihr
Tel: 89.49.03.13, Fax: 89.47.92.87
19 Rooms
Double from 300F to 420F
Open all year
Credit cards: all major
No restaurant
Region: Alsace: Michelin Map: 242

The Moulin de la Gorce is set in rolling farmland. This 16th-century mill has been converted to a lovely countryside hotel and a superb restaurant. In the various buildings clustered along the edge of a quiet pond and brook are luxurious, antique-furnished bedrooms with tapestries hung on the walls. (The tapestries are hand-painted replicas from a factory in Rambouillet, and are for sale.) The wallpapers and materials chosen for the decor are sometimes overbearing, but the rooms all have private bath or shower and are very comfortable—a few open onto a grassy terrace. The restaurant, intimate in size, is romantically furnished in soft pastel tones. Tables are set before a lovely fireplace and the restaurant's atmosphere is surpassed only by the unusually beautiful presentation of each course. The care and attention to detail that the Bertranet family strive for is evident throughout. There are currently only six rooms in the mill, but the Bertranets have built an additional three in an adjacent building. This is a lovely retreat, that might be a bit difficult to find. Please note that the Bertranet Family asks that overnight guests take one meal a day at the hotel. *Directions:* From St Yrieix La Perche travel on D704 northeast out of town in the direction of Limoges, 10 kilometers, and then turn right and travel 2 kilometers to La Roche l'Abeille. La Roche l'Abeille is located 39 kilometers to the south of Limoges.

MOULIN DE LA GORCE
Hôtelier: Mme & M Jean Bertranet
878 00 La Roche l'Abeille
Tel: 55.00.70.66, Fax: 55.00.76.57
8 Rooms, 1 Suite
Double from 480F to 700F, Suite from 1300F
Closed January
Credit cards: all major
Restaurant
Region: Sud-Limousin, Michelin Map: 233

During the Middle Ages the Château d'Isenbourg was the cherished home of the prince bishops of Strasbourg, and more recently, owned by wealthy wine growers. On the hillside above the town of Rouffach, the château is still surrounded by its own vineyards. There are forty bedrooms, nine of which are modern additions that overlook either the vineyards, the wide plain of Alsace or the castle park. A number of rooms are exceptionally elegant with massive, hand-painted ceilings. Room 2 is an especially beautiful apartment. Room 14 is as expensive, and is also impressive in its furnishings. The kitchen is the domain of the château's remarkable chef, Didier Lefeuvre. You can appropriately savor a delicious meal and fine Alsatian wines (select from the château's own reserve) in the vaulted 14th-century wine cellar or on the panoramic terrace. An open-air luncheon is offered in summertime. Between October and January you might want to plan your stay around one of the musical evenings that the hotel sponsors. The soirees begin at 7:30 pm over a cocktail and the concerts begin punctually at 8 pm, followed by a candlelit dinner. An outdoor and indoor swimming pool, whirlpool, sauna, fitness room, and tennis court are welcome additions. *Directions:* Travel a kilometer south from Colmar on the N83 in the direction of Cernay. Exit at Rouffach *Est*. The Château d'Isenbourg is located just to the north of town.

CHÂTEAU D'ISENBOURG
Hôtelier: M Daniel Dalibert
68250 Rouffach
Tel: 89.49.63.53, Fax: 89.78.53.70
40 Rooms
Double from 730F to 1560F
Open mid-March to mid-January
Credit cards: MC, VS
Restaurant, pools, tennis
Region: Alsace; Michelin Map: 242

Beyond the ruins of a medieval arched gateway, the Hôtel de la Pélissaria nestles at the foot of the village of St Cirq Lapopie which cascades down the hillside high above the Lot River. This delightful inn is enhanced by its artistic owners, the Matuchets. Fresh and simple in its decor, the inn's whitewashed walls contrast handsomely with dark wood beams and sienna tile floors. Thick stone walls and shuttered windows frame the idyllic scene of the village and the river. The restaurant is small, so it is wise to make dining reservations when you reserve rooms. Marie-Françoise offers delicious regional cuisine from an *à la carte* menu. It is incredible how efficient and creative Marie-Françoise can be from the confines of her small kitchen. François' talents are in the field of music. A piano and stringed instruments decorate the intimate, candlelit restaurant, and his own recordings stage a romantic mood. St Cirq Lapopie is truly one of France's most picturesque villages. With only a handful of year-round residents, this hamlet of steep, narrow, winding cobbled streets, sun-warmed tile roofs, mixture of timber and stone facades and garden niches is a postcard-perfect scene. It is wonderful to find an inn which so perfectly complements the beauty of this hamlet. *Directions:* St Cirq Lapopie is located 33 kilometers east of Cahors (D653 and D662).

HÔTEL DE LA PÉLISSARIA
Hôtelier: Marie-Françoise & François Matuchet
St Cirq Lapopie
46330 Cabrerets
Tel: 65.31.25.14, Fax: 65.30.25.52.
6 Rooms, 2 Suites
Double from 400F to 500F, Suite from 650F
Open mid-April to mid-November
Restaurant closed Thursday & Friday
Credit cards: MC, VS
Restaurant
Region: Lot; Michelin Map: 235

The wine town of St Emilion was dressed with banners, filled with music and laughter and visited by all the dignitaries of the region on a warm day in late September to commence the *vendage*—the beginning of the wine harvest. The day was captivating and we fell in love with the town. Crowning a hillside with vistas that stretch out to the surrounding vineyards, St Emilion is a medieval village of tradition, long considered the capital of the Bordeaux wine region. The Hôstellerie Plaisance opens on to the square, in the shade of the church, and its walls have echoed over the centuries the church bells commemorating the start of the wine harvest. To stay here, you couldn't be more central to the activity and the town's events. The hotel has only twelve rooms which are modern in their comfort and decor and many have views extending out over vineyards and tile rooftops. The dining room is lovely and extremely popular with travelers and businessmen, with tables set against windows whose views appear to plunge over the valley. Service is gracious and accommodating. The Plaisance is the place to stay in town and St Emilion is the most charming town of the Bordeaux wine region. *Directions:* St Emilion is located 39 kilometers east of Bordeaux. Take N89 east to Libourne and then travel on D936 in the direction of Bergerac. St Emilion is signposted to the north off D936.

HÔSTELLERIE PLAISANCE
Hôtelier: Samira & Louis Quilain
Place du Clocher
33330 St Emilion
Tel: 57.24.72.32, Fax: 57.74.41.11
10 Rooms, 2 Suites
Double from 580F to 790F, Suite from 1300F
Closed January
Credit cards: all major
Restaurant
Region: Bordeaux; Michelin Map: 234

Just outside of St Emilion on the road to Libourne, you find the Château Grand Barrail sitting majestically amongst the vineyards. Its cream stone facade and silver gray turrets are impressive against a sea of green vines. We were fortunate to see the property within a few weeks of its opening and marveled at the luxurious, sumptuous surroundings the renovation had wrought. For al fresco dining, the terrace patio bows outward and overlooks an expanse of green lawn—an ideal spot to linger over lunch or dinner on a warm day. The restaurant is elegant and the chef has perfected a menu to complement some of the world's finest wines. Seven bedrooms and two suites are found in the main château. These rooms are spacious and handsomely decorated in rich tones of beiges, burgundies, greens and gold and set under old beams. Some have turrets and all have lovely vineyard views. A second "château" that will house an additional 19 rooms and a pool is planned for 1994 completion. Take an afternoon stroll through the vineyards to your famous neighbor Château Figeac, and enjoy wine tasting. Because so many guests purchase wine, the château offers cellar "boxes" for you to store your wine purchases. *Directions:* From St Emilion follow D243 in the direction of Libourne.

CHÂTEAU GRAND BARRAIL
Hôtelier: Daniel Texier
Route de Libourne
33330 St Emilion
Tel: 57.55.37.00, Fax: 57.55.37.49
26 Rooms, 2 Suites
Double from 700F to 1600F, Suite from 1950F
Open all year
Credit cards: all major
Restaurant, pool
Region: Bordeaux; Michelin Map: 234

St Jean Cap Ferrat is an engaging and picturesque port village on one of France's most exclusive residential peninsulas just a few kilometers from Nice and Monaco. Nestled above the harbor, overlooking a maze of yachts is La Voile d'Or, a hotel that is larger than those we usually recommend but having looked at many of St Jean Cap Ferrat's hotels, we found this to be the very nicest, and although expensive, good value for money. La Voile d'Or is a member of Concorde hotels and offers the warm welcome, polished service and elegant decor that we expect of members of this prestigious group. We particularly enjoyed the airy restaurant with its wonderful cuisine. *Au port* the activity and scenes of the Mediterranean village are framed by the floor to ceiling glass windows of La Voile d'Or. The marina with its many yachts and fishing boats is simply a part of the hotel's decor. Inside soft Provençal pastels and countryside furnishings create a relaxed atmosphere. On a peninsula below the hotel and restaurant, a gorgeous pool is surrounded on three sides by the sparkling blue water of the Mediterranean. *Directions:* Just west of Nice, take the Avenue Semeria off the N98 in the direction of St Jean Cap Ferrat. Sign posts will direct you to the port where a one way street will take you up to the La Voile d'Or located just above the marina.

LA VOILE D'OR
Hôtelier: M Lorenzi
06230 St Jean Cap Ferrat
Tel: 93.01.13.13 Fax: 93.76.11.17
45 Rooms
Double from 890F to 3400F
Open March to October
Credit cards: none accepted
Restaurant, pool
Region: Riviera; Michelin Map: 245

Hôtel de Chantaco is a lovely Spanish villa, purposely built as a hotel, in a quiet location on the outskirts of the picturesque port town of St Jean de Luz. Set against a backdrop of greenery, the hotel with sandy-colored stucco, dark green shutters and heavy tiled roof presents an attractive picture. The lofty entrance hall leads to a large sitting room with lots of comfortable beige sofas, and a large restaurant. The bedrooms are found up the broad marble staircase. Several bedrooms have French windows that open onto tiny terraces that overlook the flower filled courtyard, and the hotel's lovely swimming pool. A few have large tiled terraces. All are decorated in a similar style, in soft beige or peach with classic decor and smartly appointed bathrooms. The hotel faces the Chantaco golf course, one of the oldest and most challenging courses in France. It also serves as a base for exploring the attractive seaside resorts that line the Atlantic and exploring the Basque and Pyrenees regions. *Directions:* Leave the Autoroute A63 at *St Jean de Luz Nord*, then travel east on Avenue de Chantaco on D918. Continue half a kilometer to the small lake and the golf course.

HÔTEL DE CHANTACO
Hôtelier: Claude Libouban
Golf de Chantaco
64500 St Jean de Luz
Tel: 59.26.14.76, Fax: 59.26.35.97
24 Rooms 4 Suites
Double from 950F to 1750F, Suite from 1350F
Open April to November
Credit cards: all major
Restaurant, pool
Region: Basque; Michelin Map: 234

This stately gingerbread Victorian (Napoleon III if you're French) home sits in a manicured garden in a lovely residential suburb of the picturesque seaside town of St Jean de Luz. Roger Larralde purchased the home to prevent an apartment complex from being built next to his family's holiday home, and converted the building into a jewel of a hotel. The entrance hall with its displays of 1930's glassware leads to the spacious living room graced by delicate Victorian furniture. Here guests help themselves to drinks from the honor bar and contemplate the menu offered by the teeny little restaurant found just across the garden, in the romantic little pavilion beyond the swimming pool. The bedrooms are all decorated with beautiful antiques, many from the art deco period, and complemented by lovely fabrics and immaculate marble bathrooms. If you are looking for a romantic hideaway ask for one of the two luxurious suites on the grounds. From the front gate it is just a 2-minute walk to the beach and a 10-minute stroll into town—a tremendous advantage in summer when the narrow streets are clogged with cars. *Directions:* Leave the Autoroute A63 at St Jean de Luz *Nord*, turn right at the third light signposted *Quartier du Lac*. The hotel is on your right.

HÔTEL PARC VICTORIA
Hôtelier: Roger Larralde
5 Rue Cepé
64500 St Jean de Luz
Tel: 59.26.78.78, Fax: 59.26.78.08
12 Rooms, 2 Suites
Double from 900F to 1200F, Suite from 1200F
Open April to mid-November
Credit cards: all major
Restaurant, pool
Region: Basque; Michelin Map: 234

La Chapelle St Martin is a small gray-washed manor that rests on a velvet green lawn. Although there is very little exterior ornamentation (even the shutters are painted to blend with the facade) the interior decor is very ornate and detailed. Colorfully patterned wallpapers, complementing carpets, paintings hung in heavy gilt frames, lavish chandeliers, tapestries and miniature statues decorate the rooms of the hotel. Known for its restaurant, La Chapelle St Martin serves meals in three elegant, small dining rooms. The setting and service is formal, with lovely porcelain, crystal, china and silver used to enhance the presentation of Chef Yves Leonard's masterful creations. La Chapelle St Martin is only a few minutes from Limoges, a city famous for its porcelain. Although many guests venture from Limoges for dinner, the manor does have rooms to accommodate overnight guests. The bedrooms are decorated with the same flavor as the restaurant and public rooms. Very spacious, the bedrooms are all with private bath and look out onto the hotel gardens and greenery. The surrounding farmland and two ponds complete the storybook atmosphere of La Chapelle St Martin. *Directions:* From Limoges take N147 signposted Poitiers to D35 signposted St Martin du Fault. The hotel is 12 kilometers from Limoges.

LA CHAPELLE ST MARTIN
Hôtelier: Jacques Dudognon
St Martin du Fault
87510 Nieul
Tel: 55.75.80.17, Fax: 55.75.89.50
10 Rooms, 3 Suites
Double from 750F to 1500F, Suite from 1400F
Open March to January
Credit cards: all Major
Restaurant closed Monday, tennis
Region: Limousin; Michelin Map: 233

La Colombe d'Or is located opposite the main square at the gates to the fortified town of St Paul de Vence. The hotel is attractive and elegant in its rustic ambiance. Antiques, worn over the years to a warm patina, are placed on terra-cotta floors, set under rough wooden beams before open fireplaces, walls are washed white contrasted by heavy wooden doors. Throw pillows, wall hangings, and flower arrangements introduce colors of rusts, oranges, browns and beiges. The hotel also boasts a fantastic collection of art. In the past, a number of now famous painters paid for their meals with their talents—and now the walls are hung like a gallery and the reputation of the inn dictates that the value of the art complements the cuisine. The restaurant of La Colombe d'Or is both excellent and attractive. Dine either in the intimacy of a room warmed by a cozy fire or on the patio whose walls are draped with ivy at tables set under the shade of cream-colored umbrellas. In the evening, stars and candles illuminate the very romantic setting. The entrance to the fortified town of St Paul de Vence is just up the street from La Colombe d'Or. After a day of sightseeing, return to La Colombe d'Or and enjoy its refreshing pool set against a backdrop of aging stone wall and greenery. *Directions:* St Paul de Vence is located 20 kilometers northwest of Nice. From the Autoroute A8 either from Cannes or Nice, exit at Cagnes sur Mer and then travel north on D6 and D2.

HÔTEL LA COLOMBE D'OR
Hôtelier: Mme & M Roux
Place de Gaulle
06570 St Paul de Vence
Tel: 93.32.80.02, Fax: 93.32.77.78
15 Rooms, 10 Suites
Double from 1100F, Suite from 1300F
Closed November to mid-December
Credit cards: all major
Restaurant, pool
Region: Riviera; Michelin Map: 245

Le Hameau is an old farm complex set on the hillside just outside the walled city of St Paul de Vence. The whitewashed buildings, tiled roofs aged by years of sun, shuttered windows, arched entryways, heavy doors and exposed beams all create a rustic and attractive setting. The bedrooms of this inn are found in four buildings clustered together amidst fruit trees and flower gardens. Each building has its own character and name: L'Oranger, L'Olivier, Le Pigeonnier and La Treille. Three of the largest bedrooms have a small room for an infant and a balcony (Rooms 1 and 3 have twin beds and Room 2 has a double bed). Room 11, with antique twin beds and a lovely view onto the garden, was my favorite. I was very impressed with the quality of this provincial inn. Monsieur Xavier Huvelin is a charming host and is graciously attentive to the needs of his guests. Le Hameau does not have a restaurant, but a delicious country breakfast can be enjoyed in the garden or in the privacy of your room. A lovely new pool is an inviting place to lounge with magnificent views of St Paul and the Riviera as its backdrop. Le Hameau is highly recommended as a wonderful inn and a great value. *Directions:* St Paul de Vence is located 20 kilometers northwest of Nice. From the Autoroute A8 either from Cannes or Nice, exit at Cagnes sur Mer and travel north on D6 and D2.

HÔTEL LE HAMEAU
Hôtelier: Mme & M Xavier Huvelin
528, Route de la Colle
06570 St Paul de Vence
Tel: 93.32.80.24, Fax: 93.32.55.75
14 Rooms, 3 Suites
Double from 350F to 550F, Suite from 650F
Credit cards: all major
Open February to mid-November and Christmas
No restaurant, pool
Region: Riviera; Michelin Map: 245

High atop a hill, set against the blue Riviera sky between Cannes and Monaco, the medieval village of St Paul de Vence is bounded by tall ramparts. Its narrow streets are lined with little houses and in the very heart of the village you find Hôtel le Saint Paul. The charming mood is set as soon as you enter the hotel and see the cozy lounge—appealingly decorated in a French country Provençal theme. Because the hotel is built within the shell of a 16th-century home, the rooms are not large, yet each is tastefully decorated and offers every amenity such as beautiful linens, fluffy towels, terry cloth robes, refrigerator, televisions, and fine soaps. This is not your standard unimaginative hotel where every room is the same, here each has its own personality. Two of our special favorites are a corner room, decorated in pretty Provençal, Pierre Deux-style print fabrics, and an especially romantic room, tucked under the eaves on the top floor with views out over the quaint tiled roof tops. One of the guest rooms has a small terrace. Another bonus, the vaulted restaurant serves gourmet meals on the sheltered, flower-decked terrace in the summer. *Directions:* St Paul de Vence is 20 kilometers northwest of Nice. Exit the A8 at Cagnes sur Mer and go north on the D6 and D2.

HÔTEL LE SAINT-PAUL
Owner: Olivier Borloo
Hôtelier: Joanna & Yann Zedde
86, Rue Grande
06570 St Paul de Vence
Tel: 93.32.65.25, Fax: 93.32.52.94
16 Rooms, 2 suites
Double from 1050F to 1275F, Suite from 1375F
Open all year
Credit cards: all major
Restaurant
Region: Riviera; Michelin Map: 245

L'Espérance is a pilgrimage site for lovers of gourmet cuisine. Marc Meneau's domain now encompasses three buildings: L'Espérance, a traditional grand home extended to the rear into an enormous glass conservatory that houses his famous restaurant; Pré de Marguerite, a single-story contemporary restaurant in a modern building with grassy grounds where a modern wing of elegant rooms with private patios border a swimming pool; and Le Moulin, a lovely old mill. Bedrooms throughout are luxurious, but come in three distinct styles: traditional (L'Espérance), traditional with contemporary chic (by the pool), rustic (in the mill). Relax and study the menu in the salon, subtle in its soft beiges, with gray leather furniture. The elegant restaurant looks out onto the garden through floor-to-ceiling windows. Tables are set with soft pastel linens, stunning flower arrangements, elegant crystal and silver. Marc Meneau is a tall, handsome man, who sports a tie under his chef's whites and welcomes guests before attending to his culinary creations. His lovely wife, Françoise, supervises the attentive, professional waiters. She bustles about to extend greetings, pour wine, assist with the service and offer a welcoming smile. Marc Meneau reappears in the lounge after dinner to relax with guests over coffee. *Directions:* L'Espérance is located 3 kilometers southeast of Vézelay on D957.

L'ESPÉRANCE
Hôtelier: Françoise & Marc Meneau
St Père sous Vézelay
89450 Vézelay
Tel: 86.33.20.45, Fax: 86.33.26.15
34 Room, 6 Suites
Double from 680F to 1700F, Suite from 1750F
Open all year
Credit cards: all major
Restaurant closed Tuesday & Wednesday lunch
Region: Burgundy; Michelin Map: 238

The Château des Alpilles has been renovated by the Bons to its former state of grandeur with high ornate ceilings, decorative wallpapers and tall windows draped with heavy fabrics. The public rooms are attractively decorated with period pieces. The breakfast room has been renovated and blends beautifully with the rest of the home. Upstairs, tiled hallways hung with tapestries lead to the lovely bedrooms. Soft, subdued colors such as rose and Dutch blue have been selected for fabrics and papers. Large *armoires*, beds, desks and chairs arrange easily in the spacious rooms, each with private bath, and make for a very comfortable stay. The corner rooms are especially nice with four large shuttered windows overlooking the shaded gardens that are planted with a multitude of exotic species of trees. On the top floor, the Bons suggest three smaller rooms that share a bath and toilet as ideal accommodation for children. The Bons have also renovated an adjacent farmhouse into four suites and a family apartment. In summer for a midday meal a barbecue of lamb, beef or pork and large salads are offered poolside. The rest of the year, although the Château des Alpilles does not have a formal restaurant, a menu of light suppers and a variety of wines are graciously offered. *Directions:* From Avignon travel south on N570 and N571 to St Rémy. Leave town to the west on D31.

CHÂTEAU DES ALPILLES
Hôtelier: Mme & Mlle Bon
Route D31
13210 St Rémy
Tel: 90.92.03.33, Fax: 90.92.45.17
19 Rooms
Double from 710F to 980F
Open Easter to 10 November & Christmas
Credit cards: all major
No restaurant; pool, tennis, sauna
Region: Provence; Michelin Map: 245, 246

Fairytale in its setting and the luxury of its decor, the Château d'Esclimont is a memorable and convenient choice (only 65 kilometers from Paris) for either a beginning or an end to your countryside travels. Not inexpensive, but well priced for what it offers, the Château d'Esclimont is spectacular. Hidden off a small country road, a private drive winds through handsome gates to expose a stunning château framed by trees and reflected in a beautiful lake graced with swans. Turrets, moats, stone bridges, towers and sculptured facades create a fanciful world of its regal past. Thirty rooms are located in the main château, all decorated regally with beautifully coordinating fabrics and handsome furnishings. Whether tucked into turret rounds or under the eaves of the third floor rooms looking out through dormer windows, the accommodations are spacious and equipped with private baths. Also very attractive in their decor and setting, another twenty-three rooms are found in the Dungeon, the Pavilion des Trophées and the Trianon—all stately buildings separated from the château by the moat. The Château d'Esclimont has a number of elegant rooms for dining and meetings. Although often hosting small tours and conferences, guests receive individual attention and excellent service. *Directions:* From Paris take A10 direction Chartres. Exit A10 at Ablis, take N10 to Essars where you turn towards Prunay (D101) for 6 kilometers to St Symphorien.

CHÂTEAU D'ESCLIMONT
Hôtelier: Nicole & Raymond Spitz
28700 St Symphorien-le-Château
Tel: 37.31.15.15, Fax: 37.31.57.91
47 Rooms, 6 Suites
Double from 950F to 1850, Suite from 2800F
Open all year
Credit cards: VS
Restaurant, pool, tennis
Region: Île de France; Michelin Map: 237

St Tropez is a charming fishing village that has become an exclusive resort where visitors come to soak up the Mediterranean sun—and hotels soak up your money. Accommodations are ridiculously expensive and don't begin to offer the value of countryside locations. But if St Tropez is what you want, we recommend that you stay at La Ponche, a hotel that occupies a cluster of houses in the old town, once fishermen's homes. The hotel is one of the oldest in St Tropez and has been in Simone Duckstein's family for over fifty years. Guestrooms and public rooms are tastefully decorated with colors and patterns complementary to its waterside setting and attractive against the white-washed walls. A few rooms have terraces that look across the tiled roof of its neighbors to the water (these gems are the most expensive rooms). All the bedrooms are individual in their decor, furnished with antiques and original paintings, equipped with ensuite bathroom and air conditioning (which is very welcome during the hot summer months). Artists of renown frequented this charming fishing village with its château, narrow streets, engaging plazas and enticing restaurants and cafés long before it became a resort. *Directions:* Once in the Vieux Port follow signs to the Citadelle and from there take the rue de la Citadelle two blocks to Boulevard d'Aumale which becomes the Rue des Remparts closer to the water. On arrival at the hotel a valet will park your car.

LA PONCHE
Hôtelier: Simone Duckstein & Margot Barbier
3, Rue des Remparts, Port des Pecheurs
83990 St Tropez
Tel: 94.97.02.53 Fax: 94.97.78.61
18 Rooms
Double from 950F to 1200F, Suite from 1350F
Open April to mid-October
Credit cards: all major
Restaurant
Region: Riviera; Michelin Map: 245

Located just 9 kilometers from the heart of the large city of Brive, enjoying the peace and tranquillity of the countryside, the Auberge des Prés de la Vézère is a reasonably priced country *auberge* just minutes from its luxurious and more expensive sister, the Château Castel Novel. The Parveaux family purchased this little country inn in 1989 and it has been rewarded with their impeccable taste and professional management. Savor some delicious regional cuisine in the wonderful country restaurant and enjoy an aperitif, after dinner drink or coffee in the comfortable salon around the blazing log fire in winter. Breakfast is a bountiful buffet—an ideal way to start the day. Upstairs the guestrooms are handsomely furnished and rich fabrics dress the beds and shuttered windows. All have TV, telephone and ensuite bathroom. Comfortable in size, they are not elaborate and offer excellent value for money. From Brive you can either head south to explore the gorgeous region of Perigord or explore north to Limoges. We used it as a convenient last night in the countryside before leaving our car at the station and taking the train to Paris. Traffic is less congested in Brive than Limoges, and both cities have express trains to Paris. *Directions:* From Brive, take D901 west in the direction of Varetz, then take the right branch off D901 following D148 to St Viance in the direction of Allassac.

AUBERGE DES PRÉS DE LA VÉZÈRE
Owner: Albert Parveaux
Hôtelier: Mme Giraudet
19240 St Viance
Tel: 55.85.00.50 Fax: 55.84.25.36
11 Rooms
Double from 280F to 340 F
Open May to mid-October
Credit cards: MC, VS
Restaurant
Region: Dordogne; Michelin Map: 239

Lucille and Jacques Bon welcome you to their 17th-century farmstead in the Camargue. Jacques' family were farmers who worked the rice fields of this windswept land with its stretches of marsh and wild horses, and he is passionate about the region. Lucille and Jacques' home is covered with vines, shaded by trellises of grapes and wisteria and decorated by tiled planters overflowing with geraniums. How fortunate that they have restored a wing of their 17th-century mas (home) into a luxurious inn. The guestrooms have rough exposed pine beams, and lovely old doors and windows incorporated into their new construction. We particularly appreciated the immaculate modern bathrooms and excellent lighting. The decor in their home marries heavy old wood furniture with leather chairs, giving a handsome masculine look. The Bons are an extremely gracious couple. Lucille is pretty and welcoming, Jacques is a handsome, friendly bull farmer with a large white mustache, tall and lean, hardened by years of work and riding. Cowboy, the family dog, is always by their side. Meals are served in a large country kitchen in front of an open fireplace under 19th-century beams, or in summer on the garden terrace. Days are for swimming, horse riding, mountain biking or participating in the rodeo with the magnificent Camargue bulls and horses. *Directions:* Leave Arles in the direction of Salin de Giraud (D36) for 25 kilometers. Three kilometers after Sambuc turn left.

LE MAS DE PEINT
Hôtelier: Lucille & Jacques Bon
Le Sambuc, 13200 Arles
Tel: 90.97.20.62, Fax: 90.97.22.20
8 Rooms, 2 Suites
Double from 1100F to 1650F, Suite from 1850F
Open mid-March to mid-November & Christmas
Credit cards: all major
Restaurant for guests, pool, horse back riding
Region: Camargue; Michelin Map: 245, 246

Set in the rolling foothills of the Pyrénées, in a picturebook village near the Spanish border, the Hôtel Arraya has captured the tradition and rustic flavor of this Basque region. Long ago the hotel was founded to provide lodgings for pilgrims on the road to Santiago de Compostela. Today it accommodates guests who have fallen in love with this dear inn and return time and again. The Hôtel Arraya is decorated with an abundance of 17th-century Basque antiques and is a comfortable and hospitable village hotel. The entry, lobby and breakfast nook are charming. Cozy blue and white gingham cushions pad the wooden chairs that are set around a lovely collection of antique tables. The restaurant offers regional Basque specialties to tempt you: *ravioles de xangurro, agneau aux pochas, foie de canard frais poêlé aux cèpes, fromages des Montagnes* and *pastiza*, a delicious Basque almond cake filled with cream or black cherry preserve. The bedrooms are all individual in decor and size, and are attractive with their white-washed walls, exposed beams and pretty fabrics. The hotel has been in Madame's family for many generations and guests are welcomed as friends in the traditional way, round the *zizailua*, or bench, near the fire. *Directions:* Exit the Autoroute A6 at St Jean de Luz. Follow directions to St Pée sur Nivelle on N10. After 5 kilometers turn right to the village of Ascain and then take the Col de St Ignace to Sare.

HÔTEL ARRAYA
Hôtelier: Mme & M Paul Fagoaga
Sare, 64310 Ascain
Tel: 59.54.20.46, Fax: 59.54.27.04
21 Rooms
Double from 385F to 600F
Open May to October
Credit cards: all major
Restaurant
Region: Basque; Michelin Map: 234

If business or pleasure brings you to Nantes, stay in this converted 13th-century abbey on the outskirts of town. L'Abbaye de Villeneuve might also serve as a good point to bridge the distance between a tour of Brittany and the Loire Valley. A tree-lined drive leads up to L'Abbaye de Villeneuve, a grand, two-story dwelling set a good distance from the main road. High ceilings and handsome furnishings impose a formal air and complement the mood of this stately home. Two intimate dining rooms offer guests a lovely atmosphere in which to dine. Service is very professional, befitting the elegant table settings and grand cuisine. A massive stone stairway wends its way up to the abbey's bedrooms—these accommodations are luxuriously furnished, with vast windows offering views of the grounds. Each room is equipped with direct dial phone, television and lovely, modern bathrooms. Although the grounds are lacking in color, there is a small circular wading pool on the back lawn. *Directions:* From Nantes follow signposts for La Rochelle and Bordeaux, and then La Roche sur Yon (green sign). At the second stoplight, follow signposts for Viais.

L'ABBAYE DE VILLENEUVE
Hôtelier: Philippe Savry
Directeur: M Lesmarie
Route des Sables d'Olonne
44840 Les Sorinières
Tel: 40.04.40.25, Fax: 40.31.28.45
20 Rooms, 3 Suites
Double from 490F to 935F, Suite from 1150F
Open all year
Credit cards: all major
Restaurant
Region: Brittany; Michelin Map: 232

Strasbourg is one of our favorite cities, and just around the corner from its magnificent cathedral on a quiet pedestrian street is the charming Hôtel des Rohan. Rolf and Nicole van Maenen pride themselves on keeping their little hotel in tip-top condition. On the ground floor is the foyer and a traditional salon, hung with tapestries, where breakfast is served. The bedrooms are not large and are decorated either in traditional, or, those on the top floors, with pine paneling in a more country decor. All are well equipped with either ensuite bath or shower, phone, radio, television and mini-bar. Rooms that face afternoon sun are air-conditioned. Breakfast is the only meal served and the staff is delighted to make recommendations for nearby restaurants that run the gamut from regional to gourmet cuisine. The location is ideal for exploring Strasbourg on foot. The narrow streets are a maze that winds in the shadow of leaning, timbered buildings and in the shade of the lacy trees that grow beside the river. Shops range from department stores and sophisticated boutiques to souvenir shops with momentos and postcards. *Directions:* Follow signposts first for *Centre Ville* then for cathedral. This will bring you to Place Gutenberg parking (underground). Facing the cathedral's main doors turn right. The hotel is on your right after 100 meters. Alternate parking is at Place du Château. The porter will carry your luggage to and from the parking area.

HÔTEL DES ROHAN
Hôtelier: Nicole & Rolf Van Maenen
17-19, Rue du Maroquin
67000 Strasbourg
Tel: 88.32.85.11, Fax: 88.75.65.37
36 Rooms
Double from 375F to 620F
Open all year
Credit cards: all major
No restaurant
Region: Alsace; Michelin Map: 242

La Bastide de Tourtour is situated on the outskirts of Tourtour, *le village dans le ciel*, and actually guards a position even higher than the "village in the heavens." From its vantage point you can enjoy unobstructed vistas of the surrounding countryside of Haute Provence. The region is lovely and the village, with its cobbled streets, galleries, tempting shops, cozy restaurants and inviting cafés, a delight to explore. The location of La Bastide de Tourtour is ideal and we are pleased to learn from travelers that the owners have expended some effort and money with refurbishments. A grand circular staircase, with old implements for weaving and spinning on each floor's landing, winds up to the guestrooms. Many of the Bastide's bedrooms have private terraces and enjoy panoramic views (views are a factor in determining rates). The decor and the view varies from room to room. The restaurant is attractive, with tables set under arches and beamed ceilings. When weather permits, tables are set on the terrace. *Directions:* Located 20 kilometers northwest of Draguignan. Leaving Draguignan follow signposts for Flayosc/Salernes, cross Flayosc and continue towards Salernes. After 77 kilometers take the road to the right signposted Tourtour.

LA BASTIDE DE TOURTOUR
Hôtelier: Francine & Etienne Laurent
Route Draguignan
83690 Tourtour
Tel: 94.70.57.30, Fax: 94.70.54.90
25 Rooms
Double from 640F to 1400F
Open March to November
Credit cards: all major
Restaurant, pool, tennis
Region: Haute Provence; Michelin Map: 245

Set on a headland, with garden paths weaving down to a small crescent of golden sand, Gerard and Danielle Jouanny opened this large lovely home, Ti Al-Lannec, as a hotel in 1978. The Jouannys offer a warm welcome rarely found in hotels, so it feels more like staying with friends at the seaside than in a hotel. Each bedroom has a different pretty wallpaper with coordinating drapes and bedspread. Family accommodations have two bedrooms, one for parents and one with bunk beds for children. My favorites were those with *salon en verandah* meaning that each has a small sitting area with doors that open to a tiny balcony so that whatever the weather you can enjoy the fantastic view of sand, ocean and rocky promontories. The large windows of the restaurant share the same glorious view. The sitting rooms have thoughtfully been equipped with jigsaw puzzles, books and games to accommodate the hobbies of the guests and the unpredictable moods of the weather. In the basement is L'Espace Bleu Marine, a complete health center where you can pamper yourself with massages and wraps, work out in the gymnasium and relax in the solarium, sauna and large jacuzzi, set in a gazebo overlooking the beach. Children enjoy the outdoor play equipment and giant chess set. *Directions:* From Rennes take N12 to Guigamp and follow signposts for Lannion for 9 kilometers to Trébeurden.

TI AL-LANNEC
Hôtelier: Danielle & Gerard Jouanny
14, Allée de Mezo Guen
22560 Trébeurden
Tel: 96.23.57.26, Fax: 96.23.62.14
29 Rooms
Double from 600F to 960F
Open mid-March to mid-November
Credit cards: all major
Restaurant
Region: Brittany; Michelin Map: 230

Nestled on a picturesque bend of the Dordogne, referred to as the *Cingle de Trémolat*, is the sleepy, tobacco-growing village of Trémolat. Tucked away on a quiet street that leads into the center is Le Vieux Logis et Ses Logis des Champs. This charming hotel opens up on one side to farmland, and has a pretty back garden with a small stream. The Giraudel-Destord family has lived in this ancient, ivy-covered farm complex for four hundred years. The current Mme Giraudel-Déstord opened the family home to guests forty years ago; her charm dominates the atmosphere and she still arranges flower bouquets for the breakfast trays each morning. Her son, Bernard, continues her fine tradition of overseeing the property and demanding excellence. The bedrooms have recently been redecorated and are located in various ivy-draped buildings about the property whose tranquil views open onto the freshness of the countryside. Each room has an individual theme for its decor and everything matches, down to the smallest detail. A favorite is decorated in large red and white checks: the duvets, the pillows, the curtains, and the canopy on the four-poster bed. The restaurant is in the barn and the tables are cleverly positioned within each of the stalls. *Directions:* Trémolat is located 54 kilometers south of Périgueux. From Périgueux travel south on N139 and at Le Bugue travel southwest on D31 to Trémolat.

LE VIEUX LOGIS
Hôtelier: Bernard Giraudel-Déstord
24510 Trémolat
Tel: 53.22.80.06, Fax: 53.22.84.89
22 Rooms, 2 Suites
Double from 700F to 1260F, Suite from 1460F
Open all year
Credit cards: all major
Restaurant
Region: Dordogne; Michelin Map: 235

In the middle of a beautiful valley, with mountains towering as high as 1,500 meters on either side, the medieval town of Trigance clings to a rocky spur. The Château de Trigance is found within the walls and ruins of the ancient castle that crowns the village. The restorations and extent of the work involved to prepare this 11th-century fortress as a hotel are fully appreciated after seeing the before and after photographs. At present there are ten rooms which are tucked behind thick stone walls of the ancient fortress. The accommodation is definitely not luxurious, often a bit dark and austere with beds butted right up against the ancient stone walls, but the setting and atmosphere is unique with an authentic medieval flavor. You can now even reserve a large room in the round tower that overlooks the village. The restaurant is renowned for its fine cuisine. Monsieur and Madame Thomas are in charge of the hotel in its magnificent setting under the warm blue skies of Haute Provence and it is their personality that enhances the character and attraction of this hillside accommodation. Park on the outskirts of this walled town and Monsieur Thomas will greet you and theatrically hoist your bags on his elevator lift. The location of the château is a perfect starting point for touring the spectacular Grand Gorges du Verdon: pack a picnic and spend a day driving the canyon at leisure. *Directions:* From Draguignan take D955 signpost Castellance for 45 kilometers (north) to the hotel.

CHÂTEAU DE TRIGANCE
Hôtelier: Mme & M Jean Claude Thomas
83840 Trigance
Tel: 94.76.91.18, Fax: 94.47.58.99
10 Rooms
Double from 590F to 900F
Open mid-March to mid-November
Credit cards: all major
Restaurant
Region: Haute Provence; Michelin Map: 245

A beautiful drive winds up to this magnificent, gray-turreted château and the first impression is captivating. The Château de Castel Novel offers superlative service and accommodation and, to top it off, the cuisine is superb. This is the country of such delicacies as *foie gras*, truffles, veal and a delightful variety of mushrooms. Jean Pierre Faucher, who served his chef's apprenticeship in the region and at some of France's finest restaurants, offers you a wonderful menu. The bedrooms are cozy and beautifully maintained. They are few in number, and I found as they were shown to me, that each one became my "favorite." They are all marvelous, but different. One is impressive, if you like to sleep in a turret; another has a pair of magnificent, spiraling wood four-poster beds; and yet another has twin beds, two balconies and a lovely view. The Parveaux family have added ten attic rooms in an annex, La Metarie du Château. These rooms are less luxurious in furnishings, but are offered at a reduced rate. Built in the 14th and 15th centuries, the Château de Castel Novel is set in a garden of fifteen acres with a swimming pool, tennis courts and a practice area of three holes for golfers. The hotel is professionally and graciously managed by Albert Parveaux and his charming wife, Christine. *Directions:* Travel 10 kilometers to the northwest from Brive la Gaillarde on D901 in the direction of Objat.

CHÂTEAU DE CASTEL NOVEL
Hôtelier: Mme & M Albert Parveaux
Varetz, 19240 Allassac
Tel: 55.85.00.01, Fax: 55.85.09.03
32 Rooms, 5 Suites
Double from 690F to 1330F, Suite from 1330F
Open mid-May to mid-October
Credit cards: all major
Restaurant, pool, tennis
Region: Dordogne; Michelin Map: 239

Vence is a quaint little town of narrow streets, intriguing passageways and tempting craft and specialty shops. Look for the largest tree in Vence and there you will find L'Auberge des Seigneurs. This is a delightful inn, located on a quiet side street at the center of Vence. The inn is charming in its decor and country ambiance—heavy old beams are exposed in the ceilings and walls are whitewashed. Copper plates, pans and bed warmers adorn the walls, Provençal fabrics cover the tables and lovely antiques decorate every nook and cranny. Wooden doors, rich in their patina, a large stone fireplace and striking flower arrangements complete a scene in the restaurant and salon that is intimate and cozy. Evenings the restaurant comes alive, mellow with the soft flicker of candlelight. Diners talk in hushed conversation at clustered tables and Madame Rodi orchestrates excellent and gracious service, tossing salads tableside, pouring wine and tending chicken grilled on the open fire. Up a creaking stairway are ten delightful, small rooms. Inexpensive in price, the bedrooms are a true bargain—comfortable and simply decorated with pretty country prints. *Directions:* From Nice travel southwest on N98 to Cros de Cagnes and then travel north on D36 to Vence. Vence is located 22 kilometers to the northwest of Nice.

L'AUBERGE DES SEIGNEURS ET DU LION D'OR
Hôtelier: M & Mme Pierre Rodi
Place du Frêne
06140 Vence
Tel: 93.58.04.24, Fax: 93.24.08.01
10 Rooms
Double from 330F to 350F
Closed mid-November to mid-December
Credit cards: all major
Restaurant closed Sunday evening & Monday
Region: Riviera; Michelin Map: 245

Looking up from the town of Vence you can see the Château St Martin sitting on the hillside on the site of an ancient Templars castle. The Château St Martin, built in traditional style in 1936, stands behind the old drawbridge, tower and wall which date back to Roman times and give the hotel a feeling of the past, while a beautifully located swimming pool and tennis courts provide the pleasures of the present. The accommodation is extremely luxurious and many of the rooms are so large that they are referred to as suites. If you prefer solitude, there are also small Provençal country houses on the estate. A well-known cook is in charge of this most famous kitchen. All products from the estate are at his disposal: fresh eggs, fruit and vegetables picked daily and oil from one thousand-year-old olive trees. Sample his splendors at tables set on a wide, outdoor terrace and enjoy a 100 kilometers vista down to the Côte d'Azur, although indoors, an elegant restaurant looks out through floor-to-ceiling windows and enjoys the same breathtaking panorama. The Château St Martin is for those seeking sheer luxury and the finest of service. *Directions:* From the Cagnes sur Mer exit off A8 take D36 to Vence. At Vence follow signs for *Autres,* avoiding the town center. Follow signs for Courseguoules (or Col de Vence) and you find the hotel high above the town about 3 kilometers north of Vence.

CHÂTEAU ST MARTIN
Hôtelier: Geneve family
Directrice: Mlle A Brunet
06140 Vence
Tel: 93.58.02.02, Fax: 93.24.08.91
14 Rooms, 10 Suites
Double from 1160F to 2250F, Suite from 2530F
Open mid-March to mid-November
Credit cards: all major
Restaurant, pool, tennis
Region: Riviera; Michelin Map: 245

Considered to be one of France's most picturesque villages, Vézelay is a "must" today just as it was in the Middle Ages when it was considered an important pilgrimage stop. Perched on the hillside overlooking the romantic valley of the Cousin, Vézelay is a wonderful place to spend the afternoon, enjoy a countryside picnic or, if afforded the luxury of time, to linger and spend the evening. A popular choice for a moderately priced hotel is the Poste et Lion d'Or, a hillside hotel that sits on the main road by the square. Poste et Lion d'Or is rumored to have existed as a post house in the Middle Ages, accommodating those who awaited the opening of the village drawbridge. Public rooms are uninspired in their traditional decor. The bedrooms in the main building are attractively decorated, several have handsome antiques, all have satin bedspreads and are accompanied by modern gray marble bathrooms. An ivy-clad annex houses less expensive rather shabby rooms with decidedly old-fashioned bathrooms. *Directions:* Vézelay is located 15 kilometers from Avallon. From Avallon take D957 west in the direction of Vézelay.

HÔTEL POSTE ET LION D'OR
Hôtelier: Remillet Family
Place du Champ de Foire
89450 Vézelay
Tel: 86.33.21.23, Fax: 86.32.30.92
49 Rooms, 1 Suite
Double from 300F to 580F, Suite from 820F
Closed mid-February to mid-March
Credit cards: all major
Restaurant
Region: Burgundy; Michelin Map: 238

Hôtel le Pontot, a fortified house with a walled flower garden, sits amongst the winding medieval streets of the walled hilltop town of Vézelay. George Thum, the American owner, leaves the running of the hotel to the personable Christian Abadie, but, he is usually on hand to help unilingual English speaking guests with their reservations and questions. On warm days guests breakfast off Limoge china, with silver service, at little tables set in the garden; in inclement weather breakfast is served in the elegant blue salon. Curving stone steps lead up to the bedrooms and the comfortable lounge. The traditionally decorated bedrooms are furnished with antiques and have small modern bathrooms. We especially enjoyed the bedroom that contains Monet's easel, and the spacious suite with its blue silk coronet draperies above its twin beds. For complete privacy request the suite in the former kitchen: its stone floor, huge fireplace and old utensils give a rustic feel and you can scramble up above the oven to the extra little bed where the servants once slept. There are some delightful restaurants in the village and guests often dine with Marc Meneau in nearby St Père sous Vézelay. *Directions:* Vézelay is located 15 kilometers from Avallon on D957. From the town's main square turn up the hill towards the Basilica, park in the first carpark on your left. The hotel is on your left.

RÉSIDENCE HÔTEL LE PONTOT
Hôtelier: Christian Abadie
Place du Pontot
89450 Vézelay
Tel: 86.33.24.40
7 Rooms, 3 Suites
Double from 550F to 840F, Suite from 700F
Open Easter to November
Credit cards: MC, VS
No restaurant
Region: Burgundy; Michelin Map: 238

Le Prieuré was built as an archbishop's palace in 1322 and became a Priory in 1333. Now it's a charming hotel at the heart of this inviting medieval village. Ivy clings to its warm stone exterior, green shutters dress its windows and sun-baked tiles adorn the roof. The hotel has expanded and changed over the years and now has twenty six rooms and ten suites, many of which have lovely terraces housed in a modern, nondescript annex. Air conditioning has been incorporated throughout—a welcome luxury in the hot provençal summers. Le Prieuré is decorated with beautiful antiques, adding charm and beauty to the ambiance and setting. When blessed with the balmy weather of Provence, dine on the terrace surrounded by foliage and soft lighting in the subtle elegance of a summer night. Marie-France and her son François are your gracious hosts and their presence lends a personal and special touch to the very competent and professional service. *Directions:* Leave Avignon towards Nîmes and immediately after crossing the Rhône River (both branches) turn right towards Bagnols sur Cèze on D980 for about 2 kilometers. The hotel is in the heart of the village, next to the church.

LE PRIEURÉ
Hôtelier: Marie-France & François Mille
7, Place de Chapître
30400 Villeneuve les Avignon
Tel: 90.25.18.20, Fax: 90.25.45.39
26 Rooms, 10 Suites
Double from 800F to 1300F, Suite from 1500F
Open mid-March to November
Credit cards: all major
Restaurant, pool, tennis
Region: Provence; Michelin Map: 245, 246

Once a Cistercian abbey, the Château de Gilly is surrounded by an expanse of grounds transected by a web of moats, with origins that trace back to the 6th century. Just north of Beaune, at the heart of Burgundy, the château guards a quiet location near Château de Vougeot, home of the Chevaliers de Tastevin. You can drive up over one arm of a moat to the entry of the Château de Gilly which was magnificently constructed to blend with two wings of the fortification that date back to the 17th century. Beautifully renovated, the interior of the château is rich in furnishings and comfort. Hung between dramatic beams, handsome tapestries drape the old stone walls. Lofty corridors, dramatic with vaulted ceilings, tile and stone floors lead to ground floor bedchambers and narrow, steep stairways wind up to rooms tucked under the heavy old eaves and beams. Quality fabrics and incredible 14th- and 18th-century paintings decorate the spacious rooms, and bathrooms have been incorporated with thoughtful modern comforts. Descend to an underground passageway that leads to the magnificent dining room. Dressed in deep red fabrics, candlelight, crystal, silver, and heavy tapestries the restaurant is elegant. *Directions:* Travel 22 kilometers north of Beaune on N74. Just before Vougeot, watch for a small road and sign on the right, directing you east to Gilly les Citeaux and the château.

CHÂTEAU DE GILLY
Hôtelier: Jean Louis Bottigliero
Gilly les Citeaux
21640 Vougeot
Tel: 80.62.89.98, Fax: 80.62.82.34
39 Rooms
Double from 810F to 1360F
Closed February
Credit cards: MC, VS
Restaurant
Region: Burgundy; Michelin Map: 243

Key Map

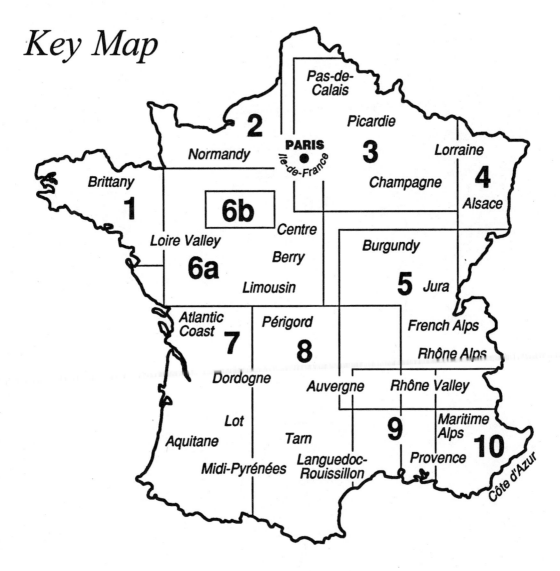

Map 1

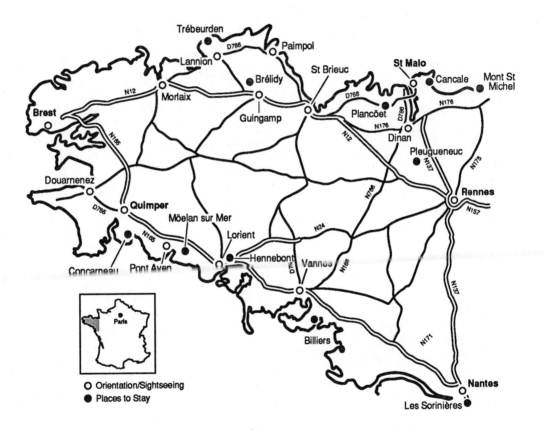

Trébeurden

D786

Paimpol

Lannion

St Brieuc

St Malo

Cancale

Mont St
Michel

N12

Brélidy

Morlaix

D768

N176

Brest

Guingamp

Plancöet

D786

N185

N176

Dinan

Pleugueneuc

N12

N137

N175

Rennes

Douarnenez

N786

N157

D786

Quimper

Möelan sur Mer

N786

N165

Lorient

N24

N137

Concarneau

Pont Aven

Hennebont

Vannes

Billiers

N171

Nantes

Les Sorinières

Paris

○ Orientation/Sightseeing
● Places to Stay

Map 2

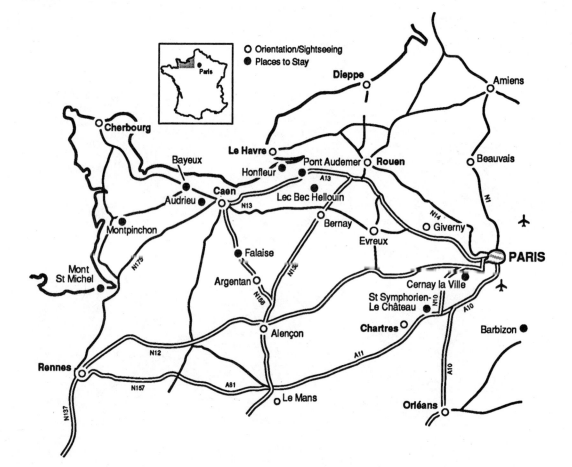

Orientation/Sightseeing
Places to Stay

Dieppe

Amiens

Cherbourg

Paris

Le Havre

Beauvais

Bayeux

Honfleur

Pont Audemer   Rouen

Audrieu

Caen

Lec Bec Hellouin

N13

A13

N14

N1

Montpinchon

Bernay

Giverny

Evreux

Mont
St Michel

N175

Falaise

PARIS

Argentan

N138

N13

Cernay la Ville

St Symphorien-
Le Château

A10

N10

Rennes

N12

Alençon

Chartres

Barbizon

N137

N157

A81

A11

Le Mans

Orléans

A10

266

Map 3

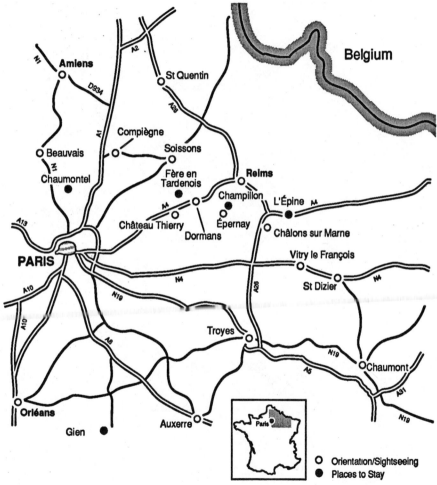

Belgium

N1

Amiens

D934

St Quentin

A2

A28

A1

Compiègne

Soissons

Beauvais

N1

Chaumontel

Fère en
Tardenois

Reims

Champillon

L'Épine   M

M

Épernay

Château Thierry

Dormans

Châlons sur Marne

A13

A26

Vitry le François

PARIS

N4

St Dizier

N4

A10

N19

A10

A6

A5

Troyes

N19

Chaumont

A31

Orléans

Auxerre

N19

Gien

Paris

○ Orientation/Sightseeing
● Places to Stay

Map 4

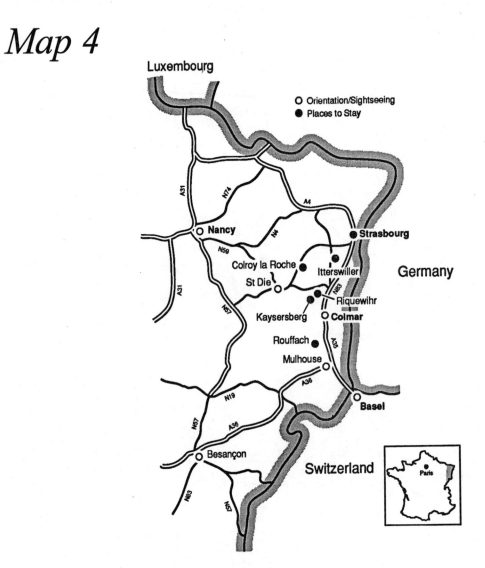

Luxembourg

○ Orientation/Sightseeing
● Places to Stay

A31

N74

A4

○ **Nancy**

N59

N4

Colroy la Roche ● **Strasbourg**

● Itterswiller

Germany

St Die ○

N83

● Riquewihr

Kaysersberg ○ **Colmar**

Rouffach ●

A35

Mulhouse ○

A36

A31

N57

N19

○ **Basel**

N57

A36

Besançon ○

Switzerland

●
Paris

Map 5

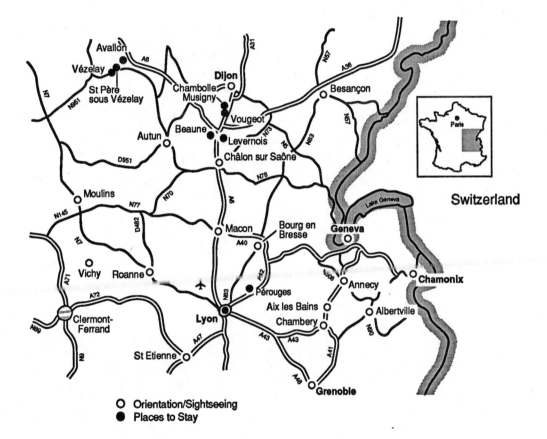

Avallon

Vézelay

St Père
sous Vézelay

Chambolle
Musigny

Dijon

Besançon

Vougeot

Beaune

Autun

Levernois

Châlon sur Saône

Moulins

Macon

Bourg en
Bresse

Geneva

Lake Geneva

Switzerland

Paris

Vichy

Roanne

Annecy

Chamonix

Clermont-
Ferrand

Pérouges

Aix les Bains

Albertville

Lyon

Chambery

St Etienne

Grenoble

○ Orientation/Sightseeing
● Places to Stay

Map 6A

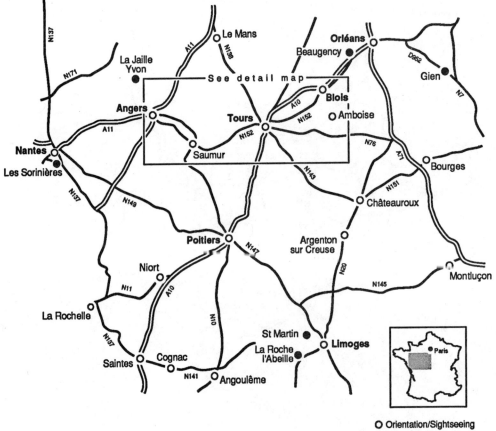

Map 6B

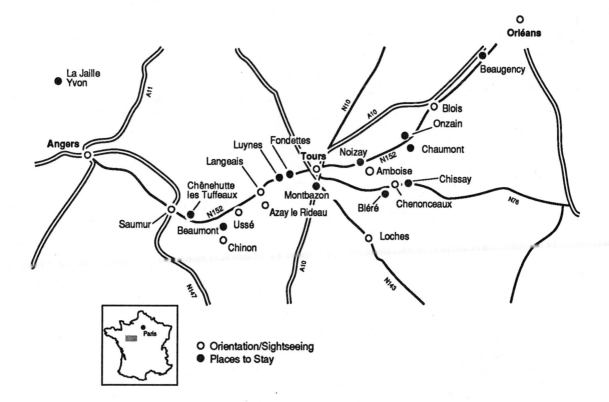

La Jaille
Yvon

Angers

Orléans

Beaugency

A11

N10   A10

Blois

Onzain

Fondettes

Luynes

Noizay

Chaumont

Langeais

Tours

N152

Chênehutte
les Tuffeaux

Amboise

Chissay

Saumur

N152

Montbazon

Bléré

Chenonceaux

N76

Beaumont

Ussé

Azay le Rideau

Chinon

Loches

A10

N143

N147

Paris

○ Orientation/Sightseeing
● Places to Stay

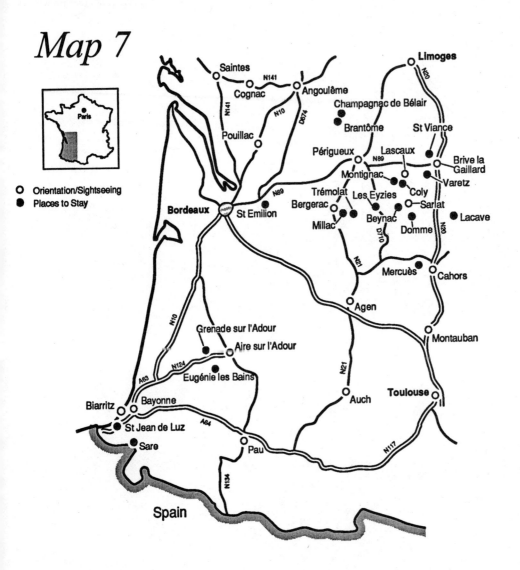

Map 7

Orientation/Sightseeing
Places to Stay

Limoges
Saintes
N141
Cognac
Angoulême
Champagnac de Bélair
Brantôme
St Viance
N141
N10
D674
Pouillac
Périgueux
Lascaux
Brive la Gaillard
N89
Montignac
Varetz
Trémolat
Les Eyzies
Coly
Bergerac
Beynac
Sarlat
Millac
Domme
Lacave
Bordeaux
St Emilion
N89
N21
D710
N20
Mercuès
Cahors
Agen
Grenade sur l'Adour
Montauban
Aire sur l'Adour
N10
N124
Eugénie les Bains
A63
N21
Biarritz
Auch
Toulouse
Bayonne
St Jean de Luz
A64
Sare
Pau
N117
N134

Spain

Map 8

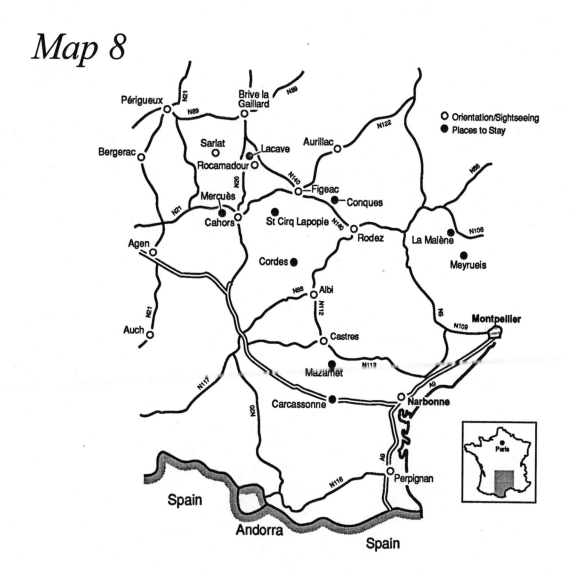

Périgueux — N21 — N89 — Brive la Gaillard — N89

Sarlat
Lacave
Rocamadour
Aurillac — N122

Bergerac

○ Orientation/Sightseeing
● Places to Stay

N88

N140

Mercuès
Figeac
Conques

N21

Cahors
St Cirq Lapopie — N140 — Rodez — La Malène — N106

Agen

Cordes ●
Meyrueis ●

N21

N88 — Albi
N112

Auch

Castres

N8

Montpellier
N109

N113

Mazamet

N117

Carcassonne
Narbonne
A9

N20

A9

N116 — Perpignan

Spain

Spain

Andorra

Paris

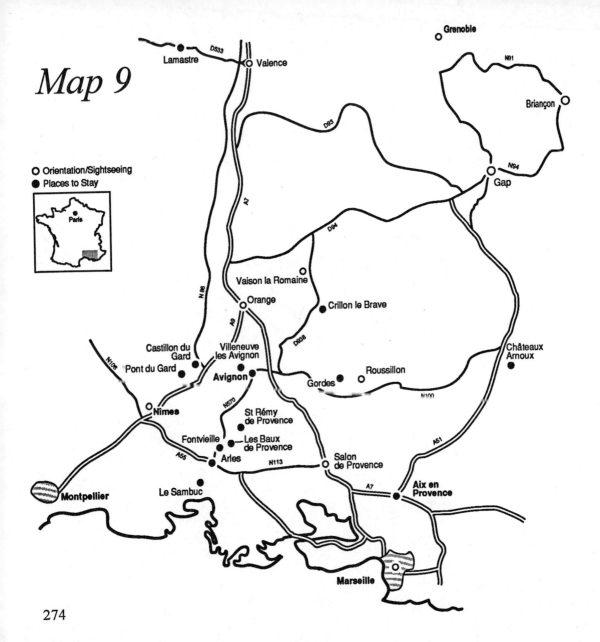

Map 9

Orientation/Sightseeing
Places to Stay

Paris

Grenoble

N91

Briançon

Lamastre   D533   Valence

N94

Gap

D93

A7

D94

N86

Vaison la Romaine

A9   Orange

Crillon le Brave

Castillon du Gard   Villeneuve les Avignon

D938

N106   Pont du Gard

Avignon

Châteaux Arnoux

Nîmes

N570   Gordes   Roussillon

N100

St Rémy de Provence

Fontvieille   Les Baux de Provence

A55   Arles

A51

Montpellier   Le Sambuc   N113   Salon de Provence

A7   Aix en Provence

Marseille

Map 10

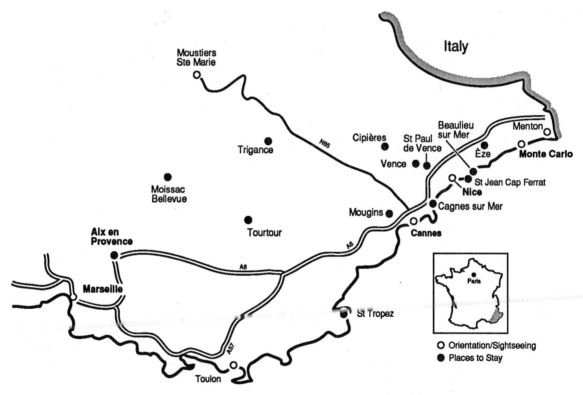

Italy

Moustiers
Ste Marie

Cipières

St Paul
de Vence

Beaulieu
sur Mer

Menton

Trigance

N85

Vence

Èze

Monte Carlo

Moissac
Bellevue

St Jean Cap Ferrat

Nice

Mougins

Cagnes sur Mer

Aix en
Provence

Tourtour

A8

A8

Cannes

Marseille

Paris

St Tropez

A57

O Orientation/Sightseeing
● Places to Stay

Toulon

Index

DISCOVERIES FROM OUR READERS

If you have a favorite hideaway that you would be willing to share with other readers, we would love to hear from you. The type of accommodations we feature are those with old-world ambiance, special charm, historical interest, attractive setting, and, above all, warmth of welcome. Please send the following information:

Your name, address, and telephone number.

Name, address, and telephone number of your discovery.

Rate for a double room including tax, service, and breakfast

Brochure or picture (we cannot return material).

Permission to use an edited version of your description.

Would you want your name, city, and state included in the book?

Please send information to:

KAREN BROWN'S GUIDES
Post Office Box 70, San Mateo, CA 94401, USA
Telephone: (415) 342-9117 Fax: (415) 342-9133

Karen Brown's Country Inn Guides

The Most Reliable & Informative Series on Country Inns

Detailed itineraries guide you through the countryside. Every recommendation, from the most deluxe hotel to a simple B&B, is personally inspected, approved and chosen for its romantic ambiance and warmth of welcome. Our charming accommodations reflect every price range, from budget hideaways to the most luxurious palaces.

Order Form for Shipments within the U.S.A.

Please ask in your local bookstore for KAREN BROWN'S GUIDES. If the books you want are unavailable, you may order directly from the publisher.

California Country Inns & Itineraries $14.95

English Country Bed & Breakfasts $13.95

English, Welsh & Scottish Country Hotels & Itineraries $14.95

French Country Bed & Breakfasts $13.95

French Country Inns & Itineraries $14.95

German Country Inns & Itineraries $14.95

Irish Country Inns & Itineraries $14.95

Italian Country Bed & Breakfasts $14.95

Italian Country Inns & Itineraries $14.95

Portuguese Country Inns & Pousadas (1990 edition) $6.00

Spanish Country Inns & Itineraries $14.95

Swiss Country Inns & Itineraries $14.95

Name _____ Street _____

City _____ State ____ Zip _____ Tel: _____

Credit Card (MasterCard or Visa) _____ Exp: _____

Add $3.50 for the first book and .50 cents for each additional book for postage & packing. California residents add 8.25% sales tax. *Order form valid only for shipments within the U.S.A.* Indicate number of copies of each title. Send form with check or credit card information to:

KAREN BROWN'S GUIDES
Post Office Box 70, San Mateo, California, 94401, U.S.A.
Tel: (415) 342-9117   Fax: (415) 342-9153

Karen Brown's
French Country Bed & Breakfasts
The Choice of the Discriminating Traveler to France
Featuring the Most Charming Bed & Breakfasts

**KAREN BROWN'S
FRENCH
Country Bed & Breakfasts**

UPDATED AND REVISED • THIRD EDITION

French Country Bed & Breakfasts is the perfect companion guide to *French Country Inns & Itineraries*. Whereas the French hotel book features delightful small hotels and inns, the French bed & breakfast guide has our personal selection of wonderful places to stay in ancestral homes, country farmhouses, and cheery cottages. All the pertinent information is given: a detailed description, driving directions, sketch, price, owner's name, whether meals are available, telephone and fax numbers, amount of English spoken, and dates open.

French Country Bed & Breakfasts does not replace *French Country Inns & Itineraries*—together they make the perfect pair for the traveler who wants to enjoy the comparatively low prices offered by traveling the bed & breakfast way. Both feature places to stay with charm, warmth of welcome, and old-world ambiance: *French Country Bed & Breakfasts* features delightful places to stay in homes, while *French Country Inns & Itineraries* features small hotels and inns PLUS the added bonus of Paris hotels, and countryside driving itineraries, handy for use with the bed & breakfast guide. Each book uses the same maps so it is easy to choose a combination of places to stay from both books adding great variety to where you spend the night.

KAREN BROWN wrote her first travel guide, *French Country Inns & Chateaux*, in 1979, now in its seventh edition. Thirteen other books have been added to the series which has become known as the most personalized, reliable reference library for the discriminating traveler. Although Karen's staff has expanded, she is still involved in the publication of her guide books. Karen, her husband, Rick, and their children Alexandra and Richard, live on the coast south of San Francisco at their own country inn, Seal Cove Inn, in Moss Beach.

JUNE BROWN hails from Sheffield, England, has an extensive background in travel, dating back to her school-girl days when she "youth hosteled" throughout Europe. June lives in San Mateo with her husband, Tony, and their children Simon and Clare.

BARBARA TAPP, the talented artist responsible for all of the hotel sketches and delightful illustrations in this guide, was raised in Australia where she studied in Sydney at the School of Interior Design. Although Barbara continues with freelance projects, she devotes much of her time to illustrating the Karen Brown guides. Barbara lives in Kensington with her husband, Richard, their two sons, Jonothan, Alexander, and daughter, Georgia.

JANN POLLARD, the artist responsible for the beautiful painting on the cover of this guide, has studied art since childhood, and is well-known for her outstanding impressionistic-style water colors which she has exhibited in numerous juried shows, winning many awards. Jann travels frequently to Europe (using Karen Brown's guides) where she loves to paint historical buildings. Jann lives in the San Francisco Bay area with her husband, Gene, and their two daughters.

SEAL COVE INN—LOCATED IN THE SAN FRANCISCO AREA

Karen Brown Herbert (best known as author of the Karen Brown's Guides) and her husband, Rick, have put seventeen years of experience into reality and opened their own superb hideaway, Seal Cove Inn. Spectacularly set amongst wild flowers and bordered by towering cypress trees, Seal Cove Inn looks out to the ocean over acres of county park: an oasis where you can enjoy secluded beaches, explore tide-pools, watch frolicking seals, and follow the tree-lined path that traces the windswept ocean bluffs. Country antiques, original-watercolors, flower-laden cradles, rich fabrics, and the gentle ticking of grandfather clocks create the perfect ambiance for a foggy day in front of the crackling log fire. Each bedroom is its own haven with a cozy sitting area before a wood-burning fireplace and doors opening onto a private balcony or patio with views to the distant ocean. Moss Beach is a 35-minute drive south of San Francisco, 6 miles north of the picturesque town of Half Moon Bay, and a few minutes from Princeton harbor with its colorful fishing boats and restaurants. Seal Cove Inn makes a perfect base for whale-watching, salmon-fishing excursions, day trips to San Francisco, exploring the coast, or, best of all, just a romantic interlude by the sea, time to relax and be pampered. Karen and Rick look forward to the pleasure of welcoming you to their hideaway by the sea.

Seal Cove Inn, 221 Cypress Avenue, Moss Beach, California, 94038, U.S.A.
telephone: (415) 728-7325   fax: (415) 728-4116